DISCARD

WHISPERS OF REBELLION

Carter G. Woodson Institute Series
Deborah E. McDowell, Editor

Whispers

of

NARRATING GABRIEL'S CONSPIRACY

Rebellion

Michael L. Nicholls

University of Virginia Press   *Charlottesville and London*

University of Virginia Press
© 2012 by the Rector and Visitors of the University of Virginia
All rights reserved
Printed in the United States of America on acid-free paper

First published 2012

9 8 7 6 5 4 3 2 1

LIBRARY OF CONGRESS CATALOGING-IN-PUBLICATION DATA

Nicholls, Michael L.
   Whispers of rebellion : narrating Gabriel's conspiracy / Michael L. Nicholls.
      p.   cm. — (Carter G. Woodson Institute series)
   Includes bibliographical references and index.
   ISBN 978-0-8139-3193-7 (cloth : alk. paper) — ISBN 978-0-8139-3206-4 (e-book)
   1. Slave insurrections—Virginia—Richmond Region—History. 2. Slavery—Virginia—
History. 3. Prosser, Gabriel, ca. 1775–1800. 4. Conspiracy—Virginia—Richmond
Region—History. 5. Trials (Conspiracy)—Virginia—Richmond—History—19th century.
6. Richmond (Va.)—Trials, litigation, etc.—History—19th century. I. Title.
   F234.R59N55 2012
   306.3'6209755—dc23

                                                                    2011027532

For Linda

Contents

Acknowledgments

History is built primarily from the archives, and historians rely heavily on archivists and librarians. At the Library of Virginia, Brent Tarter kindly chased down documents and sent copies to me in Utah as my research progressed. I enjoyed and benefited from our conversations during the lunch hours we shared at the library in Richmond. Minor Weisiger, Chris Kolbe, and the staff in the manuscript reading room were gracious and helpful. I received similar courtesies from Frances Pollard at the Virginia Historical Society, and from Susan Riggs at the Swem Library at William and Mary. The interlibrary loan staff at both the Library of Virginia and the Merrill-Cazier Library at Utah State University expeditiously handled my many requests, while the volunteers and staff at the Family History Library in Salt Lake City patiently dealt with the questions of a historian. Queries about documents were quickly attended to by Steve Tuttle of the South Carolina Department of Archives and History, Bruce Kirby at the Library of Congress, and Steve Stathis of the Congressional Research Service, each of whom sent me copies of requested documents.

Historians also rely on other scholars. During some memorable meals in Richmond and through e-mails, Phil Schwarz shared insights and sources about the conspiracy from his own documentary project. I was happy to reciprocate, but I clearly remain in his debt. I also profited from the help and direction given by the late Emory Evans, Martha King, Richard Kohn, Kevin Lett, John McCusker, John O'Keefe, Billy Smith, Angela Smith, Thad Tate, and Henry Wiencek. Warren Billings, Jon Kukla, Sally

Stassi, Ethlyn Byrd, and Elizabeth Chadwick helped me trace the Sully portraits of Thomas Henry Prosser and Lucy Bolling Hylton Prosser, which now reside in Louisiana. I thank them for their help and attention during this quest, even though reproductions of the portraits were not included in the final manuscript. Bill Nelson carefully created the maps. Carolyn Doyle, with good humor and great skill, translated my Word-Perfect files into Word and made them intelligible to the Press. There, Richard Holway and Ruth Steinberg shepherded the manuscript into a book. A portion of the research was supported by a sabbatical grant from Utah State University, and I incorporated some early research conducted under a grant from the AT&T Foundation to the Colonial Williamsburg Foundation for a history of African Americans in early Virginia towns.

Other scholars provided valuable criticisms which strengthened the book. My colleagues in FREAC, the Front Range Early American Consortium, offered valuable suggestions at an early stage. Ron Hatzenbuehler, Matt Mason, Heath Mitton, and Jim Sidbury read a version of a chapter, which was transformed into a journal article, and couched their cautions and criticisms in encouragement. But two colleagues deserve special thanks. From afar, Ira Berlin read the first draft of the manuscript, and at Utah State University, Len Rosenband graciously read more than one draft. Both offered comments and suggestions that helped with the organization of the book, its style, and my argument. None of those named here bear any responsibility for the remaining deficiencies. My thanks to each and every one.

This book is dedicated to Linda, my wife and closest friend, who is the most loving and patient person I know.

Abbreviations and Short Titles

Auditor's Item 756	Auditor of Public Accounts, Item 756: "Condemned Blacks, Executed or Transported" (microfilm), FHL
Auditor's Item 758	Auditor of Public Accounts, Item 758: "Insurrections, 1800-01" (microfilm), FHL
Council Journals	Virginia, Council of State, Journals, Acc. no. 35356 (microfilm), LVA
Egerton	Douglas R. Egerton, *Gabriel's Rebellion: The Virginia Slave Conspiracies of 1800 and 1802* (Chapel Hill: University of North Carolina Press, 1993)
ExLB	Executive Letter Book (microfilm), LVA
ExP I	Executive Papers of James Monroe, Series I: Chronological Files, Acc. no. 40936, LVA
ExP II	Executive Papers of James Monroe, Series II: Subject Files—Gabriel's Insurrection, Acc. no. 40936, LVA
FHL	Family History Library, Salt Lake City, Utah
Henrico Judgements and Ended Causes	Henrico County Court Judgements and Ended Causes 1800, box 70, Commonwealth Causes: September–October, 1800 (Gabriel's Rebellion), LVA
LVA	Library of Virginia, Richmond
VHS	Virginia Historical Society, Richmond
WMQ	*William and Mary Quarterly*

WHISPERS OF REBELLION

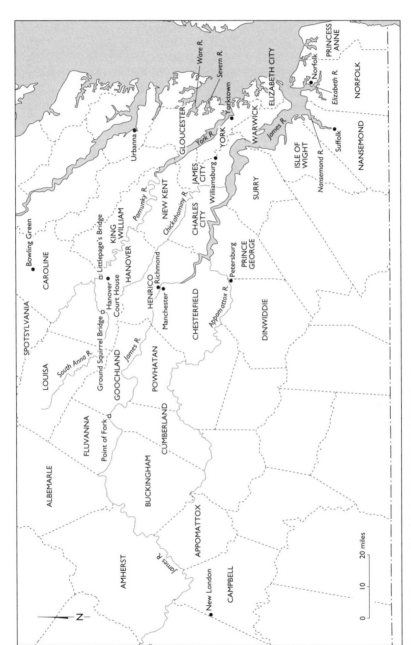

Map 1. Southeastern Virginia in 1800. (Map by Bill Nelson)

Introduction

O n Saturday morning, 30 August 1800, two slaves revealed the existence of a scheme to seize Richmond, Virginia, that very night and destroy slavery. They identified one "Gabriel," a slave blacksmith, as its leader. But the uprising never occurred. That evening, a tremendous "gust," marked by a massive downpour, flooded roads and bridges and prevented any rendezvous by the potential insurrectionists. Consequently, neither the geographical extent of the plot nor the number of insurgents in the conspiracy was revealed. In fact, the initial task for Republican governor James Monroe, beyond sending out some patrols, was to determine if the conspiracy even existed. As events unfolded, the plot proved to be the greatest direct challenge the young state had faced. Local courts tried more than seventy men, of whom at least twenty-five were executed at the gallows for their part in the plot. The cost for mustering and providing for the state militia in response to the alarm, and in compensating owners for executed or exiled slaves, totaled thousands of dollars. How the governor and the state council handled the crisis tested republican political ideals and carried implications for the political future of Republicans like James Monroe, not to mention the presidential hopes of Thomas Jefferson.

For nearly a century, the history of Gabriel's scheme received little attention beyond short accounts appearing in newspaper columns during the sectional crises and Civil War. But in 1890, the state of Virginia published volume 9 of the *Calendar of Virginia State Papers*, which included in whole, in part, or as abstracts, many of the state's records of Gabriel's

Conspiracy. It was an aspect of the effort authorized by the Virginia General Assembly in 1872 to calendar and preserve the piles of disordered documents stashed in the state capitol, a task originally entrusted to William Price Palmer, a retired doctor and devotee of Virginia history. Born in Richmond in 1821, he was educated at the University of Virginia and had taken his medical degree at the University of Pennsylvania. A lieutenant in the Richmond Howitzers during John Brown's raid, Palmer became a captain at the outbreak of the Civil War, but ill health kept him confined to duty in and about Richmond. Even before then, he had immersed himself in Virginia history, and in 1857 had been elected the corresponding secretary of the Virginia Historical Society. He remained active in the Society's leadership into the 1890s. The state's calendaring project was daunting, but through his efforts, the first five volumes of the *Calendar* were launched, before his health ultimately forced his surrender of the massive project to others. Palmer continued his interest in history, however, publishing occasional newspaper essays before his death in 1896, among them a series on the history of slavery in Virginia. On 7 December 1890, the *Richmond Times* published his first installment on this subject, a set of columns, interestingly, that focused on slave rebellions. For his account of Gabriel's Conspiracy, he apparently relied on the just-published volume of the *Calendar,* in which he may have had an early role as the state's records were sorted and identified for the project. In all, he devoted four installments in the *Times* to the episode, which appeared between 21 December 1890 and 11 January 1891. His account seems to be the first to utilize the cache of public documents to tell the story of the conspiracy.[1]

Palmer concluded that once slaves became numerous in Virginia, they posed a threat to whites because they began to consider, "at some time or other shaking off the shackles of slavery" and "of getting rid of their masters and possessing themselves of the country." Simultaneously, he believed that "the negro is by nature docile and affectionate, but at the same time easily moved by passion. His dormant emotions once aroused, no restraint of reason or morals stands between him and the executing of his will." Thus it was, Palmer believed, "that he sometimes was betrayed into acts of violence against the whites," usually by "one more intelligent, more self-reliant than his fellows," one who "would stir up among them a feeling of discontent." This leader's "naturally ardent imagination would picture to himself and a few credulous followers visions of enjoyment," if they were only free. Palmer complained that these "empty hopes" were fed "by indulgence," and he took particular note of the "unworthy stupor" and "want of vigilance at the seat of government," which he believed marked the years between fears of an uprising that gripped the state in 1793 and Gabriel's plot in 1800.[2]

But neglectful state leaders were only part of the problem that contributed to Gabriel's Rebellion. For Palmer, slave masters in 1800 were equally at fault. Their slaves "wandered about without hindrance. . . . On Sundays they roved at liberty over the entire country, visiting friends, attending religious meetings and gathering at will where they might choose." As long as the laborers were at their tasks in the mornings and enough help remained to meet the domestic demands of the white household on Sundays, the near freedom and frolics of Virginia slavery could continue. Masters and mistresses were "careful only to know that their slaves were systematically at their work [and] gave themselves no concern as to what they did in the meantime." Such laxity provided the chance "to concoct almost any evil designs without being even suspected by their indulgent owners."[3]

It comes as no surprise that in Palmer's account the conspiracy did not pick up steam until Gabriel was selected as the leader. Once chosen, he sent out recruiters, ordered arms made or gathered, and appointed additional officers. "It is curious to note how many of Gabriel's deluded followers applied for positions under his command, and how careful he seems to have been in making selections from among them," he wrote. Palmer explained the general plan of attack, and added, "We cannot but be surprised at the show of military foresight exhibited by this untutored slave at the beginning of his first and last campaign." He observed the "remarkable sagacity" Gabriel's planning exhibited, and condemned white lassitude and whites' unwillingness to believe that their trusted slaves could be "unfaithful . . . unless wrought upon by some outside influence," or that their slaves were capable, "in the nature of things, of organizing a serious rebellion." Palmer was also taken by the secrecy sustained in the period leading up to the day of the intended attack. He attributed this cloak "to that Masonic instinct so common among negroes when they are particularly interested in the affairs of their own race."[4]

Although Palmer claimed the slaves' desire to be free and to possess their masters' property was long standing, he also described relations between master and slave as "characterized by fidelity on the one side and affectionate solicitude on the other." He further asserted that at the time of the insurrection, "the utmost confidence existed between the two races." This kind of relationship, he supposed, reinforced the inability of whites to believe their slaves capable of insurrection, and created the opportunities for the conspirators to lay their plans.[5]

But in the end Palmer argued that anyone familiar with the facts of Gabriel's Conspiracy "must come to the conclusion that the negro mind in the South had, for an indefinite period been acted upon by some outside means. The plans adopted, the plausible reasons given why the scheme would succeed, and the provisions made against a possible failure could not have originated in the brain either of Gabriel or any one of his followers." Foreigners—whether forced refugees from the West Indies or the "two Frenchmen" mentioned in slave testimony—were the "immediate fomenters and directors of the movement." Absent from his explanations of the causes of the conspiracy were any claims of the influence of Revolutionary ideology or the election of 1800, of Jeffersonian republicanism or evangelical Christianity, and especially of the possibility that enslaved black men in Virginia could have concocted and carried out the conspiracy themselves to obtain the freedom he recognized they desired.[6]

For nearly a century, few historians of slavery seem to have known of Palmer's pioneering effort to portray Gabriel's Revolt, buried as it was in the 1890–91 columns of a newspaper. Nor was it apparently consulted in the form of his scrapbook of unidentified newspaper clippings, a volume held in the Richmond Public Library before its deposit in the Virginia Historical Society in 1975. In fact, few made any sustained efforts to explore the conspiracy to the extent Palmer did. Plots never implemented, after all, attract little notice. Although Ulrich B. Phillips spent two pages on the event, it was included in a chapter on "Slave Crime" in his extensive *American Negro Slavery*. His account relied on Thomas Wentworth Higginson's short article drawn from newspaper accounts and first published in the *Atlantic Monthly* in 1862, and the even briefer attention given to it in two recent monographs. Phillips did examine the vouchers for executed and transported slaves in the Virginia State Library, but not the *Calendar of State Papers* or the manuscripts comprising them. He recognized the considerable attention that Gabriel's Conspiracy provoked in 1800, but dismissed its threat by stating that either the betrayal of the plot or the storm "would probably have foiled the project"; it did not require both.[7]

Herbert Aptheker gave the conspiracy more attention two decades later in *American Negro Slave Revolts*. He did rely on the *Calendar of State Papers*, supplemented by correspondence, newspaper accounts, and the documents Monroe submitted to the legislature and subsequently inserted in the *Journal of the Senate*. Fighting the prevailing but erroneous assumptions of slave docility, Aptheker sought to build the case for a conspiracy spread wide and deep. But, in the midst of his extensive survey, he did not dwell long enough in the documents to sort out duplications or records that did not derive from the conspiracy, or to resolve anomalies in the sources. As a result, Aptheker's figures for the number of men executed, pardoned, or transported, the costs of the conspiracy, and even the date he gave for Gabriel's execution, are unreliable. At the same time, he made no claim to provide a full account of the aborted rebellion. Unlike Palmer, both Phillips and Aptheker portrayed Gabriel and his followers as laying their own plot and not dependent on white instigators, although Aptheker allowed that some whites might have joined.[8]

Other scholars of slavery and the early national era continued to touch on Gabriel's Conspiracy within their discussions of larger topics, but none stopped to offer as full an account of the event as Palmer had. In Winthrop Jordan's magisterial *White Over Black: American Attitudes toward the Negro, 1550–1812*, for example, the conspiracy served as evidence of the "Cancer of Revolution" following the upheaval in St. Domingue. Jordan wrote that Virginians were "shaken by the magnitude of the Gabriel plot" because it "jarred their picture of slavery and themselves," coming as it did when their "gradual amelioration of slavery" should have, to their minds, diminished the threat of revolt. Consequently, "as much as any single event it caused the sons eventually to repudiate their founding fathers' principles." He noted how the Federalists used the alleged influence of Jacobinism on the conspiracy against Republicans during the election of 1800, but also repeated Aptheker's inflated estimate of the number of men executed and the latter's erroneous date for Gabriel's execution, derived from an inaccurate news report.[9]

The first account that approached the extent of Palmer's newspaper columns appeared in 1972 as the concluding chapter in Gerald Mullin's *Flight and Rebellion: Slave Resistance in Eighteenth-Century Virginia*. Mullin had used the phenomenon of running away to explore issues of resistance and acculturation, and had found a disproportionate number of slave artisans among the advertised runaways he examined. When he explored Gabriel's plot, actually utilizing many of the manuscript sources, including the ones presented in the *Calendar of State Papers,* he found blacksmiths like Gabriel and his brother Solomon in the vanguard, confirming his hypothesis that the most acculturated individuals—the artisans and craftsmen, in his view—were those most likely to actively resist their enslavement. In terms reminiscent of Palmer, he described slavery in the late eighteenth century as "permissive, confused, and disordered." Unlike Palmer's depiction of the conspirators, however, Mullin portrayed Gabriel and his co-conspirators as "rational and calculating men," their goals "essentially political." But the insurrectionists were also divided, the leaders mostly "autonomous," highly acculturated men, who had to recruit followers from among the more "religious men" of the plantations and quarters. Gabriel was a man of the Revolution's ideology of natural rights, but the men he needed to carry out his strike against Richmond were those whose receding African cultural roots and beliefs still "leavened their Christianity," their ideology. Gabriel would have failed not because he was inherently incapable, as Palmer would have it, but, according to Mullin, because the blacksmith neglected to exploit the "vital force" of revivalism and instead made his "appeal in political and secular terms." He reported the statement that a white man named Charles Quersey had encouraged revolt a few years earlier, but doubted whether enough recruits really existed and whether the proposed tactics and military leadership could have actually carried the day. Thus, Mullin implied, for white contemporaries to label the downpour as "providential" was an exaggeration, because the plot was already doomed to failure.[10]

Finally, just over one hundred years after Palmer published his columns, a study eclipsed them in length and scope, and also utilized the undated clippings in the Palmer scrapbook pertaining to the event. In 1993, Douglas Egerton published *Gabriel's Rebellion: The Virginia Slave Conspiracies of 1800 and 1802,* and devoted two-thirds of the book to Gabriel's plot. Egerton also portrayed Virginia slavery as being in "a dangerous state of chaos," and quoted one of the clippings of Palmer's columns in support of his portrayal of the loss of mastery over the slave population at the end of the century. At the same time, he argued that a process of tightening the system had begun in 1796, after the publication of St. George Tucker's *A Dissertation on Slavery with a Proposal for the Gradual Abolition of It in the State of Virginia.* Of course, Egerton did not subscribe to Palmer's views of black inferiority, nor did he deny the ability of Gabriel and his cell to formulate and carry out their plans. He aimed to correct other popular portrayals of Gabriel as a messianic character with long locks, even as he claimed that black Virginians had become "emboldened by Revolutionary theory and radical Christianity." Like Mullin, his portrait of Gabriel's ideology was essentially political, but one more boldly drawn, presenting him as a "black jacobin [who] labored to gather together 'the most redoubtable democrats in the state' to destroy the economic hegemony of the 'merchants,' the only whites he ever identified as his enemies." If Palmer asserted that Gabriel and his followers needed white instigators and planners, Egerton's interpretation included the expected support of white urban craftsmen, who shared an artisan republicanism with Gabriel the blacksmith. In his view, a common ideology, white planners, and an expected white turnout transformed the plot into a class revolt rather than a racially focused slave uprising against white Virginians. Where Mullin saw a divide between the secular outlook of the leaders and the religious orientation of needed followers, Egerton found a similar gap, and added a geographical dimension emphasizing the difference between the urban-connected and -influenced world of Gabriel and the rural plantation existence of many of his recruits.[11] Since its appearance, Egerton's dramatically presented tale has served as the account most often cited in subsequent histories of the era.

Other scholars have continued to turn to the plot, but none to fully recount it. In 1997, James Sidbury came closest, in *Ploughshares into Swords: Race, Rebellion, and Identity in Gabriel's Virginia, 1730–1810.* But the span of years in the title foretold what Sidbury bluntly exclaimed in the opening line of his introduction: "This book is not about Gabriel's Conspiracy." Instead, Sidbury imaginatively used the information in the records arising from it, coupled with a specific focus on Richmond, to explore slavery and the changing identities and the meanings of race for slaves and free people of color, particularly in the generation following the Revolution. He argued that a millennial Christianity helped frame their world. He also related how the scare was presented in fiction or captured in memory, the latter especially among subsequent generations of African Americans, and a theme also touched on by Egerton.[12]

Since the 1990s, other historians have cited Gabriel's Conspiracy for larger purposes, some more extensively than others. The lengthier treatments have consisted of a book chapter or an essay. For example, Walter Rucker devoted a chapter to the plot in *The River Flows On: Black*

Resistance, Culture, and Identity Formation in Early America. Arguing for the importance of African roots to the cultural crucible of resistance by slaves in early America, he described the bridges, streams, and springs where Gabriel and the conspirators sometimes gathered as "ritual spaces," and he claimed that the presence of ironworkers within the plot's leadership to be evidence of specific influences of their West African heritage, the latter an expansion and refinement of an earlier observation of James Sidbury. In doing so, Rucker rejected Mullin's model of acculturation and resistance, rightly objecting, for example, to the implication that a blacksmith's skills were only European in origin. At the same time, he questioned Egerton's class interpretation of the plot, but continued to rely on Aptheker's numbers, preferring them to Egerton's corrections. William Merkel assessed Thomas Jefferson's response to the episode by examining his actions in the light of the Virginia General Assembly's request for help in deporting slave criminals and free people of color. Framing his discussion within Jefferson's evaluation of St. George Tucker's proposal for eventual manumission and removal, he explored Jefferson's uncomfortable acquiescence in executing slave rebels, though justified in their rebellion, through the doctrine of "necessity or self-preservation." Taking a different tack, Robert Ferguson offered the meditations of a literary historian who viewed the plot as a repressed story of failure in the midst of the successes of the "founding" and the early republic. He gave a close reading of a statement attributed some years later to one of the defendants at his trial, and noted the historical distortions created by excluding unwanted parts of the past. Most recently, Lacy K. Ford has argued that the failed conspiracy pushed Virginia's political leaders and citizens toward measures, like colonization and the interstate slave trade, that would "whiten" Virginia and reduce the dangers of insurrection. He also questioned Egerton's argument about the artisan coalition that undergirds his class interpretation of the revolt, but otherwise relied heavily on Egerton's account. Clearly, with the work of Egerton in place, none tried to fully reconstruct the actual event.[13]

With the attention already paid to the plot of Gabriel and his followers, those familiar with historical accounts of the era may wonder why another history of Gabriel's Conspiracy is needed. I initially assumed the same when beginning to explore the history of African Americans in Virginia's newly emerging towns. I greeted the publication of Professor Egerton's bold, richly detailed, and engaging study as an important source for a planned chapter on slave resistance, until my research in the archives, reinforced by the published questioning of other historians about specific points in the book, raised doubts about his handling of the evidence throughout his narrative. I finally decided to systematically reexamine the sources, and concluded that key points of Egerton's interpretation were built more on the shifting sand of suppositions than on the hard rock of archival evidence. Patient, broader, and careful research slowly allowed me to construct a more accurate chronology and outcome of specific episodes, and even a different characterization of some of the key individuals involved. Moreover, exploring the plot within its local geographical context in order to understand the connections of the conspirators revealed other clues and shaped my understanding of the scale, nature, and dynamics of the conspiracy.

The insights of other historians of slavery have also had an important influence on my specific reading and understanding of Gabriel's plot. One is the reminder of Thomas J. Davis of the law of conspiracy: when two or more individuals, slave or free, agreed to commit any unlawful act, they violated the law, whether they carried through with their plan or not. Hence, what might be considered just "loose talk"—agreeing to steal a pig, poison a mistress, torch a barn, or rise in rebellion—was in fact criminal conspiracy. It was—and still is—a fairly easy charge for the prosecution to prove. Consequently, as James Sidbury has observed, most of the trial records, the core of the evidence of the conspiracy, are essentially accounts of recruitment. Since agreeing to rebel was all that had to be proven, the record of one's joining in the plot, not why or what the conspirators envisioned beyond their freedom, comprises the bulk of the recorded trial testimony. Much less evidence emerges of specific personal or ideological motives, or visions of the future.[14]

Thus, in spite of the remarkable trove of documents produced by the crushing of the conspiracy, they are usually frustratingly quiet or incomplete, especially for efforts seeking to delve into the ideology of Gabriel and his followers, an important concern of many historians. As Peter Kolchin concluded about slave revolts in the United States in general, they were simply "too fleeting to provide many clues to the social attitudes of the slaves." Still, as Winthrop Jordan wryly noted, historians are sorely tempted "to search for ideologies at the cost of overlooking less well-articulated systems of values." He observed that scholars have often assumed that "slave rebels ought to have been revolutionaries and that revolutionaries have to have ideologies." Instead, he asserted that "for slaves freedom seemed an immediate goal to be accomplished abruptly, not a theoretical condition." He warned that without paying close and careful attention to the sources of a plot, limited though they usually are, "we are left treating a specific slave conspiracy as part of a trend or movement more of our making than of the slaves involved." Or, as David Brion Davis has phrased it, in a different context, a "tendency to write history in the constant shadow of 'what should have happened,' from the perspective of the late twentieth century."[15]

Jordan demonstrated in his masterful analysis of an 1861 plot at Second Creek in Mississippi how a careful reading of the sources surrounding that conspiracy, along with an emphasis on the local physical world those men inhabited, can yield great dividends, in spite of the vagueness, anomalies, gaps, and inconsistencies that initially seem to dog the evidence. The same is true for Gabriel's Conspiracy. What emerges from the record is not just the conspirators' goal of freedom, but their assessment of the challenges they faced and their efforts to surmount them within the scope of their experiences and with the men and materials at hand. As Walter Johnson has noted, "Collective resistance is, at bottom, a process of everyday organization, one that, in fact, depends upon connections and trust established through everyday actions: covering for a friend, slowing down on the job, stealing things and sharing them, providing for runaways when they were 'out,' taking a beating, or telling the right story in the right language at the right time." These actions bound individuals together against what they commonly faced: their enslavement. This reality also raises the importance of place and space. The appearance of Anthony E. Kaye's *Joining Places: Slave Neighborhoods in the Old South* reinforced my sense of the significance of the locale for understanding the center of the plot and its connections to other cells of insurgents.[16] In some ways, all histories of slaves and slavery are local, even personal. The challenge is to find and unlock the sources to that history. In turn, the measures taken by the Monroe administration to crush the effort are best approached within the context of Virginia's leaders' experience with slave unrest, the necessity of relying on an ill-prepared militia for control and protection, the intense atmosphere of the presidential election of 1800, and the political, even economic strictures of Virginian republicanism.

Although I came to disagree with several of the calculations and conclusions of other scholars who have examined Gabriel's Conspiracy and

Virginia's efforts to suppress it, my task was made easier by their work, and especially the pioneering books of Professors Egerton and Sidbury. Writing history is not a solitary creative process, but is built on the shoulders of those who have gone before. I also benefited from the accessibility of the microfilm collection of Virginia local and state records at the Family History Library not far away from me in Salt Lake City. The explosive expansion of the Internet and its service as a tool to find published works, archival holdings, maps, and indexes, even images of manuscript sources, many mounted by genealogists, expedited and expanded my efforts. These technological advantages were not available to this extent even a few years ago. Retirement also freed me from grading essays and papers and attending to the committees and concerns of the university and our students, and gave me the time to probe the manuscript records in depth and to reexamine them, sometimes several times, as seeming contradictions appeared. Still, as all historians know, not all can be completely sorted out, and I have offered an explanation for my use of undated documents at specific times for the development of the narrative, and for other issues arising from the sources. I do believe, however, that what follows is a more accurate and deeper rendering of the conspiracy than offered by previous scholars, though errors likely remain.

This narrative of Gabriel's Conspiracy tries to present both the conspirators and the Virginia state authorities within the context of their time and place. Jordan noted that "people involved in these most particular events need to be taken seriously as individuals with their own agendas and concerns, living as they did in situations very different from ours and, indeed, participating in a culture that, no matter how much it influenced our own, no longer exists."[17] Without doing so, one cannot comprehend the decisions made by both groups of men before the conspiracy was blown and in its subsequent repression. Chapter 1 emphasizes the geographical and political contexts of the conspiracy. It traces the sinews of the conspiracy as they were strung among enslaved men who worked near the Brook, a neighborhood framed by a watershed north of Richmond, and the physical and human connections these men had with other parts of central Virginia, mostly those along the stage road that crossed their neighborhood. It emphasizes the face-to-face world of their circles and their dealings with the whites who trod through these spaces and often shaped and reshaped them. The chapter also sets the political context for Virginia's political rulers as the country faced foreign foes and internal political dissension on the eve of the presidential election of 1800, when political rhetoric and bombast ran rampant. Chapter 2 explores how the conspiracy was put together; how Gabriel and other plotters exploited the crevasses in Virginia's system of slavery to build the cadre of followers needed for the revolt; and how they raced against time and the increased dangers of disclosure that dragging out their preparations would bring. Chapter 3 traces the unraveling of the plot after it was betrayed and almost immediately destroyed by the incredible storm that hit the Richmond area, and the Monroe administration's initial reactions to the plot. Chapters 4 and 5 follow the legal processes and trials of the conspirators and their executions, acquittals, or exiling, and the quandaries confronting the state in defending itself and prosecuting insurgents whose plot had failed to materialize. Chapter 6 studies the public, executive, and legislative responses in Virginia to the plot, and the Commonwealth's efforts to prevent future uprisings. An afterword follows the return of men to the Brook in the aftermath of the plot, and looks ahead to the impact of the conspiracy on attitudes toward slavery and the nature of Virginia's slave society.

Because I did not want to clutter the narrative with such details, scholars are directed to the notes at the back of the book for the corrections I have made to past accounts and the different conclusions I have reached from them.

1 } The Brook and the Road

Two geographical features dominate Gabriel's Conspiracy. One is a waterway known as the Brook. The other is the stage road that crossed it, called Brook Road. In 1800, Brook Road headed north out of Richmond and in about five or six miles reached the Brook, which rose northwest of the capital city of Virginia. Once called variations of Ufnam Brook, and today known as Upham Brook, it generally descended in an easterly direction. It emptied into the Chickahominy River, the northern boundary of Henrico County, not far from the Meadow Bridges, which sat six miles or so north and a little east of the city. The fact that residents of the county simply referred to the area surrounding the creek and its tributaries as "the Brook" suggests its topographical and social importance. White men and women in the neighborhood of the Brook held the majority of the enslaved men accused of the conspiracy. For example, west of the road and before its descent toward the Brook Bridge lay the lands of one of them, William Young, and adjacent to his tracts sat a schoolhouse with a spring, one of many that fed the run. Young was part owner of the schoolhouse lot, perhaps a patron in a state which had only recently begun to provide any support for public education. He also owned a mill in a fork of the Brook above where the road crossed the stream. Among his near neighbors were members of the Williamson and Price families, including Dabney Williamson and Sally Price, and the heirs of Jacob Smith, all individuals who held conspirators. Farther upstream than Young's lands, the main run of the Brook was nourished by several branches that partly drained the ridge that often bedded Three

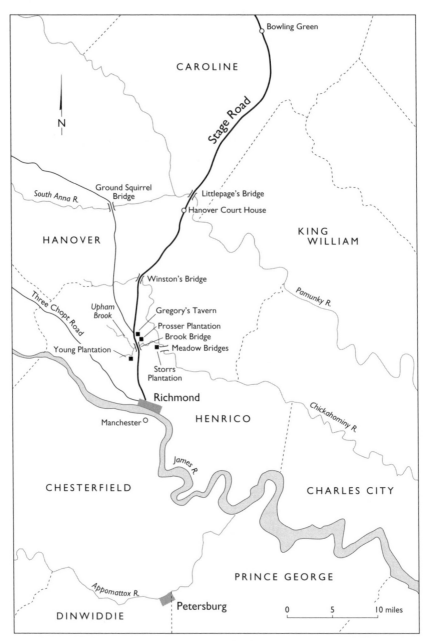

Map 2. The center of conspiracy. (Map by Bill Nelson)

Chopt Road. This thoroughfare struck out to the west from Richmond, spanned a tributary of Tuckahoe Creek called Deep Run, which gave its name to nearby coal pits, and entered Goochland County just as it crossed Little Tuckahoe Creek. By then, the road was about fifteen miles or so northwest of the capitol. Near Three Chopt Road, but much closer to Young's and the Brook drainage were the habitations, or quarters, of John Buchanan and John Mayo. Their lands and the slaves who worked them were more a part of the Brook community than the neighborhood surrounding the distant reaches of the sources of Tuckahoe Creek, which drained south into the James River.[1]

Other residents of the Brook with slaves involved in the plot resided to the east of Young's land near the stage road and stream. They included Allen Williamson, Thomas and William Burton, Thomas Woodfin, and Izard Bacon. Bacon's near neighbor, Gervas Storrs, lived farthest downstream, closer to where the Brook emptied into the Chickahominy. Although he had no slaves accused, he had recently been appointed a justice on the Henrico bench, and would play a crucial role in the judicial proceedings against the conspirators. Also included in this part of the neighborhood were some of John Brooke's tracts and the lands of Drury Wood, which he would soon start subdividing into small parcels, probably because their closer proximity to the Richmond side of the community could more easily capture the opportunities created by the capital's growth and expansion. These men would each have a slave accused of joining the plot.[2]

From a crow's eye, the Brook Bridge appeared to buckle the neighborhood together, the road and the causeway connected to it looking like a belt stretching between Richmond and the Chickahominy. Predominantly on the north side of the stream, but not too far from Young's, were the lands, mills, and home of Thomas Henry Prosser, the unmarried twenty-three-year-old son and recent heir of Thomas, who had once served as sheriff, coroner, and county justice of Henrico after his permanent expulsion from the House of Burgesses in 1765, when he sat for Cumberland County. He had also inherited Gabriel and other plotters. Close, too, were Nathaniel Wilkinson, a former sheriff and the current ranking justice and county treasurer, and Captain Roger Gregory, whose tracts abutted each other's and Prosser's at various points. Before his death in 1798, Thomas Prosser had repaired or rebuilt Brook Bridge at public charge, and had served as the surveyor or road supervisor between it and Winston's Bridge farther north. The latter structure carried Brook Road over the Chickahominy as it continued as the stage route running through Hanover County, and eventually across Caroline County and on toward Fredericksburg. Prosser's Tavern sat closer to the Brook, perhaps still located in an old store of Thomas Prosser's, as it had been in the late 1780s, and apparently run by George Watson in 1800. On the tavern grounds, Gervas Storrs conducted the election in the Brook District for the county's overseers of the poor that summer, and in an adjacent field, a deputy sheriff would hang five of the conspirators that fall. Farther along the road, about seven or eight miles from Richmond, sat Gregory's Tavern, a newer establishment where a portion of the local militia's arms were stored. It was still operated that summer by Thomas Priddy, who had succeeded Thomas Prosser as the supervisor of the section of the road between the two bridges. Gregory, Prosser, and Wilkinson were neighbors with the Mosby, Sheppard, Owen, Allen, and Burton families, among others. Their slaves, some of them conspirators, worked the higher grounds and the often wet lowlands between the Brook and the Chickahominy. In fact, some had the skills to create drainage ditches or kennels that sometimes served as both property boundaries and channels to remove excess water. Flowing from the west into the North Run of the Brook were the Hungary and Rocky Branches, or Creeks, whose outstretched fingertips almost touched the Deep Run coal pits. A Baptist meeting house near the Hungary Branch served this part of the neighborhood as a site of religious gatherings, and while masters and mistresses worshiped and prayed, it unknowingly to them provided slave men with a recruiting ground for the conspiracy.[3]

Two important roads split or forked from the Brook Road north of the bridge. One headed east to cross the Chickahominy at Wilkinson's Bridge and provide a convenient route to Hanover County between Winston's Bridge above and the Meadow Bridges below. Most directly from Winston's, but also from Wilkinson's Bridge, roads joined in Hanover County to take the traveler through its narrowest part, past Hanover Court House and on to Littlepage's Bridge at the Pamunkey River. Over its back, northbound travelers crossed into Caroline County adjacent to the North Wales plantation of absentee Charles Carter and just downstream from South Wales, his quarter in Hanover, homes to plotters. About six or seven miles farther north, the road passed a tavern at White Chimneys, and another fourteen or fifteen miles brought one to Bowling Green, the site of the Caroline County courthouse. Several of the conspirators would be incarcerated and tried there, recruits who lived and worked close to Littlepage's Bridge and nearer to the Henrico neighborhood of the Brook than to the Caroline County seat.[4]

The second tangent to the road soon emerged beyond Gregory's Tavern. But this road angled west and bridged the North Run of the Brook above the mouth of the Hungary Branch. It also crossed the curving Chickahominy, apparently near a now almost forgotten Michams Lick, to enter Hanover. It connected Richmond and Henrico to Louisa and other Central Piedmont counties via the Ground Squirrel Bridge over the South Anna River several miles into Hanover. This bridge was thought to fall within the perimeter of the conspiracy in southwestern Hanover. All these roads and bridges, mostly built and maintained by the black male slaves residing near them, served as important conduits and links, and sometimes as meeting places, for the plotters. The conspiracy, however, emerged and centered in the neighborhood of the Brook among the black men who were held or hired there.[5]

In 1787 Henrico officials had divided the county for tax purposes, using the road that ran from Richmond to the Meadow Bridges as the district boundary. Their decision placed the neighborhood of the Brook in the western, or upper, segment of the county. In 1800 the tax commissioner returned an upper-district list of some 451 free tithables, or men above the age of sixteen. Not all were white, for among them were at least sixteen free men of color. His tax tally also counted, but did not name, 1,105 black tithables, or enslaved men and women aged sixteen and older, most owned but some hired by the planters, farmers, and the few coalmine operators of the district. An additional 177 enslaved children between twelve and sixteen years old also worked in the upper part of Henrico, the commissioner noting their existence to enrich the state's coffers, as the law prescribed.[6]

The slaves who resided in the neighborhood of the Brook produced wheat, corn, some tobacco, and hay. They raised cattle, plowed and carted products to market with horses and mules, and butchered the often free-ranging hogs, once in a while without permission. Millers ground the grain into meal and flour and sawed logs into timber, while others smithed and coopered, ditched and fenced, weeded and hoed, chopped wood, tended the livestock, ran errands, and worked their own garden plots. They also served the families that held them in bondage, doing the domestic drudgery of cooking and waiting, washing and cleaning, and nursing and caring for young children. They raised their own families, too. Late on Saturdays, after their work and if permitted, some men trekked to Richmond or to other plantations, some beyond the boundaries of Henrico, to rejoin family and acquaintances—their "connections," in the language of the day. Others slipped away without permission, sometimes equipped with fraudulent passes of their own or of someone else's drafting. Some women had to await the arrival of their husbands from other plantations or from Richmond, Manchester, or places where they might be hired or held. On Sundays, if not at the call of the master or mistress, these slaves might gather to worship, to bury their dead, to gossip, to play quoits or cards, to fish, and even to feast on the fish when the run was on. In the summer of 1800, a few of the men of the Brook moved about these gatherings recruiting other men for the conspiracy.[7]

They knew each other as they knew their masters. Within their neighborhoods, they recognized who belonged, who could be trusted, who was strong, who was defiant, or who was a stranger, or unreliable, or weak. They also grew up and lived in a mature slave society and understood slavery—it was what it was—but understanding was not acquiescence. And they sometimes glimpsed the power of the state that framed their enslavement, its abilities to communicate and to mobilize its militia, and its authority to prosecute slave crimes in its county courts of oyer and terminer. Presided over by justices who dispensed justice without juries, their decisions capable of inflicting the death penalty for some felonies, they were a mark of Virginia's slave system. Another, not unique to the state, were the slave patrols pulled from the militia. While not a constant presence, the irregularity of their monthly riding made them more effective, and perceived unrest sent them into the night with greater frequency, always at taxpayer expense. Moreover, every person, white or black, if physically able, could take up a suspected runaway or inform a master or authorities of suspicious activities. But most often, slaves felt the threat or cut of the master's whip and his power to sell the recalcitrant, the latter made more effective by the bonds of family and affection that had spread and deepened over time. Even the possibility of becoming free, which had become legally much easier in the aftermath of the Revolution, and which had been most heavily used by the Society of Friends, many Methodists, and some Baptists, Episcopalians, and enlightened rationalists, contributed to a master's power and the shaping of a slave society that functioned sufficiently well to encourage most white Virginians to keep it and to seldom question it except in the abstract. Even so, their system did not leave whites at ease, sheltered in a fantasy that they had nothing to fear. They could see it could not prevent the existence of an underground economy of runaway labor and purloined goods, which many whites believed the growing numbers of free blacks, and even some whites, exploited. Nor could it prevent the grimaces of frustration and the angry mutterings about imagined blows for freedom, protection of loved ones, and in some cases, revenge and retaliation, that were sometimes overheard, if infrequently undertaken. The whisperers may have been quietly noted, too, creating mental lists or points of conversation of "the usual suspects." In the late spring of 1800, a group of men decided to act, not just conspire, to transform their whispers into a direct attack on Richmond and their enslavement.[8]

Virginia's slave society was more mature than the state's political system and that of the new nation. The state existed under the Constitution of 1776, which instituted a dominant legislative branch composed of an annually elected House of Delegates and Senate. The governor, in 1800 James Monroe, was annually chosen by these two houses of the General Assembly, and was advised by a Council of State, whose eight members were also elected by the House and Senate. Indeed, so were the members of the state judiciary, though not the county justices. The justices remained a self-perpetuating body, where vacancies were filled by appointment of the executive on the justices' own recommendation. They proved to be a major exception to the Revolutionary-era republicanism that pervaded the Constitution of 1776. But transforming any ideology into institutions that effectively functioned and governed was a challenge. The journals of the Council of State during the 1790s, for example, reveal how specific events provoked discussions of the extent or limits of powers and responsibilities of the offices and branches of government. Since there was no provision for amendments, no real institutional change could occur without adopting a new constitution, so statutes refined and clarified the responsibilities of the government's branches. And, of course, the Constitution of the United States was even younger, with significant issues of federalism and civil liberty remaining untested or unresolved. Many of these issues emerged in the unfolding crises created in American relations with the two dominant European powers, England and France. The first sustained and truly contested presidential election, in 1800, encapsulated and exposed many of the divisive issues confronting the nation. Indeed, while the slave conspirators put together their plan, white Virginians followed an increasingly bitter presidential political campaign which sometimes was portrayed in conspiratorial images. Early in 1800, in a tactic calculated to deliver all of Virginia's electoral votes to favorite son Thomas Jefferson, Republicans in the Virginia General Assembly had succeeded in passing a measure that established a statewide election for presidential electors, rather than choosing electors on a district basis, which had been the case in 1796. As the spring wore on, elections in other states made a Republican victory seem more likely, leading the Federalists to raise their rhetoric of fear about a Jefferson election. Any advantage John Adams might have gained from his incumbency was finally destroyed when the Federalists themselves split along the fault of Alexander Hamilton's ultimate and openly expressed opposition to Adams's reelection. For arch-Federalists like Hamilton, and those of the Federalist press who found it useful to brand Jefferson a Jacobin, Adams had gone soft on France. His effort to reestablish peaceful relations with the European power was unbelievable and unpardonable. If nothing else, it undercut the rationale for the Federalist-inspired expansion of the nation's military forces and their rationalization for wartime restrictions on political opposition. Still, there was a chance that the Federalists might retain the presidency through the election of either Adams or Charles Cotesworth Pinckney of South Carolina, so the contest continued to generate considerable heat. Richmond, the home of John Marshall, by sending Federalist Charles Copland as its representative to the General Assembly in 1800, appeared to be a Federalist island in the midst of true republicanism. William Rind provided the Federalists with a voice through the *Virginia Federalist*, but left late that summer to found a Federalist paper in Georgetown, close to the new national capital. Consequently, residents of Richmond and Henrico were more likely to see columns that ran the political spectrum, from Richmond postmaster Augustine Davis's *Virginia Gazette*, through Samuel Pleasants Jr.'s *Virginia Argus*, to the most aggressively Republican paper, Meriwether Jones's *Richmond Examiner*. The latter especially attacked the Federalists through the venomous pen of James Thomson Callender, a refugee from the newspaper wars in Philadelphia.[9]

In 1798, in anticipation of war and hoping to eliminate a political opposition many in the country had not yet learned to accommodate, the Federalist-controlled Congress had passed a series of punitive measures, including the Sedition Act, which criminalized criticism of the government. In the early summer of 1800, the presidential campaign and the Sedition Act collided in the federal court of Richmond. In a case presided over by Supreme Court Justice Samuel Chase, the government tried James Thomson Callender, who had proved one of John Adams's harshest critics. After fleeing beatings and threats in Philadelphia, he had lambasted the Adams administration in his *The Prospect Before Us,* printed on the Richmond presses of Meriwether Jones, Samuel Pleasants Jr., and another displaced Republican printer named James Lyon. The prospect of the upcoming trial created much tension and attracted a lot of attention, although John Minor believed it would do Callender "more good than harm, [for] it will enable him to sell off his Books which otherwise he would not have been able to do." With the outbreak of the Quasi-War with France, Congress had also expanded the United States armed forces. Subsequently, a regiment of about four hundred men under the command of a Virginian, Col. William Bentley, had taken up station several months before near Warwick, four miles downstream of Richmond in Chesterfield County. It was believed they were to move on to Harpers Ferry in the spring, but they remained near the capital. In the heated political atmosphere of 1800, with the lingering old republican fears of a standing army as a sure sign of intended oppression, the encampment of the regiment raised concerns. As early as December 1799, St. George Tucker had expressed his worries over the troops near the capital, fearing that they were meant to be dispatched to courthouses to influence the election. On 15 May, Virginia governor James Monroe wondered in writing to James Madison if their continued presence was designed to intimidate any Republicans who might cause the Chase Court any trouble, or to provoke an incident that might justify military intervention. Unbeknown to him, Congress had passed, and the president had signed into law, an act that called for the disbandment of most of the earlier authorized additional forces by no later than 15 June. Coincidentally, on the very day Monroe wrote Madison, Adams ordered their demobilization.[10]

Sometime between the 10th and the 14th of June, the regiment at Warwick stacked their guns in Manchester, a village directly across the James River from Richmond, and headed home. Interestingly, the troops left with their wages paid with monies advanced from the Virginia Treasury. Edward Carrington, the federal superintendent for Virginia, had petitioned Monroe and the State Council for assistance on behalf of the regimental paymaster, who did not have sufficient small bills with which to pay the soldiers, and they had granted his request. Although Callender's trial had ended the week before with a guilty verdict from twelve Federalist jurors, and without incident, the departure of the disbanded regiment apparently worried William Berkeley, the state treasurer. He requested the State Council to supply a guard, which they immediately authorized, consisting of a local corporal and four men to be placed at the capitol to watch the Treasury for a week or so. While Berkeley apparently believed that the Treasury was at greater risk from unstated threats in the wake of the demobilization—perhaps from the soldiers themselves—Monroe and his fellow Republican politicos presumably felt relieved by their disbanding. They did not know that Gabriel and his co-conspirators had also noted the regiment's demobilization, and had happily included that information in their calculations for the intended insurrection.[11]

There was no way to guard against another threat which disrupted life in Virginia that summer. As the summer's heat and humidity smothered Norfolk, deaths began to accumulate and fears arose over the possible outbreak of yellow fever. In early July, Thomas Newton Jr., the Norfolk superintendent of quarantine, state senator, and soon to be Jeffersonian elector, reported to Monroe that the USS *Baltimore* had captured a ship and sent it into port. Three of the prize's crew had died, and it was feared that they had succumbed to yellow fever. Municipal officials wanted the ship examined, but Newton believed he could not do so without a proclamation from the governor. He stated that news had arrived of the fever prevailing in the West Indies, the source of a significant trade for Norfolk merchants and shippers. However, the next day Newton dispatched word to Richmond that yellow fever was not the cause of the deaths, and that Norfolk remained generally healthy, except for the whooping cough which plagued several children. He discounted the fear of yellow fever to the point that he thought the quarantine house, sitting on a "pleasant shore for bathing," could be leased to advantage. His real concern was that there was no person responsible for intercepting individuals who disembarked outside of Norfolk and came to town by land. At the end of the month, Newton continued to insist that in spite of more deaths there was no danger of any infection spreading and that the sufferers had died from a "disease of a violent bilious kind, which we are subject to more [or] less of every year."[12]

Newton's assurances may have initially satisfied the governor, but fears spread from Norfolk, even if the fever had not. Consequently, on 11 August, Monroe ordered the inspection of ships from Norfolk nearing Richmond. A few days later, an alarmed citizenry in Fredericksburg wanted to know if their local superintendent had the authority to inspect Norfolk vessels too. On 23 August, after conferring with the State Council, Monroe issued a proclamation requiring the determination of the origin of all vessels nearing Virginia ports. If a ship arrived from Norfolk, it had to perform quarantine for fifteen days, computed from the time of its Norfolk departure. Superintendent Newton still protested that the local inhabitants were "as healthy as any town in the state," although he did admit that the fever gripped "strangers" and "new settlers." At the same time, fearful Richmonders sought state help to establish an infirmary for any infected individuals coming to the capital. In the midst of this yellow fever scare, the first inklings of Gabriel's Conspiracy began to surface.[13]

While the white population sparred over presidential politics, speculated about the intentions of nearby federal troops, observed Callender's sedition trial, waited for news from Europe about peace negotiations, and feared an invasion of yellow fever, the men of the Brook laid their plot for "freeing the Negroes from slavery." In the late spring of 1800, an enslaved man named Sam Byrd Jr. began to draw others into a plan to "kill the white people" and seize their freedom. He belonged to Jane Clarke, a widow whose acres sat near those of William Young and John Mayo near the Brook. Byrd was likely one of the four unnamed tithable slaves whom she reported to the tax enroller that year. He was the son and namesake of a free man of color who lived in Hanover Town, a village about eight miles east of the hamlet of Hanover Court House. His mother was or had been a slave at his birth; neither her identity as his mother nor her name were captured in the record. He claimed two uncles with the same surname in Petersburg, who were also free men of color. Over the next couple of months, Byrd recruited widely for his cause, and relied partly on his kin in his efforts. Hiring his time, apparently from his widow owner, he reportedly journeyed south to Petersburg, up the James River to Point of Fork, and west to Charlottesville. He made his way east to Hanover Town, but probably failed in his efforts to reach the Catawbas in Carolina, whom he believed he could convince to join in the cause. Even so, he would claim to have found five hundred followers for the uprising.[14]

Among Byrd's earliest converts was George, sometimes called George Smith. He was held by Ann Smith, the widow of Jacob and a near neighbor of Young's. The Smith estate was taxed on seven slaves of tithable age. Referred to once as a colonel, George Smith participated in key discussions and also recruited extensively, claiming thirty-seven enlistees from around Hungary Meeting House and some fifty in Manchester. He too planned to secure his time from his mistress and use it to go to the border between Hanover and King William Counties to a place with the exotic sounding name of "Pipeing Tree," made more so to modern ears because, it was said, that was where "outlandish people" dealt with "witches and wizards" who might forewarn of dangers and disasters. Pipeing Tree was actually an old tobacco warehouse site near the Pamunkey River. Perhaps Smith was referring to Native Americans, the Mattaponi or Pamunkey people who had long lived in the area, but it is more likely that "outlandish" referred to slaves born in Africa, or possibly the West Indies. Like Byrd's trip to the Catawba, Smith's travel to consult with those he believed could peer into the future might not have been realized—he reported no warnings or blessings from them—but he enlisted two men of the Brook who would play significant roles in the conspiracy.[15]

One was named Gilbert, a man Gabriel later identified as one of the core conspirators—indeed, the only name he would disclose. Gilbert belonged to William Young, one of seven tithable slaves reported by him in 1800, and he obviously lived near Byrd and Smith. Gilbert could write, knew where his master kept a sword, owned a pistol, purchased gunpowder in Richmond so he could fire it, and promised to recruit men. He failed to win a captain's commission to lead them, however, because he stuttered. He demurred when Smith argued for delaying the revolt, supporting instead Gabriel's push for an earlier start to the insurrection. Although he admitted he was unable to kill Young and his wife himself, he was "determined" they would be slain by the men with him. He was soon taken up and imprisoned, in contrast to Gabriel and Jack Bowler, both leaders who remained at large for several weeks. He would provide the names of many of his fellow conspirators, and even of some who may not have been seriously involved.[16]

The second individual of note recruited by George Smith, assisted by Sam Byrd Jr., was Ben Woolfolk. Described as a mulatto in one newspaper account, though indicted as a "negro man slave," he belonged to Paul Graham, who held property and apparently lived in Hanover in

1800. He was identified as being from Caroline County, and indeed his family roots were there. Woolfolk, however, was hired to William Young, where he worked with Gilbert. He was to be a captain, and was entrusted to join in the recruiting in Caroline County, no doubt because of his acquaintances in the neighborhood near Littlepage's Bridge. At one time in the plotting, he was expected to lead the Caroline conscripts to the general rendezvous scheduled for the night of the attack. A glimpse of his personality or character was revealed when one of the individuals he solicited initially scoffed to Woolfolk that he was up to "his usual folly." Another estimate of him came from the lawyer assigned to defend the Henrico conspirators, who called him "the suspicious Ben Woolfolk." Like Gilbert, he would later become the source of many names, but unlike his co-worker, Woolfolk did not swing on the gallows. Instead, he became a chief witness for the state in many of the trials held in Richmond and all of those in Bowling Green.[17]

Also involved in the earliest plotting was Jack Bowler, aka Jack Ditcher, a slave of the widow of William Bowler of Caroline County and likely hired near the neighborhood of the Brook, given his frequent appearances around Prosser's place. He was a skilled ditcher, and he was huge, his 6 foot, 4 (or 5) inch frame towering over most men of his day. He was described by Richard Bowler, a Richmond tavern keeper presumably related to Bowler's owner by marriage, as about twenty-eight and perhaps the strongest man in Virginia. Bowler wore his hair long, most of it tied back into a queue, but with twists of his locks at the sides. A scar ran above one of his eyes, and his hairline sat "very low on his forehead." Over the course of the summer, Bowler amassed several pounds of gunpowder and bragged he had gathered more ammunition than two people could carry. He also claimed the support of an unnamed person with military experience gained during the Revolution who had agreed to lead the men initially into Richmond. Early on, Bowler was thought to be at "the head of the Plan," but later contended with Gabriel for command and lost it to him. It was Bowler, ironically, who first spoke to Gabriel about the plot.[18]

After authorities interrogated several of the earliest-seized conspirators, they concluded that Gabriel was the chief mover behind the intended insurrection, and so he had become by the time the conspiracy collapsed. He was a blacksmith and slave of Thomas Henry Prosser, who with two overseers worked thirty-seven tithable slaves and eleven more taxable children, one of the largest work forces in the county. Unlike Bowler,

Gabriel wore his hair short above his longish, even "boney" face, carried two or three scars on his head, spoke through two missing front teeth, and bore a court-imposed brand on his left hand. He was twenty-four but looked much older, and could both read and write. His skin was "darkish" and his brow "gloomy," even "insidious," or at least that was how Prosser saw him. He was "well made and very active," stood between 6 feet, 2 inches and 6 feet, 4 inches, depending on who you talked to, and was obviously big enough to present a commanding presence and to intimidate others. A neighbor certainly found him physically threatening. Absalom Johnson, who rented most of Nathaniel Wilkinson's lands and leased many of his slaves, had accosted Gabriel the fall before in an apparent confrontation over a stolen pig and had lost "a considerable part of his left ear" to Gabriel's uneven but effective bite. As a result, the Henrico Court tried the blacksmith for maiming Johnson and found him guilty. But instead of sending him to the gallows, they allowed him to plead his benefit of clergy, a medieval procedure that provided a means of avoiding capital punishment for the educated, a one-time privilege. It was extended to slave defendants of some capital crimes early in the eighteenth century. By then, it no longer required a demonstration of the ability to read, but still demanded branding the defendant's hand to eliminate recurrent claims of the benefit to avoid the gallows. Hence, the justices ordered Gabriel branded on his left hand to mark their judgment and prevent him from claiming the privilege in the future. Within a month, Johnson again complained about threats from Gabriel, and the court forced Prosser to post a $1,000 bond that his slave would keep the peace for one year toward the good people of Henrico, and especially toward Johnson. But Gabriel did not wait for the year to expire before breaking Prosser's bonded promise. Indeed, Absalom Johnson was named among those who were the first to be killed.[19]

Working with Gabriel at Prosser's were two of his brothers. Martin, the eldest of the three siblings, may not have been an artisan, but he was something of a preacher, and he spoke with the authority of scripture to an assembly of conspirators. Gabriel thought him too old to physically participate; it was probably his age that diminished his value in the eyes of the court when they condemned him to die. But if he was the Martin who had a son named Frank who worked as a blacksmith in Goochland County, one wonders if perhaps he might have once wielded a hammer too, for skills were often clustered in families. In fact, Solomon, like

Gabriel, also toiled at the forge. This brother took the scythe blades delivered to him by committed insurgents and refashioned each one into two cutlasses to which Gabriel fitted handles. He served the conspiracy as its treasurer, apparently holding and doling out the contributions collected for the purchase of powder and the liquor that lubricated recruiting.[20]

A third man at Prosser's observed Gabriel's gatherings, heard his conversations at the blacksmith's shop where he likely worked, and sometimes accompanied Gabriel about the neighborhood. Reported to be eighteen years old, his name was Ben and he appears in the record as Prosser's Ben, but his relationship to Gabriel and his brothers is unknown. One press account claimed he voluntarily surrendered, but a witness stated he was "taken up," an eighteenth-century term for capturing someone or something. He apparently was never charged, for he was certainly never tried and no pardon was ever issued in his name. But whether voluntarily or under another euphemism of the age called "close examination," Ben quickly "made some disclosures," an act which became known to others like Gilbert and Ben Woolfolk even before they were arrested. He served as the most frequent state witness, was especially important for the early Henrico trials, and was later freed by Prosser, but only after some Richmond residents contributed enough money to reimburse a less grateful Prosser for his freedom.[21]

The details of the plan as originally envisioned by Sam Byrd Jr., if his claim to authorship is authentic, are not known. They probably changed some during the course of the often intense discussions held among the chief plotters and while the recruiting proceeded during the summer, a process that saw Gabriel emerge as the chief tactician and general. In any event, the basic scheme was likely in place from the start: attack and take Richmond as the means to destroy slavery. In the past, the absence of any significant urban centers in Virginia may have diminished the idea of a focused attack on the institution by a large number of rebels, but by 1800 Richmond proved a tempting target. Its population had swollen in sixteen years from about 1,300 residents in 1784 to just over 5,700 in 1800. Forty percent of the capital's inhabitants were enslaved in 1800, another 10 percent were free people of color. Although not large by contemporary standards, Richmond housed flour mills, tobacco warehouses, a nearly completed and just-opened state penitentiary, the beginnings of a state armory, a powder magazine, and the capitol and the offices of state government, as well as the usual array of shops, taverns and, of course, homes. To seize if not destroy them might deal a death blow to Virginia slavery, or at least provide the bargaining chips for the freedom of those who rose in rebellion. The example of St. Domingue, joined with the published news of slave uprisings or conspiracies during the previous decade, which often recounted strategies where towns were the focus of attack, heightened awareness by both whites and blacks of the strategic importance and vulnerability of urban centers. From the neighborhood of the Brook, Richmond seemed to sit close enough to strike.[22]

By late July or early August, the conspirators had hammered out the details of their attack. In the dead of night a contingent of men (one witness set the group at fifty) would slip into Rocketts, the lower or eastern riverside extent of the town. They knew the warehouses and mostly small wooden homes and stores that predominated in the neighborhood could easily be set aflame. A fire in Shockoe bottom in January 1787 had destroyed Byrd's Warehouse and about forty or fifty houses in three hours' time, and dangerously threatened the offices of the state government, which had not yet climbed the hill. More recently, on the morning of 22 November 1798, a fire had swept through ten wooden houses and even destroyed a brick structure, although citizens managed to save two other brick buildings which had also started to burn. Only massive efforts had kept the other side of the street from igniting as well. Near the time of this fire, Gilbert, who then worked at John Young's in Caroline, had talked with a slave whose owner lived near White Chimneys. Brutus, or Julius, perhaps a man who could have had more than one master and received more than one name, had been hired to either William or John Foushee in Richmond and had run away from him, apparently to lurk about Caroline, close to home. He told Gilbert about a plot involving several enslaved men, including himself, to torch Richmond for the plunder they might gain. When news of the 1798 conflagration soon arrived, slaves like Gilbert linked this fire, perhaps mistakenly, to Brutus's reported scheme. Among the sufferers was Charles Purcell, a silversmith, who lost his house, almost his wife, and perhaps his stock. Either upon hearing of Gilbert's statement about the fire, or more likely if it figured in the trial of Brutus in Richmond on 25 September 1800, Callender and others concluded the slaves had been responsible.[23]

Fire has always been one of the weapons of the weak, and none of this was lost on the conspirators. This part of the plot might have originated with Armistead, a slave of William Galt of Richmond, who suggested to

George Smith and Gilbert that the wooden houses "at the other end of town," presumably Rocketts, should be set on fire, leaving the brick buildings as their own. But at that point George disagreed, arguing that they would need all the houses for themselves. By August, however, a consensus had been reached to start the attack by creating the diversion of burning the lower part of the town.[24]

As in the case of earlier Richmond fires, the conspirators expected a massive response from Richmond's male citizens to put out the blaze. If accidental fires produced such panic and destruction, they could imagine what the embers or flint and steel of fifty purposeful men could ignite. As most of Richmond's nearly one thousand adult white men scrambled toward the lower part of town to attack the flames, the core contingent of several hundred insurrectionists would move in from the Brook, overwhelm the few guards at the penitentiary or the capitol where some of the state's arms were stored, seize the magazine, and capture, if not kill, Governor James Monroe. Now more fully armed, they would destroy the exhausted firefighters as they returned to their homes. In addition, the plotters anticipated reinforcements would come into the town from the Manchester side of the river, some of them expected from as far away as Petersburg. If this strategy failed, they mentioned vague plans about redeploying toward Hanover Town or lower down the peninsula to Yorktown, where they would make their stand against the state's forces that would surely be raised against them.[25]

Over the summer months, this cadre of conspirators worked individually and in concert with each other to recruit the phalanx of insurgents needed to carry out their plan. They also had to find ways to arm them and to keep the conspiracy from being discovered. The longer they waited to attack, the better their chances of gathering weapons and men. But the longer they took, the greater the likelihood that the conspiracy would be revealed as word of the plot seeped beyond their most trustworthy recruits. But they decided to risk their lives for the freedom they calculated they would gain.

2 } Are You a True Man?

For three or four months, the cell of conspirators built and spread their plot around the Brook and up and down the Road. They gathered recruits; pilfered tools to be reshaped into weapons; pooled their monies, probably gathered from tips, market sales, and found and stolen coins; and purchased liquor for recruiting and powder for guns. And they did this without attracting the attention of private citizens or public authorities. Only a few records hint at when specific meetings, trips, and conversations took place. Even when the talk turned earnest remains unknown. The criminal informations filed by the Commonwealth's attorney for Henrico County generally charged defendants with conducting illegal conversations between 1 July and 1 September, a range of dates apparently intended to adequately bracket the activities of the conspirators. But it was surely underway before then. Ben Woolfolk was not among the very first to be recruited, and he claimed to have been approached "sometime last spring." Citing his testimony at the trial of George Smith, one newspaper reported that Woolfolk had been recruited by Smith about 1 July, but this was likely a repeating of the first date listed in the criminal information. Woolfolk's recorded testimony at the trial certainly contained no such claim. Assuming it was part of Gabriel's plot, the charge against a Louisa County plotter named Ben listed his criminal collusion as having taken place on 16 June 1800, a date so specific that there must have been some evidence for it. If so, it indicates the plan had matured enough to have been spread into a nearby county two weeks before the first date appearing in the Henrico informations. Hence, it is most probable that the transformation from loose talk to a serious undertaking began in late April or early May. However, contrary to later accounts which relied on an abstract of a misdated letter in a nineteenth-century calendar of Jefferson's correspondence, the government of Virginia would remain ignorant of any of this until after the first week of August. As James Thomson Callender observed, the plot had "been kept with incredible secrecy for several months."[1]

No matter when it began, to wrest their freedom from the white population required a sizable force. The plan needed men, especially physically able ones. It also demanded arms, secrecy, and a credible probability of success, perhaps the latter more than anything else when it came to recruitment. But these challenges were all intertwined. Without the sense of success, few would join, the risks of making or stealing weapons and tools would not be taken, and keeping the conspiracy a secret would be less important. The scheme would be dismissed as just more of the bravado of gathered men sometimes overheard by other slaves and whites alike, but with little expectation of implementation. Thus, recruiting required discretion and discernment. Enough details had to be revealed to engage attention and raise the hope of success, but not so many as to threaten the plot's undertaking, especially if a potential insurgent rejected the solicitation, or joined but then got cold feet. Betrayal was highly possible; its cost deadly. In this regard, it was especially important to keep secure until the last moment the actual day the uprising would begin, for as long as it remained unknown or undetermined, the half-hearted would be less likely to reveal the plot. Indeed, it appears that the decision when to launch the attack on Richmond was the last major tactical issue the group confronted, and one reached with some disagreement. Clearly, recruitment could not be a blanket endeavor, but required carefully contacting men whose judgment and connections could lead to other like-minded and able individuals. At the same time, finding men in sufficient numbers would force these solicitations beyond the Brook and the net of local connections, a central concern of this study.[2]

James Sidbury keenly observed that the records from the trials of the conspirators—the core sources containing the details of the conspiracy—reveal more about recruitment than about the plotters' intentions. After all, to "consult, advise, or conspire to rebel, or make insurrection" was a felony, and was all the state had to prove to the unanimous satisfaction of the sitting justices in order to find a defendant guilty of "conspiracy and rebellion." Hence, the trial records recount gatherings, reveal who recruited whom, and hint at what was said to get a man to join. Recognizing these records for what they are helps to avoid what Winthrop Jordan warned against: interpreting a "specific slave conspiracy as part of a trend or movement more of our making than of the slaves involved." Consequently, to attribute a specific political ideology to the plotters, as Douglas Egerton does when he ascribes to Gabriel an artisan republicanism, or to claim Gabriel believed he could expect the support of Virginia's "redoubtable democrats," goes beyond the evidence and reveals more a historian's vision than Gabriel's. Moreover, realizing that the testimonies and confessions are foremost records of recruitment accounts not only for the content of much of the testimony but for some of the anomalies in it as well. For example, some recruits expected that they would kill all white people without exception, while others sifted out from their intended targets the ones thought more friendly to liberty or to themselves. Is it possible that different scenarios were presented to different individuals? Or that, in order to secure their commitment to this extraordinarily dangerous undertaking, potential recruits were encouraged to interpret in their own way phrases like "conquer the white people and possess ourselves of their property"? The records suggest as much.[3]

The process of winning men willing to put their lives at terrible risk was a delicate one, and, not surprisingly, one that first spread among the kin and close acquaintances of the core collaborators. Gabriel, for example, enlisted his brother Solomon, and did so in a direct manner. In response to a series of questions from Solomon about goals, tactics, leadership, and contingencies, Gabriel stated that the forces to be raised would "conquer the white people," leaving the men who vanquished them with their property. The tactic would be to attack in the night; the recruits led by a man "from Caroline" who had been at the siege at Yorktown during the War for Independence. Gabriel even named Jack Bowler as the "head of the Plan." A bond of trust obviously existed between the two brothers for Gabriel to spread the details so openly before Solomon.[4]

In efforts to enlist those beyond blood ties, recruiters took a less-direct approach. Hence, when George Smith first solicited his neighbor Ben Woolfolk about the conspiracy, he "asked if he would join a free-mason Society." Woolfolk rejected his query with the curt response that "all free mason's would go to hell." Smith clarified his question by saying that it was actually "a society to fight the white People for their freedom." Hearing this, Woolfolk said he would give the invitation some thought. Later that week, Woolfolk met with Smith and Sam Byrd, and about a week or ten days after the initial query, engaged again in intense discussions about the plot when George Smith reappeared accompanied by Sam Byrd and Jack Bowler. By that time, Woolfolk had joined, and apparently soon began to serve as a recruiter himself. Not surprisingly, Woolfolk used a similar approach when he first talked to Abraham, a slave of Thomas Burton who lived near the Brook: he invited him to join "his Society." Abraham dismissed the scheme as another of Woolfolk's "usual folly," an indication that he knew the recruiter well enough to be skeptical about any proposal from him. Woolfolk protested that he was serious and revealed that the group "was a combination to kill the white People." Once he understood the purpose, and perhaps that it was not "his" (Woolfolk's), Abraham joined, promising to keep the conspiracy secret and pledging to be ready when contacted again. The evidence does not indicate that he asked for time to ponder the proposal, or that he required further persuasion. Woolfolk may have been an effective missionary for the cause, but since no other witnesses appeared against him at his trial, Abraham may have had no further involvement with the conspirators. Indeed, his ready conversion may have been his way of quickly getting rid of Woolfolk. At the same time, he apparently kept his pledge of secrecy. More deliberate was the response of Michael, a slave of Judith Owen. He was approached directly by Gabriel to join in the cause, but his initial response was to demur until he "would see the business progress well." Gabriel later made him a sword, which Michael said he would be ready to deploy by the time the uprising was to begin, a decision either influenced or bolstered by the weapon itself.[5] Clearly, men evaluated their chances as they responded to recruiters, and sized up each other.

The importance of personal connections for the initial contact further emerges from the evidence of the recruitment of Jacob, a slave of Thomas Woodfin, whose place was closer to the mouth of the Brook. He joined a gathering at a schoolhouse at the invitation of a man named Ben, who, if Prosser's Ben, lived closer to him than Ben Woolfolk. The man who recruited him, Jacob explained, had "mentioned to him the war against the White People." He came to the gathering to learn more, but felt "great concern" when his recruiting officer failed to appear. Woolfolk tried to assuage his worries and then "communicated the plan to him." However, the edgy Jacob dismissed Woolfolk's overtures by saying he had already gathered as much from the absent recruiter. Perhaps he was disappointed not to learn more, or maybe Woolfolk's approach was off-putting. Whatever the reason, Jacob's response flustered Woolfolk, who insulted the recruit by observing "that he looked so poor and weakly" he doubted he could kill a man. A now more irritated Jacob warned Woolfolk not "to take me by my looks," and boasted, "I can and will kill a white man as free as eat." In an additional retort, he declared that he had already joined "to fight in the war against the White people," anyway. More careful was the approach of Martin toward Billy, possibly both slaves of Roger Gregory. Martin dropped that he had news that "the boys on the Brook were going to fight the white people." He told him he had joined and invited Billy to enlist. Billy rejected the overture and urged him not to get involved. He then asked Martin which men were engaged, but Martin refused to tell him, adding "he would know in time." The obverse reveals a similar caution. Watt approached Ben, both men held by Prosser, and asked about "the intended insurrection of the Negroes." Ben pled ignorance, but Watt insisted that the young man knew of it because he was "so frequently in the company of Gabriel with whom the plan was said to originate." Ben replied that if he wanted to know something he should ask Gabriel himself. Watt explained that some "enmity" separated the two men and he could do so only with reluctance. Since Ben testified that he knew of the differences between the two men at the time, he may have believed that revealing the plot to Watt entailed too great a risk. Watt later claimed to have subsequently talked with Gabriel, promising to recruit men, and even to provide some gunpowder and lead to the cause.[6]

Not enough able or trusted men lived in and about the Brook to carry the plan to completion, so the plot had to be extended geographically. Given the obvious importance of personal connections, the directions the sinews of conspiracy were pulled followed the conspirators' lines of contacts beyond their neighborhood. Importantly, the practice of hiring slaves lengthened a man's string of friends and acquaintances. Hired slaves in rural areas were mostly male and usually worked for a term of a year, traditionally from New Year's Day to Christmas. During the hire, if the distance was not too great, occasional visits home were not unusual. In addition, the splitting of families through sale; the parting of spouses, children, and acquaintances at the death of an owner; or the giving of slaves at the marriage or coming-of-age of an owner's children, stretched but did not always break the ties of kin and friends. Visits among these families also occurred, particularly late on Saturdays and on Sundays. The conspirators utilized these trips and connections to advantage.[7]

Sam Byrd Jr. revealed to Gilbert how important kin were for his recruiting efforts beyond the Brook. He relied upon the efforts of his free father in Hanover Town on the Pamunkey River border with King William County, and utilized two uncles, apparently Reuben and Jesse Byrd, to find recruits in Petersburg. The records make no mention of acquaintances among the enlistees he claimed to have obtained near the Point of Fork up the James River or in Charlottesville, but he may have had them there too. Watt, who had been at odds with Gabriel, felt confident he could raise nearly a dozen and a half men because he had numerous sons "up the Country," probably in Goochland County, where he focused and expected recruiting success. Martin's son Frank may have also been an agent enlisting men in the same county, which adjoined Henrico on the west. Michael, a slave of Thomas Goode of Chesterfield County, was married to a woman at Joseph Mosby's in the Brook neighborhood. On his trips to visit his wife, he took the Brook Road through the center of the conspiracy. He joined and became a leader of the men recruited on the south side of the James. His work may have made it easier for George Smith to claim to have found fifty willing insurgents in Manchester. Likewise, Gilbert had been hired in Caroline County in previous years, which put him in contact with other Caroline conspirators. William, or Billy, one of the plot's emissaries to Caroline, was, like Gilbert, a slave of William Young's. He may or may not have been hired in Caroline, but William Young had purchased the bulk of his property in Henrico from John and Mary Young of Caroline, the same couple Gilbert had worked for in past years. Ben Woolfolk belonged to Paul Graham, then listed in Hanover, but also stated as of Caroline County, both areas visited by Woolfolk. Graham, in turn, was related to the Thilman and Woolfolk families, who also had slaves involved in the plot. Given the interwoven texture of Virginia's slave society created by the passing, sharing, financial bonding, visiting, and sales of slaves, this should not come as a surprise. The connections among masters contributed to those among their slaves, and the relationships created by slaves, also affected, or could influence, the decisions made by owners about sales, hires, and inheritances. This was part of Virginia's society, black and white.[8]

The principal plotters spread their conspiracy not unlike some successful modern cosmetic or vitamin marketing schemes. Personal contacts were asked to recruit their own segment of the insurrection and, if they were thought able, to command them. Michael, the man from Chesterfield discussed above, provides one example, Thornton another. Thornton worked as a blacksmith at Hanover Court House and belonged to Paul Thilman of Hanover, who had recently added a tavern to his enterprises there, and who also served as the county jailer. Two other slaves in Thilman's employ, Dick and Randolph, actually attended at least one of the meetings held at Young's in Henrico, but Thornton was likely recruited by William, who made his way up the road from the Brook toward Caroline and succeeded in securing "several Negroes up there who were named by him to enlist men." Like Prosser's blacksmith shop in Henrico, Thilman's forge at Hanover may have been a site for recruiting and discussing the conspiracy while Thornton cut and hammered scythes into swords. By the time the attack was to commence, Thornton claimed a following of twenty or thirty men, gathered from his comrades in Thilman's gang and out of the men on the quarters of Charles Carter, Thomas Nelson, William Penn, and the estate of Samuel Gist. They worked not far from the road coming from the Brook, or the area surrounding Littlepage's Bridge, and were likely part of a neighborhood not unlike the Brook. Thornton figured himself a general, but would serve as a colonel "upon this occasion," and he confidently believed he could "make his men obey him." Indeed, given the skill and physical prowess reflected in a slave man's price, he probably could. He joined Gabriel, Solomon, and Price's James as the four plotters most highly valued by any court of the slaves convicted for the plot, each of them priced at $500.[9]

Similarly, John, a slave of Mary Jones of Hanover, who hired him to John Harvie, the current Henrico sheriff and one of the contractors at the state penitentiary in Richmond, diligently recruited among the men with whom he worked. When he was able to return to Hanover, he intended to continue these efforts up in Caroline County, where he likely had more ties. He was to be a captain of the men he enlisted, as was Ned, a slave of Ann Parsons, the widow of Woodson and the daughter of John Mosby Sr., who recruited among those he called the "Warehouse boys" in Richmond. He had purchased a sword from Wilshire, a slave of Mosby's grandson, Benjamin Mosby. Walking with Gabriel and carrying a stick, he demonstrated his skill with his sword by flourishing his wooden proxy. The men agreed he should be a captain, but probably less for his swordsmanship than for the men he was gathering into the conspiracy. The promise of military rank rewarded and elicited enlistments.[10]

Indeed, offering military rank fostered recruiting, but it could prove to be a difficult issue, because some thought more highly of themselves than the conspiracy's leaders did. Charles wanted to be a captain, but Gabriel saw him as nothing more than a sergeant. The disappointed man "cursed mightily about it" but to no avail, until he told Gabriel of the existence of twenty-nine stand of militia guns kept at his master Roger Gregory's tavern. Gabriel agreed to promote Charles upon the promise of taking him to the arms, and maybe finding more, a key part in the development of the insurrection. Similarly, a slave of John Mosby Sr., named Will, looked forward to killing Mosby and being a captain of infantry, a post that may have been tentatively held out to him. However, Gabriel rejected his captaincy because of his diminutive size, but made him more physically formidable and elevated his spirits by placing him in the cavalry. Assuaged, Will focused on getting Mosby's sorrel horse to ride to the mustering. Even Gilbert, one of the central planners, according to Gabriel, sought to be a captain but was rejected because he stuttered. He did not object at the time, apparently because of his deep commitment to the larger cause, but he also identified a lot of the plotters before he went to the gallows.[11]

Sometimes the conspirators stumbled in finding recruiters. Jack Gabriel, another slave at Charles Carter's North Wales quarter, had rounded up several men, enough to be considered a captain of a company. But it must have been a discouraging revelation when he informed Woolfolk a couple of weeks before the intended rendezvous, that he would only come "if he was able to travel." If he couldn't, he would send his men under the command of John Fells, another slave of Carter's. His notice became more worrisome after Woolfolk talked to Fells, who was to be a colonel, "upon that occasion." Fells told the emissary from the Brook that if the men he had enlisted would not come with him, "he would get a Horse & ride down himself." A promised or self-ascribed rank did not carry much weight if the man himself were not weighty, particularly when men's lives were at stake.[12]

The records of recruitment also suggest what was or might have been said to draw men into the conspiracy, and what they made of the chance. Obviously, the grand objective was gaining freedom. To Jack Bowler it was "a fight for our liberty," to George Smith a fight "for their freedom," and to Sam Byrd Jr., a plan for "freeing the Negroes from slavery." Beyond freedom were other rewards. Gabriel convinced his brother Solomon to join so that they could also "possess ourselves of their [the white people's] property." Many looked forward to the houses they would occupy in Richmond, and some expected a share of the money in the state treasury when it fell into their hands. While some talked in broad terms, of "taking the Country," for example, others had more personal goals. Billy itched to kill Claiborne Lipscombe for the abuse he had suffered at his hand. Lewis anticipated cutting off the heads of Dabney and Lucy Burton Williamson and getting their money. He then expected to ride Williamson's horse, Cumberland, into Richmond, where it would be handed off in favor of one he coveted that belonged to Henry Shore.[13]

To gain their freedom required that they "conquer the white people," in the words of Gabriel. Grasping what this entailed varied among the recruits and likely reflected part of the recruiting process. For the men along the Brook, it would start with the murders of Prosser, Mosby, and Johnson, but the attack would then spread to "all the White neighbors." Once gathered, the columns were to move quietly into Richmond, where the "inhabitants were to be mas[s]acred save those who beg[g]ed for quarters and agreed to serve as Soldiers with them." In one account, Gabriel is quoted as admonishing a general gathering at Young's spring that "we must slay them as we go." Another heard him say that "they would slay the white males from the cradle upwards, but the females of all ages were to be spared." Other reports, probably reflecting the numerous and varied conversations over the course of the summer, contained other caveats to the general massacre of whites. Prosser's Ben testified at the trial of Gabriel that his leader "expected the poor white people would also join him," and in his confession, Ben Woolfolk narrowed the general exclusion from murder of all white females to only those "poor white women who had no slaves." In the same confession, Woolfolk stated, "As far as I understand all the Whites were to be massacred except the Quakers, the Methodists and the French men," because the former two "were conceived to be friendly to liberty," and because the French were believed to be potential allies, given the hostilities that existed between the two nations—despite, apparently, the struggle against the colonial power in St. Domingue. Indeed, the conspirators fed on a rumor of a French army having invaded Virginia at South Quay.[14]

The exemption of some whites even reflected what had to be said to gain recruits. Quakers lived in the midst of the recruiting areas of the insurgents. They were numerous in Hanover County, where Woolfolk spent part of his recruiting efforts, and intertwined in the families of Henrico, though more heavily in the lower part of the county. Most likely, someone had a relative or an acquaintance who had been freed by a Quaker or who knew of the efforts of the Society of Friends to expel slave-owning members and support the legal suits of those who were illegally held in slavery. Similarly, Methodists took a stand in favor of emancipation after the Revolution. At their General Conference meeting in Baltimore just that May, they had urged their members to petition their state legislatures for the gradual emancipation of the slaves in their respective states. In addition, several freed people of color were living testimony to the actions its members had taken. Thus, some potential recruits may have hesitated at the suggestion of a general massacre of whites as an essential part of the plot, so the pitch may have been modified to overcome their reluctance. Interestingly, none mentioned sparing any artisans. Put directly, recruits were likely told—or heard—what they needed to hear.[15]

Suggestions that some whites would be spared reflected the concerns of some, but the most common statements as to intent contained no exceptions. Indeed, other than Woolfolk's testimony, none of the defendants mentioned sparing Quakers or Methodists, and only one additional witness among the decidedly small number of deponents, Prosser's Ben, seconded Woolfolk's exempting of French people. Instead, most testimony indicated the plot's purpose was "to fight the white people," or was "a combination to kill the white people," or "a war against the white people," or a plot "for the purpose of murdering the White Citizens," or "to kill every body," or "to slay as they went," or "to kill or be killed." Besides Lewis's desire to decapitate, King claimed he could "slay white people like sheep," while the brothers Isham and George were ready to "wade to our knees in Blood sooner than fail in the attempt." These visceral proclamations precluded any discussion of limitations on who would be killed. No evidence suggests that anyone was delegated to mark the doors of whites who were to be passed over.[16]

If some recruits narrowed the range of intended victims, some recruiters expanded the threat of death to those who would not join. Mary Jones's John, for example, told John Williamson's Daniel that "all Negroes who did not join in the insurrection would, and should be put to

Death indiscriminately," perhaps a bitter outburst after Daniel had declined his invitation to an enlistment barbecue. Isaac, a slave of William Burton, posited the same policy to another Burton slave named Daniel, but the witness also alleged that Isaac was in his cups when he made his threat. However, Mosby's Will was deadly sober when he claimed "that all the blacks who did not join would be put to death," according to John Holeman's Tobey. Still, since Toby does not seem to have been otherwise implicated in the plot, this conversation could reflect the frustration of a failed attempt at recruiting too. No trial evidence supports the often-embroidering Callender's particular report that wives of the conspirators who refused to join their husbands after the plundering of Richmond would be killed, though that may have been a rumor bandied about among whites, or possibly something Callender heard from his jailmates.[17]

These general threats may have silenced the unconverted, and in one instance may have become specific. When Thornton was pitching the plot to men around Littlepage's Bridge, Bristol, a slave of Charles Carter, and Primus, a slave of William Overton of Hanover, urged him to stop and threatened to "inform the white people" if he did not. They left, but some men chased them down, "with an intention of putting them to death." The two men gained release after convincing their pursuers they had no desire to reveal the plot.[18]

To succeed, the recruits needed confidence that the conspiracy could field and mount enough men to take Richmond. Gabriel knew he did not need thousands of men to put the plan into execution, though he would need that many to hold any gains. But to claim huge numbers in the presence of potential converts could contribute to the expectation of victory and entice the enlistment of the very men the conspiracy did need to carry the attack. Consequently, what were certainly inflated numbers of reputed or expected recruits floated through the conspirators' conversations. Prosser's Ben testified at the trial of Solomon, Gabriel's brother, that one thousand men *were* to be recruited in Richmond, six hundred from western Hanover near Ground Squirrel Bridge, and four hundred from Goochland. He claimed two hundred of an expected four hundred mounted men already had been "appointed." At Gabriel's trial, the same witness stated that Gabriel "said he had nearly 10,000 men. . . . 1000 in Richmond, about 600 in Caroline and nearly 500 at the coal pits, besides others at different places." As Ben noted, these were "nearly all the Negroes in town," which included some four hundred horsemen, the same figure Ben used in his previous testimony, but when offered then, a group that seemed distinct from the Richmond recruits. Whatever the differences in his testimony, there is little hard evidence those goals were met. Still, large numbers appeared in the spiels of other recruiters. Mosby's Will, while attempting to recruit a man he had cornered, claimed five thousand insurgents had committed. Ben Woolfolk told Gabriel he had found six hundred in Caroline, probably the basis of the figure reported above, while Sam Byrd Jr. thought he had around five hundred scattered about the many places he had visited. Other combined totals were lower. Perhaps the figure the core group hoped to garner was revealed by the two individuals closest to Gabriel. On the day scheduled for the uprising, Gabriel's brother Solomon told Pharoah, one of the two Sheppard slaves who betrayed the conspiracy, that he expected a thousand men that night and needed to finish four swords by then. Nanny, the wife of Gabriel, also counted on one thousand men to assemble on the night of 30 August. If Gabriel would have had that many, he would have been pleased.[19]

A close reading of the testimony and confessions suggests that Gabriel and his co-conspirators used, and may have even been caught up in, their own exaggerations. While it appears that they inflated numbers to increase the sense of the scale of the conspiracy in order to gain more followers, recruiters may have overstated their accomplishments to reinforce their position in the conspiracy. Some referred to lists of names, but they were seldom produced as evidence of their numbers. Nonetheless, lists did exist, although they were likely the first things thrown into the fire when the plot collapsed. When Ben Woolfolk was first recruited, Sam Byrd Jr. pulled out "his list of men," but it only had four names on it, or at least four that he remembered, and all were men of the Brook. It was early in the plot too, which may explain its stubby length. Prosser's Ben observed Gabriel and Solomon with lists "of the Names of the Conspirators," but they were never displayed outside of the inner circle and likely did not contain the names of all who had joined. Rather, it is far more likely that they noted the names of key recruiters and the numerical reports of their labors: the work of individuals like Thornton, or Michael, or George Smith, for example. Yet other rolls which were supposedly in existence were never produced. At some time, Sam Byrd Jr., the plot's self-proclaimed progenitor, told Gilbert to go to Richmond and meet a free black man named Matt Scott who was to show him a tally of his recruits. When Gilbert found him and asked to see it, Scott put him off, saying "he would let him see the list at some other time," but Gilbert said he "never saw the list." If he had, it may or may not have substantiated Scott's claim to have gained one hundred men for the cause. One wonders if Scott had bragged of his success and Byrd wanted to verify the claim.[20]

Indeed, one might question if Byrd worried about Scott's claims because of his own reporting practices. Ben Woolfolk twice stated that Byrd was asked how many men he had, once at Young's spring "in July last," the other time on "the day of the sermon at my house [Young's] which was about three weeks before the rising was to take place"—that is, on 10 August. On both occasions, Byrd claimed five hundred recruits but did not produce his list as proof, only referring to it. If Byrd twice claimed this amount, no additions had been made in over two weeks. But since Woolfolk testified that the five hundred troops Byrd had purportedly raised by July were to be turned over to Gabriel's command and the elevation of Gabriel to the generalship appears to have been decided later, Woolfolk may have misdated his statement. The claim may have been made only once, on Sunday, 10 August. If so, it was George Smith who asked him how many men he had. When Sam Byrd did not produce his list, Woolfolk reported that Smith wanted to delay the attack. Was this because Smith doubted that Byrd really had that many subscribers? Did he sense that promised recruits were added to actual enlistments in the claims being made? Without evidence of real recruits, did Smith fear they were rushing toward a date without enough men actually in hand? It is interesting that the assertions of large numbers of enrollees were often from places distant from the Brook, perhaps from local recruiters one did not know how far to trust in their reporting. Did George Smith sense this too?[21]

Gabriel and the inner circle used other tactics to enlist men, tactics that built upon a different kind of deception. At Young's spring, where one if not more key meetings were held, Gabriel invited the men willing to join the cause to stand up, while telling the uncommitted to sit down or remain seated on the ground. Price's John, who repeatedly testified about one of these gatherings, named the individuals that stood up and enlisted with Gabriel, such as Frank, Sam Graham, Sawney, Laddis, and perhaps Peter. He apparently did not recognize Sam Byrd Jr., Martin, George Smith, and Gilbert as central players in the plot when he described them standing to join Gabriel. They too stepped forward and pledged their allegiance to Gabriel and the plot, even though they were already deeply involved, leading James Sidbury to conclude they were "planted . . . in the crowd to lead the way." If they were, it comports with the tactic of inflating the number of recruits in order to build the enlistments needed to take Richmond.[22]

As the recruiting spread geographically and increased numerically, the danger of losing control and the difficulty of keeping the plot secret rose too. Sam Byrd Jr. had found followers upcountry who wanted to target the state arsenal sitting at the Point of Fork on the James River near the border between Fluvanna and Goochland Counties, where Virginia partly stored and refurbished militia weapons. Indeed, some of them sent word down by "a black man who carries the mail to Charlottesville" to delay the attack on Richmond until they took the arsenal and could march down as an armed column to assist them. George Smith and Sam Byrd rejected the proposal. Later, Gabriel did not specifically mention followers from that area in his public calculations of his forces—perhaps he wondered about Byrd's claims too—and no further mention of an attack on the upstream arsenal was made by a conspirator. Maybe the rebuff deflated the interest or dissipated the support of any plotters near the arsenal. Or perhaps this indicates that those on the periphery of the plot could be as unsure of the group at the core as the latter were of them. Lives were at stake, and trust became fragile stretched over long distances and through men who more and more were strangers, not neighbors or connections.[23]

Sustaining the secrecy needed for success also became a greater potential problem as time passed and recruiting spread. With the need to gather recruits beyond the periphery of acquaintances, or even from among those whom one did not completely trust, solemn promises were extracted not to reveal the plot. Thus, Ben Woolfolk, whose relationship with Abraham was not completely congenial, demanded that Abraham "keep the business secret and not divulge [it] to a woman." Similarly, when Woolfolk ran into King in Richmond—the slave of the state's attorney general, Philip Norborne Nicholas, and once the slave of Governor Robert Brooke—the men first joined in "an indifferent conversation." King, perhaps not at his steadiest, asked, "Do you not know me, my name is King, commonly called Governor's King." Woolfolk replied, he "did not but I have often heard my brother speak of you." King confirmed he knew Woolfolk's brother "very well." About this time, Nicholas arrived looking for King, who had been sent to (Edmund?) Randolph's to be his waiter at dinner, and re-dispatched him on his original task. Some short time later,

King returned muttering, "his language and deportment" enticing Woolfolk into approaching him about the conspiracy. "Are you a true man?" he asked. King confirmed he was. "Can you keep a proper or important secret?" King said yes. Then Woolfolk told him, "The negroes are about to rise and fight the white people for our freedom." King lit up: "I never was so glad to hear anything in my life . . . and will be ready to join them at any moment; I could slay the white people like sheep." Woolfolk then "enjoined him to keep it a profound secret . . . [and] not to mention it to or in the presence of any woman." But he then encouraged him to enlist "any sound or truehearted men," but only if he "knew them well first." He later said he took King to be sober at the time.[24]

Woolfolk's testimony provides the only statements about excluding women from the plot. Both James Sidbury and Douglas Egerton have noted the "maleness" of the enterprise and have suggested that the different spheres of men and women under slavery that had emerged, or were even West African cultural antecedents, were reasons for the exclusiveness of their Society. It may also have been seen by these men as a pragmatic reality. It was a female house slave who warned William Mosby that the washed-out plot had only been postponed. Another woman hurried to tell an Albemarle County master of four armed men who asked the way to Columbia, near Point of Fork. Isham's wife opposed his attendance at a gathering, although it is not known if she understood the proselytizing that went on there. And in February 1801, it was a woman in Manchester who warned her master about overheard whispers, suggesting the embers of rebellion had not been fully quenched in the bloody crushing of the conspiracy. At the same time, Gabriel's wife Nanny seemed fully aware and supportive of the enterprise. Obviously, different individuals, men and women, pondered the potential for success and the consequences of failure for themselves, their families, connections, and neighborhood, and reached their own conclusions.[25]

The insurrectionists knew that their war required leaders with a strategy and military acumen. "Who was at the head of the Plan?" Solomon queried Gabriel when he first approached him about the plot. His brother named Jack Bowler. "I asked him if Jack knew anything about carrying on War." Gabriel admitted Bowler did not. Solomon then asked "who he was going to employ." The conspirator said, "a Man from Caroline who was at the Siege of York-Town," who would lead the assembled recruits from the Brook into Richmond. After the town fell, was fortified, and after "exercising [training] the Soldiers the command was to be resigned to Gabriel," all within one day. Interestingly, the testimony of Prosser's Ben at the trial of Gabriel paralleled Gabriel's statement to Solomon, except Gabriel was always the one in charge.[26]

Ben mentioned no man with military experience from Caroline. Neither did John, who informed Daniel that Gabriel and Solomon stood "at the head of the business," and who portrayed himself as a recruiter in Caroline. Nor was the man ever mentioned in the evidence against William or Ben Woolfolk, both emissaries to Caroline. However, after being found guilty, in a private confession Gilbert stuttered out the name of a white man in Caroline that Richmond Alderman John Foster recorded as Charles Quersey, a Frenchman, who "frequently advised him & several other Negroes, to rise and kill the White People." But the encouragement had been given "three or four years" before, and Gilbert hadn't seen him since, although others told him that Quersey was "very active . . . in this late business." Gilbert was probably implicating Charles Dequasay, Dequazer, or Dequesa, depending on the year of the Caroline tax list. He had arrived in the county by 1784, but had left it by 1797, moving to an unspecified location in the upper end of Hanover. He last appeared on the Hanover tax rolls in 1799 and was not re-enrolled on either Henrico or Caroline tax records. With the exception of one year, he owned or held one or more slaves in Caroline between 1789 and 1796. Gilbert also mentioned that Quersey had lived with Francis Corbin at Reedy Mills. In 1798, Francis Corbin informed George Washington that he had left Middlesex County two years earlier for a healthier climate at the "Reeds," lands he had long held and which probably included a mill at Reedy Mills. Thus, Gilbert's estimate of Corbin's contact with Quersey would most probably have been in 1796. Corbin's closest post office was White Chimneys on the Road from the Brook, and thus within the reach of the conspiracy. But if Quersey ever worked for Corbin, it did not last long once the Middlesex planter relocated to Caroline, and Corbin may have provided a clue why. In 1798, Corbin solicited a regimental appointment from Washington as the federal military forces were expanded in the expectation of war with France. He confessed his lack of military experience, but noted: "Of one thing I can speak with confidence. I shall feel myself perfectly at home in fighting the French." Although Corbin did not gain his appointment, it is not likely Quersey returned from Hanover to Corbin's employ in 1800.[27]

If Bowler convinced Gabriel that an unnamed man from Caroline, perhaps but most likely not Quersey, was willing to provide the initial military command, he also told Prosser's Ben of two Frenchmen "who were the first instigators of the plot," but he did not and would not reveal their names. Similarly, it may have been from Jack Bowler, or perhaps secondhand from Prosser's Ben, that Gilbert learned of two Frenchmen who "have been very active in this Town" but whose names Gilbert "never heard" either. For whatever reason, slaves caught up in the conspiracy later named other slaves, but never the two elusive Frenchmen, leaving their identity solely in the hands of Bowler. This makes it appear as if their mention by Bowler to Prosser's Ben, and his informing Gabriel of the man who had been at Yorktown, may have been an effort in the early stages of the conspiracy to answer the question of military experience that others besides Solomon would raise. On the other hand, both of Prosser's slaves, Ben and Gilbert, both in the inner circle, were the only confederates to mention the two Frenchmen, so their reputed roles may have served a limited, even diminishing purpose in the recruiting process. For most followers, the melding of excitement, desire, and anger with men like Gabriel, Bowler, and Thornton may have been enough if the basic tactic was a surprise attack during which they would indiscriminately slay all.[28]

More important than the two Frenchmen for recruiting may have been the conspirators' use of the crisis in relations with France. Ample evidence existed of the warlike measures, actual naval conflict, and the expectation of real war with France in the months before the conspiracy took shape. Just as whites occasionally picked up black conversations, slaves certainly heard white ones, and the talk of war with France was roundly discussed in and about Richmond. Indeed, Ben Woolfolk explained that Frenchmen were to be spared because "they had understood that the French were at war with the Country for the money that was due them, and that an Army was landed at South Key which they hoped would assist them." This information came to Woolfolk, at least, from the well-traveled Sam Byrd Jr., who may have picked up the rumor in Richmond, Manchester, or Petersburg. Interestingly, during the first weekend in September, a group of slaves, one estimate numbered them at one hundred and fifty, allegedly gathered south of Suffolk in Nansemond County near the Norfolk County line. They remained there for several days, one report suggested, before dispersing only after they learned of the demise of the insurrection. Although it would be pure speculation, given the rumored French army's landing site, is it possible that they expected a rendezvous with this imagined force, "to do what those of Richmond were about to do?" South Quay was not that far away. Another said they departed to recruit more support. Had this become necessary after finding there was no French army to join them?[29]

If military experience and leadership raised questions for recruits, a more material one existed in arming them. As already noted, Solomon, Thornton, and Gabriel took the scythe blades brought to them and made them into swords. However, recruits were encouraged to find their own swords if possible. Jack Bowler reported he had made fifty spears, or pikes, by fixing bayonets on the end of sticks, and George Smith even claimed he would make crossbows. Martin ran bullets, as did Gabriel, from lead they had secured, some donated by Watt, another Prosser slave. Gabriel claimed to have worn out two pairs of bullet molds, and showed off nearly a peck of bullets, with more lead to be cast. Watt also presented Gabriel with about a pound of gunpowder, Jack Bowler gathered about six or seven pounds, and Gabriel obtained about ten more, purchased during trips to Richmond. Access to arms concerned several recruits, and even Jack Bowler queried Gabriel about them in his challenge to Gabriel's leadership. Williamson's Laddis wanted to know where they were going to get ammunition; Thilman's Dick asked after arms; and Ben Woolfolk had to promise John Fells they would be supplied. Gregory's Billy joined and said he would be a captain, "if Gabriel would find him arms." Gabriel promised, and Billy found six or seven recruits. Finding enough weapons became a more pressing issue as the summer passed, and is reflected in the promotion of the stripling Charles. As noted above, he became a captain because he could furnish some arms and promised more. The conspirators possessed at least six guns and a pistol by 30 August, with several dozen more waiting to be seized at Gregory's Tavern with Charles's direction that night.[30]

In the plan to attack Richmond, firearms were not essential in the assaults against the ill-guarded capitol, magazine, and penitentiary, but they would be crucial to kill the returning firefighters and hold their position in the capital. The plotters believed they could "rush through" the few men stationed at these state properties and seize the arms and munitions they guarded. But it was not yet clear that there would even be swords enough. Solomon later confessed he had made twelve. One witness said Gabriel claimed twelve dozen created, perhaps a number as inflated as the ranks of recruits. Clearly, adequately arming the forces remained a problem. On Friday, 8 August, at a barn raising at Prosser's, Jupiter, the slave of Nathaniel Wilkinson who suffered thirty-nine lashes for hog stealing at the Henrico Court the fall before, approached Gabriel. He reported that his efforts at finding followers in Richmond had gone well, and he asked Gabriel "how he came on in the Country." Gabriel responded that "he could make out some Arms, but not sufficient," a response that suggests that his biggest concern at the moment was arms more than men. His spirit must have risen when Jupiter revealed that "the man who kept the key would let them into the Capitol to take the Arms which were there." Gabriel had been going to Richmond on Sundays to acquire "ammunition" and to find where the arms were stashed. Now he could act. On Sunday morning, James obtained the key from Robert Cowley, unlocked the door of the capitol, and led Gabriel and Jupiter into the building. James was the slave of the clerk of the Virginia Court of Appeals and would have known Cowley well, for the elderly free black man was the Keeper of the Capitol and served as the doorman to the State Council. Once the slave of Peter Randolph, in 1785 Cowley had negotiated with Edmund Randolph for his purchase and emancipation. By 1800, the sixty-year-old-man was deeply trusted and performed many important tasks for the governor and council. Thus, James's and Cowley's paths probably crisscrossed as they went about their duties, private and public, among the courts and offices of government. As James, Gabriel, and Jupiter entered, the trio paused to invite Gilbert into the building, but he declined. Gabriel told him afterwards that he had "viewed the arms" and that James and Jupiter would have them ready on the night of the uprising. Ben Woolfolk recalled that Gabriel expected Cowley would provide a key if called on about a week before the insurrection, or if not applied for, would "hand him arms as fast as he could arm his men" when they arrived in force. Woolfolk understood, perhaps mistakenly, that Cowley himself had conducted Gabriel through every room in the capitol. Later that same Sunday, Gabriel led a meeting at Young's spring, following a funeral for an unidentified infant, where he pushed for enlistments and said they were to gather in three weeks to implement their plan. With direct access to enough of the state's arms now possible, he was anxious to move.[31]

Gabriel felt the pressures that were building. Isaac, a slave of James Allen, for example, came to the blacksmith shop and inquired of Solomon if the swords were ready. He also asked when the "Insurrection would commence." If it was not soon, he stated, he would run away, for "he was determined not to serve a white man another year." Gilbert switched his allegiance from George Smith to Gabriel because of the former's foot-dragging, another sign of impatience. In addition, Gabriel learned from the overseer of Roger Gregory that there was a "Rebellion in some quarter of the Country," which made him "anxious," according to Solomon. Most likely, he feared that unrest elsewhere would tighten local controls and make recruiting more difficult and whites more likely to stop to listen to the whispers. Someone might also let the unguarded word slip. In fact, as it turns out, a white man along the Brook, probably a member of the Locust or Lucas family, joshed with George (Smith?) that he would be happy to lead them if he could "get money" as a result of the uprising. Locust had probably overheard a conversation, and like most of them, took this one to be the banter of boastful working but presumed powerless men. But it clearly indicated the possibility of exposure, a threat that continued to mount as time passed.[32]

But not everyone had been as eager as Gabriel to push for the start of the uprising. Although it is very difficult to establish a clear chronology for many of these meetings, it appears some of the leaders met between the visit to the capitol that Sunday morning and the gathering at the spring after the funeral service later in the afternoon. George Smith, as already noted, wanted to continue to build the conspiracy, even though earlier he had thought he could have his men gathered by 24 August. Gabriel pushed to move as quickly as possible. Gilbert, anxious because the summer would soon be over, wanted it to happen before "the Weather got too cool." Gabriel proposed that his brother Martin should decide. Actually able to quote and perhaps to read scripture, Martin also created it. He artfully claimed, "there was this expression in the bible delays breed danger," falsely asserting the authority of scripture for a non-biblical proverb of ancient origin, but a phrase possibly heard in an evangelical sermon warning of the dangers of delaying one's salvation. His support for Gabriel's proposal, however, reflected the knowledge of the group of their opposition: "the country was at peace, the Soldiers were discharged & the arms all put away, there was no patroling in the Country." He then exclaimed that "before he would any longer bear what he had borne he would turn out & fight with a stick." Gilbert's aggressive claim to be ready with his pistol, however, was dampened by its need to be repaired.[33]

At this juncture in the meeting, Ben Woolfolk entered his observations, revealing some hesitancy about their preparedness. "I told them that I had heard in the days of old, when the Israelites were in Servitude to King Pharoah, they were taken from him by the power of God & were carried away by Moses." He noted that God had provided Moses with an angel "to go with him; but I could see nothing of that kind in these days." If Gabriel were a Moses, apparently no one else looked like God's angel to him. Martin responded by loosely quoting Leviticus 26:8: "I read in my bible where Gods [*sic*] says, if we will worship him, we should have peace in all our land, five of you shall conquer an hundred & a hundred a thousand of our enemies." His rejoinder addressed George Smith's apparent concern about the number of recruits and answered Woolfolk by implying that supernatural strength bestowed by God was better than an angel. He did not elaborate on the conditional nature of the divine promise. The group continued to discuss when "they should execute the plan." Finally, Martin "spoke & appointed for them to meet in three weeks which was to be of a Saturday night."[34]

From this meeting the inner group moved into the gathering of the mourners for the baby, and Gabriel invited the men down to the spring for a drink of grog. There he spoke of the plan and invited his audience to join in the cause, which was now scheduled for the night of 30 August. With three weeks to go, Gabriel urged all to recruit as heavily as they could. Jack Bowler asked challengingly what Gabriel was to do for arms, apparently as a way of putting himself forward. Gabriel could now respond with word of the arms in the capitol. Bowler then tried to claim leadership of the plot, something he had intimated to Prosser's Ben he would do, but when put to a vote, Gabriel, who had just pushed for quickly putting the plan into effect, and who had the most recruits present, received "by far" the most votes to be the General of the conspirators. Bowler was named second-in-command, bearing the title of Captain of Light Horse, although another account gives that honor to George Smith. The group dispersed on the appearance of Young's overseer, but sometime later met again at the schoolhouse, having previously agreed to assemble there. At this gathering, "a final Conclusion on the business" was reached.[35]

Over the next three weeks, recruiting continued as Gabriel had ordered. Word was sent to Hanover and Caroline of the decision to rendezvous on the night of 30 August. Sam, a runaway slave of Prosser's who wandered back into the neighborhood, learned of the plan. On 25

August, Solomon heard that "the boys in Town" were "all well and nearly ready to do the business." Scythe blades continued to be hammered into swords, Gabriel making one for Michael. Men boasted of anticipated outcomes, some contradicting others. Wilkinson's Sam bragged that with a hundred men like himself, he would "venture in town," and if they had enough men to "fill up the Capitol square they would drive the White people in the River," while Gabriel declared he would sit down and eat with the merchants after Richmond fell. Over the summer, such talk had surely marked many conversations, and it just as likely continued as a way of bolstering each other's commitment. Someone exclaimed that if any of the whites agreed to their freedom, they would not be killed, but they would still have one arm cut off. At once a bloody boast, it also revealed that the conspirators really expected the defeated whites to pay the highest price for their enslavement, for few would likely have survived the lopping. In the same vein, Woolfolk reported that Gabriel and Gilbert talked of buying a piece of white silk for a flag "on which they would have written death or liberty," though they apparently never did so. Often seen as a play on Patrick Henry's cry of "Give me liberty or give me death," the real meaning of the painted white silk may have been: You will die if you do not give us liberty.[36]

3 } The Deluge

The plotters recruited an unknown number of men, perhaps hundreds, approaching them individually or grouped at barbecues, fish fries, and church or religious assemblies, in dram shops and plantation quarters, around blacksmith forges, and along the road. They also gathered in the shade of bridges and adjacent to springs, where rum and sugar and water were mixed and passed around. During these communions, Gabriel and the men in the web of connections stretching out from the Brook, but strung primarily north and south along the Brook Road, presented their plan and built their conspiracy with the minds and limbs and anger and enslavement of the men around them. The leaders could only hope that a strong enough corps would congregate on Saturday night, 30 August, near Prosser's Tavern close to the Brook. On that day, little else could be done except finish and distribute a few swords and wait for the night and the assembling of men.

Three weeks earlier, on Saturday, 9 August, John Grammer, the Petersburg postmaster and clerk of the Hustings Court, informed Augustine Davis, the Richmond postmaster, editor of the *Virginia Gazette,* and sometime printer for the state, of the overheard whispers "of an Insurrection" which was to take place either that night or on some future Saturday night. "I mention it that you may be on your Guard," he wrote. He also indicated that Petersburg officials would investigate quietly to avoid creating a public alarm. On Monday, 11 August, the Petersburg Common Hall discussed "the existing state of things" and decided some measures ought to be adopted, "to Controul the licentiousness of Slaves and to prevent their going at large contrary to law." It ordered the constables to list all slaves over the age of twelve, to name all slaves permitted to "go at large & hire themselves or trade as free Negroes," and to identify any white vagrants. They were promised two dollars for every one they took up "that may be going at large contrary to law" and who was subsequently found guilty by the Court of Hustings.[1]

To Petersburg's white residents who were troubled by the town's growing free black population, the measure provoked a welcome, and perhaps surprising, response. On Wednesday, Daniel Coleman presented himself before the Hustings Court clerk to be re-registered. He had won his freedom in a lawsuit in 1797 when he was about forty-five years old. Sarah Scott also appeared, a thirty-eight-year-old free woman of color who had been raised in York County and had married William Scott. This was her first registration, and she became number 154 in the book which had been kept since 1794. The next day, eighteen more free people of color asked to be registered or re-entered in the book; on Thursday, seventeen more. Even on Saturday, 16 August, two individuals applied and were registered. The following week, eleven appeared before the clerk. During the last week of August, only three asked to be placed in the register, two of them on Friday, 29 August. The first of the latter presented a copy of a registration under the hand of the Essex County Court clerk dated 5 July 1799. It identified the man as free born, twenty-two years, one month, and eighteen days old, a bit over 5 feet, 8 inches tall, and a "shade lighter than black." His name was Reubin Bird. The Petersburg clerk noted, "The bearer thereof appears to answer to said register"—that is, he appeared to be the man described. The second man was older at about thirty-four, an inch taller, and carried a scar on his neck which ran under and behind his right ear. He carried an affidavit from Walker Halls of Essex County that he had been born free. Described as a "light brown Mulatto man," his name was Jesse Bird. Three weeks later, two men with these names would be arrested as the two "uncles" of Sam Byrd Jr.[2]

The 9 August warning from Petersburg reached Postmaster Davis in Richmond late on that Saturday. He relayed it to Mayor James McClurg the same evening. He called in Captain William Austin of the Richmond City Troop of Horse and Lieutenant John Dunsmore of the Light Infantry and asked them to patrol the night with men from their companies. After learning of the Petersburg rumor the next day, Governor James Monroe inquired of the mayor if he had indeed received a warning, whether it appeared credible, and if it was, what had been done to secure the city. He observed that an insurrection was a danger "of a kind much to be dreaded and against which we cannot be too well prepared." McClurg responded by indicating that the Petersburg whispers "appeared to be vague and uncertain" and that he had sought the Richmond patrol on Saturday night. He added that Captain Austin had taken the original letter to the commander of the militia to arrange for the patrols, most likely as evidence to justify them, since the mayor had no authority to order one from the militia. They found no suspicious activities about the town and had probably turned in before three black men—Gabriel, James, and Jupiter—slipped into the capitol building to spy out the public arms it contained on that same Sunday morning.[3]

Ten days later, in Hanover on 20 August, the county court of oyer and terminer heard the case of Liberty, a mulatto man about forty years old, with "fierce eyes," accused of murder. They found him guilty and ordered him hanged on 26 September, remanding him to the county's jail until his execution. There he joined Harry, "a small black fellow with a bushy head of hair." Harry was about thirty, had been found guilty of rape and ordered hanged, but in three days he would have his execution stayed by the Council of State until well into September. On Thursday and Friday, 28 and 29 August, "the Negroes in the neighbourhood of Hanover Court house . . . were very riotous and ungovernable," and on Saturday they had apparently assisted Liberty and Harry in breaking out of jail, or so the jailer Paul Thilman recounted. He requested a proclamation from the executive calling for the two men's capture. The jailer also added, with some puzzlement, that "about a week before," Paul Woolfolk had come across two slave men "armed with bayonets" and had ordered them to surrender. Seeing that Woolfolk carried only an axe, they invited him "to come on, they were ready for him. That they would go where they pleased." Unwilling to engage them, Woolfolk meekly watched them depart. The men were later seen crossing the plantations of Charles Carter in Caroline, "unmolested." Thilman concluded that "a concert" of the slaves in Hanover and Caroline to rise in rebellion could be in the works, but ignorant of any of the conspirators' ongoing efforts, he did not urge any further action from the governor. Monroe could not have had the letter long before he laid Thilman's request for a proclamation before the council. On Monday, 1 September, he had called for their convocation on Tuesday to confront a possible insurrection, but not because of the news from Hanover.[4]

Ben Woolfolk had gone to Caroline, apparently on the weekend of 17 August, with word of when the men were to gather, a trip that took place roughly one week before the confrontation involving the two bayonet-brandishing men. When he returned, he proudly brought instructions from Thornton on how to make paper cartridges, a skill no one at the Brook possessed. He may have also brought concerns about some of the expected Caroline captains, especially Jack Gabriel and John Fells. Perhaps this is what prompted another council where the debate reemerged over the date of the attack. Some wanted to delay it to 31 August to allow the men from Caroline time to get to the Brook and to take advantage of the common sight of men traveling on a Sunday. Gabriel wished to keep it on the next Saturday night and won, arguing that the enlistees already were warned of the date of the insurrection and that they had enough men for the initial assault, especially if more would soon arrive to reinforce them. On Monday, 25 August, word came to Prosser's blacksmith shop that the fifth column in town was "nearly ready," but it was apparently expected that the Richmond recruits would be prepared in time for the attack, for the news provoked no reported concern. On Friday, a drunken Isaac slurred that he had learned from Gabriel's wife Nanny that Governor Monroe had inklings of the plot and had moved all the arms from the capitol to the penitentiary; but what anyone made of that rumor as it wafted about the Brook remains unknown. Watt left that night to gather his sons and his recruits in Goochland, or so he said as he departed from Prosser's. Apparently, he would not be seen again until November, and he certainly would never again see Gabriel and some of the other Prosser slaves alive.[5]

Early the next morning, Saturday, 30 August, two men made their way from the Brook to Richmond. One was Pharoah, a man of about twenty-seven years and a very skilled scytheman. He had been bought for a handsome price by Philip Sheppard at public auction. The other was Tom, about thirty-three or thirty-four and often charged with running the plantation of Elizabeth Sheppard in the frequent absences of her sons. Once in Richmond they headed to Mosby Sheppard's counting room and knocked on the door. Mosby owned a part-interest in Tom at his mother's death and had witnessed a deed of emancipation from his brother Philip to a slave named Gabriel the year before, a man who had bought himself from the Sheppard estate of whom Mosby was an executor. Mosby was also a private in the Richmond Troop of Horse, the cavalry unit captained by William Austin. At their knock, Sheppard opened the door and admitted the two familiar faces, his visitors closing the door behind them. Then they blurted out that "the Negroes were to rise" in the neighborhood of Thomas Henry Prosser and kill him. They also intended to destroy Major William Mosby and Absalom Johnson, march on Richmond, join fellow conspirators in town, take the state's arms and munitions, and, finally, the city too. Then the two men fell silent, "appearing much agitated." In a more measured tone, Sheppard asked them when it was to take place and who was the head of it. They answered, "That night" and "Prosser's Gabriel." At this, Mosby Sheppard, apparently concluding that the greatest immediate danger existed at the Brook, left the men and rushed to find his uncle William Mosby, locating him by "ten or eleven o'clock" and giving him warning. The major, in turn, informed his neighbor Dabney Williamson and gained Roger Gregory's commitment to meet that night with what men they could collect at Gregory's—that is, Priddy's Tavern. Mosby also sent word to Captain Austin in hopes of arranging a coordinated patrolling with Williamson on both sides of the Brook.[6]

Sheppard returned to Richmond, possibly bringing Major Mosby's note to Austin, and by two o'clock had informed Monroe of what he had learned. He told the governor of his confidence in Pharoah and Tom and of his firm belief in the truth of their warning. Relying on Sheppard's word as "a respectable citizen," Monroe summoned the Richmond regimental officers, including Austin of the Richmond Horse, and arranged for guards to be placed at the penitentiary, capitol, and powder magazine. Austin's cavalrymen, apparently including Mosby Sheppard, were sent to patrol the roads connecting Richmond and the Brook. Monroe also dispatched a letter to the mayor of Petersburg. Whether the product of his own initiative or encouraged by Mayor McClurg, the governor's letter warned the Southside mayor of the alarm and suggested the city remain on guard. Noting the whispers in Petersburg earlier in the month, Monroe thought that it was probable that the just-revealed Brook conspiracy extended there too.[7]

Pharoah spent some time in Richmond and then headed home, perhaps still with Tom, passing Prosser's blacksmith shop near the Brook. Seeing Pharoah coming from the direction of Richmond, Solomon hailed him, asking if "the lighthorse of Richmond were out." Pharoah said "he had seen some at Col[onel Parke] Goodall's Tavern," an establishment called the Indian Queen, near the capitol. After hearing this, Solomon declared that "the business of the Insurrection had so far advanced that they were Compelled even if discovered to go forward with it." He may have thought the mustering of troops confirmed the rumor Nanny reportedly had voiced of the conspiracy being discovered. Of course, he did not realize that it had been revealed only hours, not days, before. Solomon turned again to his work on four swords he needed to finish "by the time of his Companys meeting that Evening," which he said "would consist of 1000 men." Pharoah strode on up the road, perhaps wondering what he had wrought. Perhaps he believed the plot doomed and feared the bloody reprisals that would sweep the countryside in its wake. Perhaps he cast an eye to the sky. Soon rain would begin to fall—if it hadn't already— from lowering clouds. Up in Caroline County, showers had started that morning.[8]

About sundown, the sky fell around Richmond and washed the conspiracy away. William Mosby, who rode through the storm, thought it "the greatest rain perhaps ever known." James Monroe called it "the extraordinary torrent of rain" and "one of the most extraordinary falls of rain ever known in our Country. Every animal sought shelter from it." It was providential, the act of "the great disposer of events." James Thomson Callender described it to the *Philadelphia Aurora* as "the most terrible storm of thunder and lightning accompanied with an enormous rain, that I ever witnessed in this state." He too attributed it to "the immediate agency of a Superior Being," although he dropped this explanation in an almost verbatim account he wrote to Jefferson the day after posting his column to Philadelphia. In Caroline County, the "great fall of rain," punctuated with thunder and lightning, earned entry in James Duvall's diary.[9]

The conspirators called it the "fall of rain and gust" and the "great fall of rain" too, but none indicated they saw it as a divine rebuke to their intentions. As the downpour continued and the Brook surged toward the bridge, Gabriel, Solomon, and Jack Bowler decided to postpone the attack for one night, according to Prosser's Ben, who attended the meeting. Prosser's Frank was there as well, or quickly learned of the decision, because he informed George (Smith?) of the postponement when he arrived and asked "why they did not start." Judith Owen's Michael also stopped by Gabriel's house after the postponement to get a promised sword; he was told to return the next night, it "being too rainey an evening for carrying their plan into effect." He left clutching his sword, leaving a promise to reappear on Sunday night. Out in Caroline and Hanover, where it had been raining much of the day, the once scheduled rendezvous at 10 p.m. at Gist's old field apparently never occurred because of the decision to begin without them. Nor did any subsequent muster attract any notice. Consequently, it is equally unlikely that Ben Woolfolk trudged there to lead the six hundred recruits he claimed to the Brook. The mounted Richmond patrollers later reported seeing figures leaving Richmond in the storm's intervals, the opposite direction slaves usually trekked on a Saturday night. Nevertheless, William Mosby, Roger Gregory, and their riders found nothing as they searched during the soggy night between Gregory's Tavern and Prosser's plantation on the north side of the swollen Brook. Mosby returned home by eight or nine Sunday morning, exhausted.[10]

That same morning, Gabriel and Jack Bowler were once again seen together. No one, however, testified that either one of them was spotted later in the day. Apparently, the Brook had dropped, since Goode's Michael managed to get to Joseph Mosby's, where his wife lived, and where he found several men, including two of the Prosser slaves, Ben and Frank. He asked Frank why the men had not moved on Richmond the night before. Frank described the weather, and Michael, who was to have led men into the capital from the Manchester side, also admitted that "the rain had prevented him from attending." Somebody arrived with the news that several had been taken up. The group quickly stashed a gun that someone possessed, and then probably dispersed. No one recounted that they still planned to gather that night to attempt what the storm had delayed; evidently, for most of the conspirators, the rain had also diluted the adrenalin needed for the attack.[11]

When William Mosby returned home, he collapsed into bed, but his rest was soon disrupted by one of his female slaves. "You must not tell," she cautioned. Have you heard that the Negroes were going to revolt? she asked. He affirmed he had, and inquired where they intended to gather. She said near Prosser's, and that they would try again that night. He queried her on how many, and she said about three or four hundred, including those from town and the country who intended to kill all before them as they swept toward Richmond. Although this account sounded much like the plan that had been relayed to him by Mosby Sheppard, and for which no physical evidence had yet emerged, what was novel and alarming was the rescheduling of the revolt. What Mosby did at this point remains unclear. Still, it is likely that he stumbled back out to resume patrolling, something Monroe had already and independently requested of the Richmond forces for a second night.[12]

On Monday, 1 September, the patrols had little to report, but Mosby "and other gentlemen of character from his neighbourhood" warned Monroe of the reality of the conspiracy. Perhaps the details in the warning given by the woman in Mosby's house, which confirmed the tale of Pharoah and Tom, convinced them. Perhaps they were inspired by a statement extracted from an interrogated captive, maybe Prosser's Ben. In any case, with their assessment in hand, Monroe could no longer act in the most minimal fashion or keep quiet the rumors. He called for the Council of State to meet at ten o'clock the next morning. He also directed those in the neighborhood of the Brook who believed in the conspiracy's existence "to apprehend and commit to prison those whose guilt they had good cause to suspect." By the end of the day, six men had been captured and brought to Richmond.[13]

With no massing of slaves observed or any other material evidence yet in hand of the conspiracy, Monroe still needed to determine whether a plot actually existed. If it had, he still needed to know if it was finished — or merely postponed. Unfounded fears could produce unnecessary alarms and uncontrolled reactions. If a plot existed, inaction could be disastrous; but if the plot was nothing more than loose talk, mustering forces could be fiscally expensive and politically embarrassing. To the Richmond mayor he suggested, "Perhaps the best course will be to lay hold of the informers, and the suspected and extort from them what can be obtained." By taking up Pharoah and Tom, "they will be secure against the suspicion" of having betrayed the revolt. He did not describe the methods to "extort" information. He also recommended that the town and county coordinate their formal inquiries, "that process be issued at the same time against all who are accused or suspected of being concerned in the affair." He thought "a magistrate or two" from both Richmond and Henrico would be sufficient. Monroe then reminded McClurg, "You will observe I only suggest this measure to your consideration." He had no authority to order these measures as governor under Virginia's constitution, which had institutionalized a republican ideal of a state executive with restricted personal power, placing many executive decisions in the collected hands of the council. McClurg replied quickly, agreeing on the "propriety & even necessity of the measures" Monroe recommended. However, he could not discover who the informer had been, "his" name having "been carefully conceal'd; and all that I know of him from Information is, that he was a negro from the country somewhere about the Brook." He pledged that if the informer were interrogated by a county justice, who would have jurisdiction, and if any names of town conspirators were revealed, he would take immediate steps to secure them. Within a day, Gervas Storrs, the justice who lived at the lower end of the Brook, and Joseph Selden, another Henrico magistrate from the upper district, began serving as an examining court, interrogating men as they were produced. Once the court was constituted, Monroe also urged the roundup of any witnesses against the conspirators and their confinement in the penitentiary, as much "for their own personal safety as to prevent their running away." Without their testimony, doubts would remain about the existence of the conspiracy, and questions could be raised about spending state monies on a specter.[14]

Along the Brook, the dragnet continued to draw in its prey. As men were netted and the conspiracy collapsed, Moses heard Gregory's Martin "curse the black people for intending to rise against the whites." When the posse of patrollers approached Wilkinson's Sam, "he gave himself up saying he was innocent, and that he could not be brought in as one of the Conspirators." Michael was chased down by a man named Glenn and an overseer named William Gentry, who had gone in vain to Gabriel's house hoping to seize the leader but who then came upon Michael carrying his scythe-bladed sword on the road. Michael fled into the adjacent woods, followed closely by Glenn, and tried to defend himself with his weapon, but was subdued even before Gentry caught up with the two dueling men. By Tuesday evening, 2 September, the patrollers of the Brook had delivered about twenty men to Richmond, seized from the plantations of Thomas Henry Prosser and his neighbors. The jail, shared between Richmond and Henrico, could not contain all of them, so the coffle was redirected to the penitentiary. Even this new facility was not ideal, since the first order of the council that very morning, in the wake of the escape of an inmate, had been to order "the grates of the cells be better secured" and the plank enclosure of the grounds completed.[15]

The sweep through the Brook did not snag all of the conspirators. Ben Woolfolk remained at large a bit longer. As men were hunted down, Gilbert, "certain that they would be detected," decided to run away and began to write himself a pass, perhaps in the form of a copy of a free black registry. He used a rule to measure his height to provide an accurate description of his stature in the forgery, and encouraged Woolfolk to run too. Lewis, probably still ready to decapitate his owners, "urged the necessity" of storming the jail to free the captured, and thought a party of one hundred men could accomplish the daring raid. He apparently did not know that most were in the penitentiary. But for the others along the Brook, it appears escaping detection did not last long. Gabriel and Jack Bowler managed to remain at large for a longer time, but Gabriel was captured in Norfolk on 23 September, and Bowler surrendered at the Brook on 9 October. Prosser's Watt, who left for Goochland on Friday, 29 August, was secured and jailed by mid-November, if not earlier. As men's names were extracted or surrendered over the next several days, orders went out for their arrest, and most seem to have been taken quickly into custody.[16]

While the militiamen of Henrico gathered up conspirators, Monroe met with his assembled council on Tuesday morning as requested. With little evidence yet in hand, they perused a report on the state of the penitentiary, authorized a reward for the capture of the escaped felon, and, as noted, ordered the tightening of the facility's security. Next, they assented to the recommendation of the Henrico County court for the reappointment of John Harvie as sheriff for the ensuing year, and then turned their attention to the most pressing reason Monroe had summoned them to council chambers. Monroe told them what he knew, which still wasn't much, but given their response, they surely recognized the thoughtfulness of the conspirators in their choice of the key targets to attack. Consequently, they advised that a guard of sixty men be mustered for the protection of Richmond and the penitentiary, where the bulk of the arms were kept. In addition, they wanted the superintendent of the arsenal at the Point of Fork warned, and a force of fifty—twenty-five men each from the counties of Goochland and Fluvanna—sent there as an additional guard. Furthermore, they desired that all of the militia commanders in the state should order out "regular patrols." The council then authorized rewards of $100 each for Harry and Liberty, who had escaped from Hanover jail. One wonders if they mulled over Thilman's news of the two bayonet-wielding men and his concern about a possible combination of slaves in Hanover and Caroline as they left the council chamber.[17]

"Same day in the afternoon," the council met again, likely on the basis of more information, but not yet of more prisoners arriving from the

Brook. The councilors "advised" that a force of sixty men from the Henrico militia should be sent with specific instructions to search for weapons and to patrol around "the plantations of Messrs Wilkerson [sic] and Prosser where it is suggested the conspiracy originated." Monroe was empowered to utilize the Richmond Horse "to execute his orders on this occasion," and to call out additional men if warranted. Then the council authorized what Monroe had earlier suggested: "that the Magistrates be permitted to commit witnesses or informers of the plot to the Penitentiary for their security." They then adjourned again, and Monroe began immediately to implement their instructions.[18]

He ordered Colonel David Lambert to establish the sixty-man guard with officers from his Richmond regiment, with a dispatch of twenty-five men to the penitentiary, fifteen to the powder magazine, ten to the capitol, and ten to the jail. They were to be in place by six that evening and serve until sunrise. Their weapons were to be issued from the supply in the penitentiary and surrendered to replacements, an indication of the under-armed status of the state forces, if not of a practical policy of not loading too many muskets. Monroe drafted orders to militia colonels in Goochland and Fluvanna Counties for each to direct twenty-five men as guards to the Point of Fork, and a warning to Major Robert Quarles at the arsenal. The next morning, Robert Cowley, the man the conspirators expected would open the capitol to them, galloped west to Point of Fork with Monroe's message to Quarles and returned with the major's acknowledgment. Someone else delivered Monroe's instructions to Colonel John Mayo, commander of the Henrico militia, to station fifty men at Watson's or Prosser's Tavern every night starting at six o'clock, with watches until sunrise. They were also to secure their arms from the stock in the penitentiary, surrendering them to the men who replaced them. The force was to use the tavern as a hub for patrols to be sent out during the night "to such places as the officer shall deem best."[19]

The party marching the prisoners into Richmond late on Tuesday brought some scythe-bladed swords they had found too. Now the state possessed the physical evidence of the plot in these weapons, "well calculated for execution." Their capture put an edge of urgency to Monroe's orders: the circular to all the militia commanders regarding patrols, and the delivery of arms from the penitentiary to the local militia men called into service. On the next day, he remembered, or was reminded, that the arms once carried by the federal regiment he feared, but left in

Manchester at its demobilization, could be at risk, and so he dispatched more orders and requests. One order went out to place a watch of twelve men under a sergeant to guard them in the meantime. He followed this with a missive to Colonel Mathew Cheatham of the Chesterfield militia requesting a troop of twenty-five who would be put in rotation with the initial guard organized in Manchester.[20]

While Monroe scribbled and dispatched, magistrates Storrs and Selden interrogated. One of those examined was Prosser's Ben, the eighteen-year-old who worked in the blacksmith shop with Solomon and Gabriel and who was among the earliest to surrender or suffer capture. Even before Gilbert and Woolfolk were apprehended, they knew he had made "disclosures," unless they mistook him for Pharoah and Tom. The two justices probably built on his statements, perhaps extracting more from him and gaining confirmation from others. His role is best revealed by the testimony he gave at most of the early trials in the Henrico court. Although specifics from these early interrogations did not leak, the general plot became known and rumors started to spread. On Saturday, Petersburg recorder William Prentis wrote Monroe requesting him to compare the names of four black men against "a list of a number of blacks concerned in the affair at Richmond" which he heard Monroe possessed. When the letter reached Monroe is not clear, and his reply on the following Monday has not survived, but none of the men Prentis named appear in any other record derived from the conspiracy, and no further action appears to have lain against these four men in Petersburg.[21]

There is no surviving written communication from Storrs and Selden to Monroe or the council before Monday, 8 September, when they reported that their examination had "clearly proven [Gabriel] to be the main spring & chief mover in the contemplated rebellion." But that lack of official intelligence had not prevented the council from acting. Two days before, on Saturday, the 6th, the council had already decided, "on further consideration of the conspiracy & insurrection among the Negroes," to advise the governor to move all gunpowder from the public magazine to the penitentiary and to have the arms belonging to the United States in Manchester transferred there for safekeeping. They also "advised" the governor to suspend the return of arms sent in from the county militias for refurbishing and repair under a program begun that summer. This made it easier to meet their directive for the arming of Richmond's "citizens" upon the order of any member of the executive, that is, the governor and council. They increased the guard for the city to one hundred men, to be comprised of militia or volunteers, and invoked the Militia Act to empower Monroe to call out the forces of Henrico, Chesterfield, and Richmond to the extent he believed the crisis warranted. And they authorized his arranging for their material support. In addition, the Richmond artillery was also to be supplied with powder and ball. Once again, Monroe issued the orders to carry these measures into effect, and wrote more messages to Chesterfield County regarding the status of the federal arms, including one calling for the parading in Manchester that evening of as many men as could be mustered. This time, he dispatched Robert Cowley across the James River to Chesterfield with the orders respecting those forces.[22]

Monroe also made the plot more public and the state's response appear more formidable in Richmond. He ordered the Richmond Horse to parade in full complement at 5 p.m. at Capitol Square, one of many measures, as James Sidbury has noted and Monroe later justified, that served as a display of state power to reassure its citizens and intimidate its slaves. On the heels of this, John Boyce, sometime editor, clerk, and schoolmaster, made first mention in his diary of the conspiracy. He recorded "an alarm this Evening on account of intelligence that the negro's were expected to rise." He cryptically entered, "Bob Cooley[,] stop'd by the Guard at the Watch House about a quarter before ten o'clock[,] said he had been over the River on a message from the Governor & was going home. [He] was not detained[,] he rode very fast[.] I was not present."[23]

On Monday, 8 September, with Gabriel now established as the head of the conspiracy, the governor and council decided on a reward of $150 for his capture. When they deliberated the next day, they raised the prize to $300 and held out the promise of freedom to up to five of his "accomplices who shall be instrumental in apprehending him." The proclamation appeared in newsprint beginning 12 September. Next, in response to information just received from Alderman John Foster and a delegation from the Richmond Common Hall, the council authorized Monroe to "take measures for apprehending all those who have been charged . . . and are out of the jurisdiction of the corporation of" Richmond.[24]

John Foster, rope maker and alderman, and probably the Richmond counterpart to Storrs and Selden, had interrogated men and apparently took his findings to Mayor McClurg. Foster had compiled a list of names he had gathered from two sources. One was Gilbert. Foster interrogated him at the penitentiary and gained the names of Ann Smith's George and Charles, and Thomas Woodfin's Jacob, all of Henrico. To these were added Moses at the coal pits at Tuckahoe, Jack Bowler, William Galt's Armistead of Richmond, Paul Thilman's or Paul Graham's Randol, and Paul Graham's Sam in Hanover. Foster indicated that Gilbert believed Sam could provide the names of more than forty more. Two other men appear to have been identified by Gilbert too, though this is not entirely clear. They were Bob and John, the slaves of Sally Price. Bob worked for her out in the Brook, while John toiled for Hugh Shelton in Richmond.[25]

Having obtained the name of someone who was close at hand, a trap was set for Price's John. It was probably Shelton who sent him to Foster's "lumber house," or storage shed, for a bar of iron. After John stepped into the building, men quickly closed the door behind him and seized and secured the surprised man. They accused him of being part of the conspiracy, which he denied, and they threatened him with prosecution unless "he would make some important discoveries." Any physical abuse he suffered at their hands was not part of Foster's evidence, but the threat of execution clearly pervaded the interrogation. Ultimately, John reversed himself and described a meeting about a month before at Young's where Gabriel and Bowler recruited men after a "religious meeting," probably the funeral of the infant child on 10 August. He said "a great number of the Negroes from Richmond" attended, but he did not know who they were. He named Young's Sawney, Gilbert the confessor, and Ben, probably meaning Ben Woolfolk, who was hired by Young. He accused George Smith of being "very active" in the cause, mentioned a man named Billy Chicken, who was apparently already in custody, and listed Paul Graham's Sam as "being concerned." He stated that Bowler was second-in-command to Gabriel. Foster's information provoked a hastily called meeting of the Common Hall, which met in the security of the Senate chamber in the capitol, where he presented his evidence. The Hall concluded after hearing from Foster that two men in particular, "whose names it is thought unproper at present to spread upon record are deeply involved in the guilt of the intended insurrection and capable also of giving . . . information respecting their accomplices," leaving the names to be reported orally. But it also realized that, in spite of the threat those accused posed to the capital, nearly all of them resided outside Richmond and beyond the municipality's jurisdiction. Consequently, the Hall sent Foster to Monroe with his information, and a committee to the governor seeking his aid in rounding up the men accused by Gilbert and John, which was granted by the executive council.[26]

With authorization from his council and with Foster's list in hand, Monroe wrote to secure some of the accused. He confidentially ordered Paul Thilman in Hanover to arrange the arrest of Randal, or Randolph, who reportedly belonged to him or possibly Paul Graham, and Sam, who did belong to Graham. He correctly noted that one witness had accused Randolph and two had named Sam. Thilman was to utilize a magistrate in Hanover or Caroline, depending on where the slaves were, and to carry out this order "with alacrity . . . due diligence and discretion." On 11 September, two days later, Monroe wrote to Robert H. Saunders in Goochland and requested the arrest of Moses at the Tuckahoe coal pits. Other instructions regarding these accused men have not survived, but may not have been necessary if they were found, as Billy Chicken was, to be already in custody.[27]

Meanwhile, Monroe received mixed messages about the conspiracy. From William Bentley, the regimental commander of the demobilized federal regiment whose arms had been stacked in Manchester, and which arms the state now wanted secured in the penitentiary, came an unenthusiastic reply. On 8 September, he claimed that since receiving Monroe's "recommendation" for the removal of the arms, he had made "diligent inquiry into the grounds of the alarm . . . on this side of the [James] river." After discovering no evidence of unrest from Chesterfield through Powhatan, his home county, and into Cumberland, he concluded no plot existed. The few "people of Color" in that corridor of counties who admitted to anything asserted their knowledge came only from the spreading news of an alarm in the area of Richmond. He saw no need to move the arms, but said he would if the public safety required it. As it turned out, getting these arms into the safety of the penitentiary would prove to be long and costly. Bentley's reluctant response could not have been well received by Monroe, nor could Bentley's conclusion regarding the existence of the conspiracy. If others shared his view and the "intended insurrection" proved little more than loose talk, the increasingly aggressive, and thus expensive, actions taken by Monroe and the council could prove politically embarrassing. On the other hand, it may have been reassuring that the conspiracy did not appear to have spread that far.[28]

While Bentley thought fear of a conspiracy unwarranted in the counties of his inquiry, fear reigned to the south in Petersburg and its

neighborhood. Initially, Joseph Jones, the Collector of the Port of Petersburg and a militia general, did not make much of the rumors either, and
expressed that in writing to Monroe on the same day Bentley had sent
his negative appraisal. But soon after dispatching his letter, Jones talked
with Benjamin Harrison, a delegate to the General Assembly from adjacent Prince George County. Harrison claimed that one of his slave men,
on condition of anonymity, flatly stated that an uprising was intended,
named "several slaves and mulatoes . . . and mentioned the names of two
white men as being concerned." Jones learned from another, unnamed
citizen that an elderly black man, a preacher whom he had questioned
about the affair, denied that he ever preached anything but faithful service to God and master, but he admitted that some counseled otherwise.
Speaking as if the plot existed, the old preacher reportedly urged a harsh
retribution by the whites, for without it, he argued, there would only be
encouragement: "Kill every one they found concerned," he allegedly said.
Jones became alarmed at these revelations and now wrote Monroe endorsing, in effect, the elderly parson's proposal. "Where there is any reason to believe that any person is concerned they ought immediately to
be hanged, quartered and hung up on trees on every road as a terror to
the rest." He advised a declaration of martial law, "for if they are tryed by
the Civil Law, perhaps there will be not one condemned. . . . Slay them
all where there is any reason to believe they are concerned, let them be
Whites, Mulattoes, or negroes." Massive violence "would put a total stop"
to it; leniency would ultimately kill more slaves, and "a great many more
of us." Then, in language that sounds eerily familiar today, Jones ended
his letter with a quote, saying, "This is one of those kind of cases that 'we
must do wrong or right that good may come of it.'" Just as he started to
seal the letter, one arrived from Monroe, which calmed him down a bit.
But in his postscript he advised, "I do think it wd be well not to be lulled
too much."[29]

Elsewhere in his letter to Monroe, the general reported that Petersburg
officials had jailed six men, "but they hardly know what to do with them.
The Town magistrates I believe want to hear from you." Indeed, William
Prentis was writing to Monroe at the same time, inquiring whether "the
investigation on Thursday [4 September]" had produced any information important to Petersburg, "as the people of this town labour under
great fear and apprehensions." He acknowledged Monroe's letter of the
day before, which had apparently failed to provide any confirmation of

any involvement of the four men mentioned in his earlier letter. Now he wanted the bearer of this communication, Captain William Hill Sergeant, to present to Monroe the city's concerns in person. Sergeant also carried a list of the names of the six jailed men, who "are supposed to have some knowledge of the intended insurrection," to check against the evidence Monroe had in hand. These six men were not the same as the first four suspects. Four of them were leaving a documentary trail, though not of conspiracy. James Vaughan lived in the section of Petersburg cut out of Prince George County and was a successful free barber in his mid-forties. He was likely the man who went to prison in 1807 for murdering his wife. David White belonged to the estate of a woman named Murray and had been arrested in the aftermath of the Petersburg census as a slave permitted to go at large by his wife, Polly Spruce, who hired him from the estate. The court had prosecuted her for her illegal indulgence. Dick White, the brother of David, was named too. Polly Spruce would purchase him from the Murray estate in January 1801 and free him. Another of the suspects, Charles Timberlake, was a troublesome slave of John Bell, or at least so in 1805 when Bell tried to ship him off to the West Indies to be sold. Cyrus Skinner, and a man identified just as Jonathan, remain nearly historically anonymous. Captain Sergeant returned with no additional information relating to the town or affirmation of the involvement of the six men, and none of them would be tried.[30]

The angry and fearful in Petersburg demanded harsh repression, even state-sanctioned murder, or desperately tried to discover the terrorists in their midst. And they continued to patrol their town. On 13 September, the Town Hall noted "that (at this time) it is essentially necessary for the safety of the town that a night watch shou'd be continued for another year." In other places, following the orders from the governor, patrols increased in size and frequency. In Goochland County, for example, men who had not been dispatched to guard the arsenal at Point of Fork patrolled every day but two between 6 September and 16 September, logging a total of at least 739 man-hours, a commitment far out of proportion to normal practices. How the patrols conducted themselves remains unrecorded, but in northern Virginia, James Rush reported to John Mason that the patrols authorized by Monroe had put "power in the hands of ignorant and arbitrary Characters," which he claimed "will be frequently abused."[31]

Meanwhile, James Monroe continued to organize and direct the defense of Richmond. On 9 September, he told the colonel of the Chesterfield militia that his whole regiment should be mustered, that their services would be needed for at least a week, and to send one hundred men over to Richmond to parade on Church Hill, apparently on the afternoon of 10 September. The next day, he communicated much the same to the Richmond regiment, ordering the total mobilization of the unit and wanting the whole regiment paraded on the Capitol Square that afternoon at 4 o'clock. An artillery company was to position itself there in the night, with a cannon whose firing would serve as the city's alarm. Just as Gabriel and his recruiters tried to create the impression of large enlistments by claiming lists with hundreds of men, Monroe had to stage the appearance of an impregnable Richmond to calm fears and destroy any hope for an actual attack. In fact, the town did not seem to have enough functional arms to defend itself without resorting to those of rural areas which were accidentally present. The state was woefully short of powder, and in the initial responses had to borrow some. Men were drawn from each company and detached to the penitentiary to produce cartridges, while others were sent to speed up the refurbishing of weapons. But with the parade of hundreds, the beat of drums, the tramp of feet, the clop of hooves, the display of colors, the rattle of sabers, and the glint of bayonets, the state displayed its power to citizens and slaves, a veneer over the actual scramble to make itself militarily capable of suppressing a major slave insurrection.[32]

The governor also prepared "General Orders" for the 19th Regiment of Richmond when drawn up on the capitol grounds. He assigned various numbers of men to the penitentiary and the capitol. He provided for sentinels at outlying points, along with a guard to watch the back side of town. He positioned another unit at the jail, where some of the incarcerated were, with patrols to be sent up the Shockoe Valley, to Rocketts, and to other locations. Those not assigned to guard duty that night were to retire, prepared to deploy on any alarm to either the Market House or Goodall's Tavern, depending on where they lived. They were all expected to return to the Capitol Square at 9 a.m. the next morning, 11 September, to relieve the guards. When they did, Monroe, "the Commander in Chief on this emergency," announced that he had appointed three aides-de-camp and required that all officers and men obey their orders. They were Alexander McRae, a member of the State Council and an intensely loyal Republican; Meriwether Jones, the devoutly Republican editor of the *Richmond Examiner;* and Philip Norborne Nicholas, the acting attorney general, appointed by Monroe earlier in the year at the incumbent attorney general's death. He also provided that reinforcements from the Chesterfield regiment would be quartered at the Richmond tavern of Richard Bowler.[33]

While Monroe organized the militia as Virginia's commander-in-chief, the magistrates of Henrico did the state's legal business, preparing the cases against the accused men incarcerated in the state penitentiary and Henrico jail. On 11 September, with the obvious presence of troops in the town, the Commonwealth's attorney for Henrico County, George William Smith, presented criminal "informations" against thirty men for "conspiracy and insurrection," based on the evidence gathered by Gervas Storrs and Joseph Selden. By the time the Henrico trials would finish in early December, almost that many more would be charged and tried, as well as a handful in Richmond City and Caroline, one in Louisa, and possibly another in Dinwiddie County. With the first round of indictments in hand, the justices of the Henrico County Court of Oyer and Terminer immediately opened the trials against the men accused of conspiracy.[34]

4 } Revenge or Justice?

W hen the captured men arrived at the penitentiary, they were examined by Gervas Storrs and Joseph Selden and if thought complicit in the plot were transferred to the jail to await trial. From there, they stepped the short distance to the Henrico County courthouse to stand individually before the bar as both person and property. As they did so, the trial testimony began to reveal the nature and extent of the whispers and boasts, some rough numbers of those involved, and the subplots and plans, though never completely nor perfectly, because the law of conspiracy did not demand that. The evidence also exposed the crevasses in Virginia's slave society, which the plotters were able to exploit as they put their scheme together. As one after another defendant moved from jail to court and again to jail, or in some cases, returned to the custody of their owners, if acquitted, the fate of those found guilty ultimately moved into the hands of Governor Monroe and the state councilors. Their decisions sent men on to the gallows, released them to masters and mistresses under pardon, or left them to sit in jail under a reprieve, awaiting a final disposition. The results of these executive deliberations were not always immediately known, or accurately reported by the press, leading to confusion then, as now, as to who secured pardon or reprieve, and when and where the guilty were executed or, in some cases, finally exiled from Virginia. In terms of understanding the conspiracy, this was the process that produced what evidence exists of the conspiracy as created, lived, and crushed. It also reveals the roles played by slave deponents, for and against the defendants, especially three key witnesses for the Commonwealth: Prosser's Ben, Price's John, and Graham's Ben Woolfolk.

On 9 September, Governor Monroe thanked James Madison for help in hiring an overseer for his plantation. He passed on other news, informing Madison of the insurrection scare and stating that around twenty-five men suspected in the plot had been incarcerated and would be tried the following week. The governor thought the evidence that the plan involved men in "Henrico, parts of Hano[ve]r & chesterfield," was "satisfactory," and declared it "at an end if it was ever contemplated." He also noted that his wife had gone to spend time with family in Caroline County with their daughter Elizabeth and toddler son Spence, the latter "much improved." The parents hoped that "by moving him abt. he will . . . get the better soon of those diseases of childhood & recover his strength." Monroe also wrote to Thomas Jefferson on the same date, but apparently only after learning more details about the progress of the investigation, perhaps from the Richmond Hall delegation and John Foster. He again mentioned the "great alarm" caused by the discovery of the conspiracy, but to the vice president he now relayed that "Abt. 30 are in prison who are to be tried on Thursday and others are daily discovered and apprehended in the vicinity of the city." He added, "I have no doubt the plan was formed and of tolerably extensive combination." From what the magistrates had told him, most would be condemned. He promised to keep Jefferson informed of any new developments.[1]

As Monroe had indicated to Jefferson, the trials opened two days later, on Thursday, 11 September, when Gabriel's brother Solomon stood before seven Henrico justices sitting as a juryless court of oyer and terminer. Under Virginia law, at least five justices would hear the evidence against the defendant and listen to court-appointed defense counsel, any defense witnesses, and the accused himself, if the defense desired. Then, beginning with the youngest judge, each would individually and publicly declare his decision. Conspiracy and insurrection were felonies and carried the death penalty. The convicted could not avoid the gallows by pleading one's benefit of clergy, though the court could recommend the extension of mercy to the executive, which might result in a pardon. To convict, however, the justices had to be unanimous in their verdict. One vote in favor of the defendant brought acquittal, which is probably why General Jones wanted them tried in military courts under a declaration of martial law. And of course, the court could also find the defendant not guilty. This was not to be Solomon's fate. He pled not guilty, "and was fully heard in his own defense by James Rind, Gent. counsel assigned him." The court heard the witnesses who had been "charged, sworn and examined." Then the justices pronounced him guilty, ordered him hanged the next day "at the usual place," and sent him to the jail for what was expected to be his last night.[2]

Prosser's Ben and Sheppard's Pharoah had testified against Solomon. Pharoah recounted his conversation with the blacksmith on his way home from informing Mosby Sheppard of the conspiracy. Ben gave a lengthier and more dramatic statement, telling of the plan, the number of recruits, and of Solomon's sword making, naming Gabriel as the planner and mentioning that "2 White french men was the first instigators of the Insurrection, but whose names he did not hear." He also stated that Lewis Barret had been "spoken of as one of the Towns Negroes concerned." It is not clear if he had earlier spilled all of these details to Storrs and Selden, the two investigating magistrates, neither of whom sat on the trial.[3]

Having disposed of Solomon's case, the court heard the evidence against Will, a slave of John Mosby Sr. Once again, Prosser's Ben testified, telling of Will's bringing two scythe blades to Solomon, of his rejection as a captain of infantry but of his appointment to the cavalry. Ben also said that in the melee of murder, all whites would be killed except French men, "none of whom were to be touched." Toby, a slave belonging to John Holeman, said Will had told him of supplying the blades to Solomon and of his place in the horsemen. He added that all blacks who did not join would be killed by the five thousand men who would storm Richmond. The judges declared Will guilty, ordered him hanged on the morrow, and dispatched him to the jail.[4]

And so it went. John Williamson's Daniel and William Winston's Charles swore of the recruiting efforts of Mary Jones's John, who had been hired by John Harvie at the penitentiary. Prosser's Ben and William Burton's Daniel told of conversations with Isaac, also a slave of William Burton's, of his getting the promise of a sword from Gabriel, of his determination "to kill or be killed," of his commitment to the "murdering of the White Citizens," and of the threatened killing of those blacks who refused to join. Prosser's Ben remained to be rejoined by Pharoah in recounting the quest of Judith Owen's Michael for a sword, although her slave Ned testified that Michael had informed Gabriel he would engage only if he saw "the business progress well." William Gentry capped the state's case with his account of Michael's futile swordplay and capture. Next, Prosser's Ben once again took the lead against Ned, a slave of Anne Parsons who recruited among the men working in the Richmond warehouses and listed his captain's rank. Wilshire, a slave of planter and tobacco inspector Benjamin Mosby, swore he sold Ned a sword so he could guard the warehouse where he lived and worked, but the court heard Ben more loudly. The justices individually declared each of these four men guilty, scheduled their hanging for the next day, and remanded them to jail. Roger Gregory's Billy was next, but because of the time, the court adjourned until 10 a.m. on Friday, having tried and condemned six men.[5]

Early the next morning, jailer William Rose rang his "day light bell" to "signal my Servants to rise to Duty." Its ring, he reported to Monroe, moved "the unfortunate Criminals to a sense of their approaching Fates, and the whole Jail was alive to Hymns of Praise to the Great God and true (I hope) Penitence instantly began." His letter covered a petition from Solomon to the governor hoping for "a respite for a few days from the execution of the just and awful sentence . . . as he is ready . . . to make numerous discoveries concerning the late atrocious Conspiracy." Solomon's petition was in the hand and probably the words of James Thomson Callender, who now shared the jail with the condemned. When the cart or wagon came to carry the convicted to the gallows, Solomon remained to tell what he would. The five other men, Will, John, Isaac, Michael, and Ned rumbled off in the midst of "the whole force in service in the city (infantry and horse)" toward their deaths.[6]

At the gallows, the soldiers formed a circle around the site, "to keep off the croud during the execution." Within the ring rode Colonel John Mayo with two queries in mind. His slave George had disappeared a year before and Mayo believed he had been harbored on the Brook. He first inquired about his slave, but he gained no information. He then interrogated the prisoners—in their last moments of life—whether any white men were involved, as had been rumored. All denied the fact, although Michael seemed a bit hesitant. Mayo bore down on him, and Michael finally named John Stockdill, or Stockdell, a man Mayo knew had been dead for two years. He pressed Michael further, who then claimed "that he had heard from some of the boys" that Mr. Billy Young was the head of some men and had promised five dollars to those who would join. As Mayo withdrew, he and deputy sheriff John M. Sheppard, who oversaw the executions, exchanged their doubts about Michael's statement. With that, the men were hanged. Mayo later claimed he had grilled others subsequently sent to the gallows, who all denied Young's involvement, and stated he finally had it "explained to me" that Michael had confused planter William Young with his slave William or Billy Young.[7]

As Solomon sat in jail mentally composing what he might say, and as five men strangled under the gallows, the Henrico Court opened at mid-morning to try whom they could before day's end. They picked up where they left off with Gregory's Billy. Prosser's Ben served as the state's only recorded witness, saying "Billy was one," and told of his recruitment by Gabriel and of the convert's willingness to recruit if made a captain. The court found him guilty. Martin, the scripture-quoting older brother of Gabriel, next stood before the bar. Ben testified he had enlisted with Gabriel but his brother declared him too old, to which Martin allegedly responded he could make bullets, and did. Price's John, appearing for the first time as a sworn witness, told of Martin's agreeing at a spring where grog was served to join Gabriel to "fight the White People." He too was pronounced guilty. The court next heard Prosser's Ben swear that Roger Gregory's Charles had convinced Gabriel to make him a captain after promising to take him to the arms in Gregory's Tavern, while another slave named Patrick testified that at the same tavern, Charles had asked him "if he was a man." He wanted "to talk with a man, he would pay him well," a statement the court apparently took to be a recruiting effort. They agreed he was guilty. Next to be brought before them was Prosser's Frank, who Price's John identified as one of the men at Young's spring who enlisted under Gabriel, "to fight the White People." Prosser's Ben claimed he was a recruit of Gabriel and had been present at the brief meeting of conspirators on the Sunday morning after the storm. The court found him guilty as charged. Gregory's Martin became the next defendant. A man named Billy, possibly also a slave of Gregory, said Martin told him he had joined the "boys on the Brook." Prosser's Ben admitted that he did not know that he had, and a man named Moses swore in the man's defense that after the conspiracy was discovered, he heard Martin "curse the black people, for intending to rise against the whites." The judges unanimously acquitted him. William Burton's George, like Gregory's Billy before him, appeared but would have to wait for his legal ordeal, the court adjourning until the next day, Saturday, 13 September. As the judges left, they could see they had convicted four more men—Billy, Martin, Charles, and Frank—each of whom they ordered to be executed on Monday, 15 September, and had acquitted Gregory's Martin. Perhaps they felt some magnanimity; they surely believed that justice had been served.[8]

That Friday, Monroe had met with the council early enough to issue a reprieve to Solomon until Monday, 15 September, and to reject the extension of mercy to the five other men convicted the day before, who soon headed to the gallows. When the executive met again in the afternoon, they also authorized the payment of forty dollars as partial reimbursement to Paul Thilman, the rest to be split between "two Negroes as farther encouragement for their service" in capturing Harry, who had escaped from the Hanover jail, although Liberty remained an escapee. Monroe then dashed off a note to the mayor of Williamsburg. Someone in Hanover claimed to have spotted Gabriel asking the way to Jamestown. He wanted patrols ordered out to intercept the fugitive and for the mayor to pass the information on to the James City County militia commander and to Mr. [John] Ambler at Jamestown.[9]

The first public notices of the collapsed conspiracy also appeared on Friday, 12 September. Monroe's proclamation for the capture of Gabriel made its initial appearance in the *Richmond Examiner*, edited by one of his aides-de-camp, Meriwether Jones, and in the *Virginia Gazette and General Advertiser*, edited by Augustine Davis. The latter also carried the first news account of the conspiracy. It reported that thirty or forty men had been arrested, that Gabriel had "induced many poor, ignorant, and unfortunate creatures to share in his nefarious and horrid design," and that six had been found guilty and sentenced the day before. Davis hoped the plot, "so deeply planned, and long matured . . . entirely exploded." In the Richmond jail, James Thomson Callender, who served as a sort of contributing editor for the *Examiner*, put pen to paper, but sent his column to the *Aurora*, the Philadelphia Republican paper edited by James Duane, who would print it on 23 September. That Friday night, a young woman named Elvey Garthright was murdered, her body thrown under Bottom's Bridge, the span over the Chickahominy between Henrico and Charles City County on the road from Richmond to Williamsburg. She had been carrying two dresses she had sewn with her sister, which were not with her body when it was discovered the following Sunday. Although a rider reported seeing a black man carrying a bundle within a half hour after Garthright had left her sister's home, the unknown man was never seen again, and interestingly, no one seems to have tried to connect this incident to any of the slaves still at large associated with the conspiracy.

Perhaps this reflected a desperate desire that the plot was limited to the upper area of Henrico around the Brook and the populace hoped, along with Davis, that it was over. But when the story appeared in the papers a few days later, could Monroe have wondered if the unknown man could be Gabriel working his way down to Jamestown? If so, he left no indication he did. Nor did he know, by the time he might have seen the account, that Gabriel had already slipped across Henrico to the James River and boarded a ship to Norfolk.[10]

On Saturday, 13 September, the governor met his privy councilors again and examined the cases of the four men found guilty the day before and whose executions were scheduled for Monday. The council declined staying the execution of any, advising that "the law be permitted to take its course, they not appearing to be proper objects of mercy." Meanwhile, a sick Adam Craig sought relief of a lesser sort through the influence of Philip Norborne Nicholas, the acting attorney general and another of Monroe's aides-de-camp. The clerk of the Henrico Court, the Richmond Hustings Court, and its Common Hall, Craig had been ill for the last few days and feared his health would prevent his leaving his house for several more. He pled for an exemption from military duty for his two deputy clerks and another man who "does the running business in the County office." Craig's sickness and his deputies' service in the guard the previous two days had forced the closing of the clerk's office. As had happened during the crackdown in Petersburg the previous month, "numbers of free Negroes and Mulattoes have been constantly applying for their registers," which he was obligated to provide, and which they especially needed in the intense atmosphere of the crisis to avoid imprisonment. Furthermore, he expected the county and city courts and Richmond Hall to sit all the next week. For these reasons, he begged "a temporary discharge from duty" for his assistants, a request likely granted. Monroe was also queried in writing by Storrs and Selden about six slaves arrested "at the instance of the executive." Three were from Caroline County, the others from Richmond and vicinity. The examining magistrates wanted to know "upon what grounds they were suspected & where the testimony against them can be procured." Two of the men were named Moses, both employed by John Graham of Richmond. One may have been the Moses at the Tuckahoe coal pits named by Gilbert, who was taken up on Monroe's order of 11 September but who was never tried. Indeed, since none of these men ever faced trial as a conspirator in 1800, most were probably victims of zealous and fearful patrollers who gathered up the usual suspects. Small wonder that the free people of color in Richmond and Henrico were knocking at the door of the clerk's office.[11]

As Storrs and Selden searched for the evidence to charge the incarcerated, the Henrico justices continued the trials of the men already indicted. At Saturday's court, William Burton's George reappeared following the postponement of his trial from the day before. Prosser's Ben testified that at Gabriel's house George and his brother Isham had enthusiastically enrolled, saying "here are our hands & hearts, we will wade to our knees in blood sooner than fail in the attempt." Another slave of Burton's also appeared for the Commonwealth, but Burton himself provided an alibi for George, claiming he was employed driving his family to and from "a preachment" the Sunday of the alleged conversation. All of the judges but one pronounced George guilty, but George Williamson's vote brought acquittal. The judges next found Frank, a slave of Nathaniel Wilkinson, not guilty, Prosser's Ben apparently standing as the only witness against him. Sawney's case, next heard, had a different outcome. Ben testified that this slave, hired by William Young from the estate of William Lewis, had enlisted under Ben Woolfolk and had contributed his mite toward the purchase of grog to spur recruiting in Caroline. Price's John, who had earlier given up Sawney's name to his captors, then testified that the defendant was among those who stood up at Young's spring at the urging of Gabriel to show their commitment "to fight the White people." The court found him guilty and set his execution for Thursday, 18 September. They then put off the trial of Daniel, "as well as other slaves," until Monday, 15 September. Early the next day, Sunday, 14 September, Gabriel waded into the James River about four miles below Richmond, discarded a bayonet fixed on the end of a stick, and climbed aboard a schooner named *Mary* grounded on a bar. He claimed to be a man named Daniel but admitted some called him Gabriel. Two slave crewmen were not so sure.[12]

On Monday, as Gabriel floated down the James, the state hanged his brother Solomon, along with the four men found guilty the Friday before, on the gallows in Richmond. Callender complained to Jefferson "of their bellowing . . . below stairs," and wished that they had been executed immediately upon conviction, even though he had helped with Solomon's petition. Solomon's confession was dated the 15th, so it appears he gave it early that morning to Storrs and Selden, who forwarded it to the council, where it was read. In it, Solomon recounted his initial conversation with

Gabriel about the plot, its aims, strategies, and timing—the "discharge of the number of soldiers one or two months ago" identified as an important factor—and its leadership. He admitted to making twelve swords at Gabriel's request, and revealed that "the first places Gabriel intended to attack in Richmond were the Capitol, the Magazine, the Penetentiary, the Governor's house & his person." He did not specify whether they intended to kill or just capture Monroe. Nor did Solomon surrender the names of any other plotters but Gabriel and Jack Bowler. Everything else he knew, he took to his grave.[13]

Just as the five men executed on Friday received a guard of all the forces mustered in the town, so did Solomon, Billy, Martin, Charles, and Frank, the five who died on Monday. Monroe provided detailed instructions on the respective roles of the infantry of the 19th Regiment and the Richmond Horse: fifty men to march to the jail as an escort of the prisoners; the cavalry "to prevent the people from approaching the criminals"; the rest of the forces to fall in behind the guard as they passed to the gallows. Afterwards, all were to return in good order to Capitol Square to be discharged. There Monroe either delivered or had an officer read a statement of thanks to the troops, wherein he also provided his first public analysis of the events begun two weeks earlier.[14]

What Monroe included reveals his political sensitivity to the potential questioning of the executive's conduct in a crisis that had not physically materialized. "The trials," he preemptively pronounced, provided "incontrovertable proof that a serious conspiracy against the lives and property of the good people of this Commonwealth has existed," and whose "danger has been in great measure averted by the patriotism and good conduct" of the men mustered into service. "Checked" by the storm, and losing the advantage of surprise by the revealing of the plot, the conspirators, according to Monroe, "trembled in contemplation of the enterprize they had undertaken." Confronted by the "preparation that was made and the decision which was shewn that their effort would be in vain," they "recoiled from it." The state owed its thanks to "the great disposer of events" and the "slave who discovered the conspiracy." He then revealed that patrols would still be drawn from the Richmond Horse and that the artillery company would remain in place.[15]

When the council and Monroe met that day, they began reducing the number of activated troops but left in place one hundred fifty men defending Richmond, thirty guarding Manchester, twenty-five patrolling

Henrico, and four artillerymen sitting at the capitol. As they listened to the clerk read Solomon's statement, they were reminded, as perhaps even Storrs and Selden were in taking his confession, of Jack Bowler's greater significance as an early leader and organizer. Consequently, the council authorized Monroe to proclaim a reward of $300 for his capture, the same amount they had offered for Gabriel. They obtained a description of him from Richard Bowler on Wednesday, and the advertisement began appearing on Friday, 19 September, in the *Examiner*. Apparently still looking for additional clinching proof of the conspiracy, or, more likely, trying to grasp the extent of it, the council also authorized Monroe "to send for any person or persons who may be reported to him as capable of giving information relative to the insurrection."[16]

At the Henrico County courthouse the judges continued hearing the cases of the indicted, having not yet dealt with half of the thirty originally presented on 11 September. They resumed the case of John Brooke's Daniel and found him not guilty in an unrecorded vote. Next, Peter, described as a mulatto slave of Prosser's, listened to the duet of Prosser's Ben and Price's John and then heard the judges pronounce his guilt and order his execution on Thursday, 18 September. Nathaniel Wilkinson's Jupiter, who had appeared in the same court a year earlier for stealing the hog of Absalom Johnson, followed Peter to jail with the same death sentence hanging over his head. Prosser's Ben repeated Jupiter's conversation at the barn raising with Gabriel, when he revealed how they could get into the capitol and told of his enlisting men in Richmond. Thomas H. Prosser put a date on the conversation by stating when he had left for Amherst, "about the seventh of August," the day before the raising, and in the vernacular of the day, put a period to Jupiter's life. The judges next disposed of the case of Sam, another slave of Wilkinson's, with a guilty verdict, and set his execution on Thursday. Again, Prosser's Ben provided the key testimony, relating how Sam had bragged that with enough men "they would drive all the white people into the River," and of his enlistment under Gabriel. An unnamed white man may have testified, saying that Sam had protested his innocence when taken up. Two men, Davy and Bristoe, appeared on his behalf, but to no avail, the clerk noting only that Bristoe "said no to all inter[r]ogations." A third Wilkinson slave, and the second Daniel tried that day, followed at the bar, and he was unanimously found not guilty. Prosser's Ben provided the only testimony against him. He retold a conversation between Daniel and Solomon which offered quotations of how "the boys in Town" were "well and ready to do the Business," Ben explaining to the judges the parlance of the plotters. He also said that Gabriel claimed Daniel as a follower, "but never directly heard the prisoner make any acknowledgment to that effect." Apparently, Daniel had not attended the meeting at Young's spring or Price's John would certainly have testified, as that seemed to be his one vantage point for observing the plot.[17]

The next case proved provocative. At the last round of trials, the court had acquitted Burton's George when justice Williamson had failed to cast a guilty vote. Now his brother Isham, who had joined George in exclaiming how ready they were to wade knee-deep in blood to win their freedom, stood at the bar. It seems the testimony offered at the two trials was essentially the same, with one difference. This time, master Burton could not testify to Isham's whereabouts in the same manner he could vouch for George's during any of the activities of the day when the criminal conversations took place. The court found Isham guilty, provoking Burton and ten of his neighbors near the Brook to petition the council the next day for a pardon. They claimed "that if he [Isham] had any knowledge of the plot or Conspiracy that he has been Seduced and Perswaded into it." They feared no danger from him if he should "Return into his Master's Service." The council rejected the petition, and also ruled that none of the others convicted that same day merited any mercy from them. Thus, four more men—Peter, Jupiter, Sam, and Isham—would leave the jail with Sawney for the gallows on Thursday, 18 September, bringing the total condemned to fifteen. Writing home the next day after having just arrived the evening before from Fredericksburg, John Minor noted the ten who had already been executed and the four more found guilty on Monday. He felt deeply for them, and for those still awaiting execution, "yet the severity is necessary," he wrote. "How dreadful the situation!! to be obliged to be *cruel* and *unjust,* as the only means of self defence, *I am sick of these thoughts.*"[18]

On Tuesday, 16 September, while Minor expressed his anguish to his wife, the judges met again and continued with what Minor concluded was "necessary." They decided, "for reasons appearing to the court," to postpone the case of Gilbert, which they had put off the day before because they had lacked the time to hear his case. Perhaps he may have promised to talk, or was ill, but the postponement made Ned the next defendant. This slave of William Young was identified by Prosser's Ben as "one of the Conspirators," a man who had enlisted under Ben Woolfolk, the hired slave of Young. The six pence he put into the plot to support

Woolfolk's Caroline County recruiting were enough for the judges to deem him guilty and order his execution on Friday the 19th. Isaac, a slave of James Allen, also was sent to the gallows on the testimony of Prosser's Ben. He testified that Isaac came to Prosser's blacksmith shop and inquired of Solomon "if he had cut the Scythe Blades to fight with, and at what time it would be that the Insurrection would commence." It had to be soon, he said, or "he would go off, as he was determined not to serve a white man another year." The court grimly granted his wish by ordering him executed on Friday. Harry stepped before the bar, a slave of Thomas Austin of Hanover. Prosser's Ben testified, but the court found him not guilty. The same was true for Ned and Joe, both Austin men also facing the testimony of Prosser's Ben. But the string of acquittals ended at the trial of Laddis, a slave of John Williamson. Prosser's Ben relayed that Gabriel encouraged him to enlist Laddis, which he did, and that Laddis later "readily consented" to join Gabriel "to fight the white people," even before the meeting often referred to at Young's spring. Price's John reinforced the evidence of his involvement when he swore Laddis stood with the others at Gabriel's invitation at the spring and pledged "he would stand by him til the last." The court set his execution for Friday as well.[19]

Billy Chicken, whose name Price's John had given to John Foster, faced the justices next. By then, he had been sitting in jail since 5 September, apparently on the accusation of Prosser's Ben. The court, however, failed to convict him. The clerk did not note whether it was because of the lack of unanimity for a guilty verdict or a pronouncement in favor of this man recorded as a slave of Dabney Williamson.[20]

Then the bailiff called Ben Woolfolk, whose name had begun to appear as a recruiter in earlier testimony. He was likely picked up as the Ben at Young's on the list drawn up at the interrogation of Price's John. It was soon enough to be indicted with the others on 11 September. Indeed, Price's John testified first, claiming the presence of Woolfolk at Young's spring, his enlisting with Gabriel, his agreeing "to slay them as we go," and his holding the rank of captain. Prosser's Ben followed, recounting a trip with Gabriel to Woolfolk's before a recruiting venture to Caroline, and of hearing Woolfolk claim to have six hundred recruits he would lead to the rendezvous at the Brook. Witness Ben also revealed that Woolfolk had gathered six scythe blades for Gabriel, and "very readily agreed" with the general to "slay the white males from the Cradle upwards, but the females of all ages were to be Spared." Woolfolk quickly joined the list of those scheduled to die, though his date was set for Monday, the 22nd. Perhaps Woolfolk had blurted out he would make a confession before the court could set his death for Friday along with Ned, Isaac, and Laddis. The judges then put off the trial of Stephen until the next day. It appears that Woolfolk was returned to the hands of Storrs and Selden, to whom he began to reveal the names of his co-conspirators.[21]

Richmond newspapers appeared on Tuesdays and Fridays, and the Tuesday editions now carried more information to the public about the trials and executions than the previous Friday's issues, printed just after the first day of the trials. The *Argus* reported the executions of five men on Friday and five more on Monday, with more scheduled for Thursday. "Tis most devoutly to be wished, that these examples may deter all future attempts of this diabolical nature," prayed Samuel Pleasants. The *Examiner*, which had carried Monroe's proclamation on Gabriel on Friday, printed extracts from the militia law regarding duties and patrolling, so "no non commissioned Officer or Soldier may plead ignorance" of their responsibilities during the crisis, and then ran a rant that rose from the Richmond jail. Callender lambasted the court's failure to condemn George, the slave of William Burton, singling out dissenting justice George Williamson and calling him "a *quondam* Anabaptist preacher." "It is hoped," Callender continued, "that the natural instinctive sense of shame, which even a dog is capable of feeling, will prevent this *humane* magistrate from ever ascending the bench again." The seditious Scot reported the testimony of George's willingness to engage in a bloodbath, and claimed all present at the trial thought "his guilt of the blackest die." The column, "stated in civil, but in plain terms," Callender later explained to Jefferson—without acknowledging authorship—provoked "a prodigious racket . . . against the Editor, as if he had designed to insult the whole sect of Baptists. Thus you see that illeberal superstition, and the most narrow prejudice are not excluded from this state." He claimed George himself was a Baptist minister and that Burton later "acknowledged that his *alibi* was founded upon a mistake." But Callender also admitted to Jefferson he "could not say with what justice" the "blame" frequently cast upon Baptists "for having put impracticable notions of liberty into the heads of these fellows," had any merit. On Friday, editor Jones apologized for the sulfurous sentences from the Richmond jail, claiming that the column "was not intended to reflect upon the Baptist society generally. The Editor knows the writer of that paragraph never puts himself in the way of religious disputes." He then testified to magistrate Williamson's "much esteemed" standing within the community.[22]

While Callender immersed Baptists in his scorn, Augustine Davis ignited a political firestorm with his commentary on the testimony given at the opening trial of Solomon, where two French men were alleged to have been the "instigators" of the plot, and at the trial of Will on the same day, where the French were allegedly to be spared from the sword. Davis, the Federalist-appointed postmaster, concluded, "It is evident that the French principles of Liberty and Equality have been infused into the minds of the negroes and that the intemperate use of these words by some whites amongst us have inspired them with hopes of success." To Federalists, the phrase "French principles of Liberty and Equality" was shorthand for radical Jacobin threats to order and structure. Davis then reported the execution of five on Friday and five more on Monday, as had the *Argus*, and noted, "The trials are still going on." Testimony on the public record, but still known to only a few, suddenly became public knowledge and part of the political contest of 1800. Davis's account would be reprinted and used by Federalist newspapers throughout the country in their attacks on Jefferson's candidacy because of the vice president's perceived pro-French positions. It would provoke reactions from the fraternity of Republican editors, too. Did Davis delay publicizing the trial testimony of Thursday until after the crisis seemed under control the following week? It would seem so. In fact, it appears that this lifelong Virginian was cognizant of the importance of white solidarity in the face of slave insurgency, but thought that once the state was clearly in control he could poke at an external, French-inspired ideology to make political points, and do so without naming any particular group. Callender, on the other hand, was politically insensitive to this—indeed, to many things—and willingly attacked an indigenous and growing religious sect whose members comprised an important part of the Republican electorate.[23]

On Wednesday, as the furor over who inspired their slaves to revolt heated up, Gervas Storrs and Joseph Selden took down the confession of the convicted Ben Woolfolk. The Henrico Court postponed yet again the trial of Gilbert, and found Stephen, a slave of Thomas Wingfield of Hanover not guilty, Prosser's Ben serving as the sole witness for the Commonwealth. Meanwhile, on the information of either Gilbert or Woolfolk, Monroe ordered a justice in Hanover to arrest Sam Byrd Sr., the free father of the wide-ranging recruiter and namesake. A Caroline justice was requested to secure four slaves of Paul Woolfolk and Paul Thilman and send them to Richmond for trial, and a dozen more named for arrest and trial in Caroline, all on the accusations of Woolfolk. By 30 September, a guard from the militia would be stationed at the Caroline County jail to seal the confinement of those placed in irons inside, but their trials would not begin for three more weeks.[24]

In Richmond on Thursday morning, Monroe and the council began disposing of matters of state when William Foushee belatedly joined them, apparently bringing the trial records of the men condemned that week. The council rejected any claims for mercy, including the petition in favor of Burton's Isham, but issued the pardon to Ben Woolfolk. With that, Foushee left again and the board resumed its deliberations. With no mercy forthcoming from the council, the cart and guard came to the jail and rolled away with Sawney, Peter, Jupiter, Sam, and Isham. Their deaths brought the number of executed men to fifteen, all at the gallows in Richmond. Back in the council chambers, the feisty Alexander McRae, also one of Monroe's aides-de-camp, introduced a resolution which called for a guard of at least fifty men to be placed at the penitentiary to protect over three thousand arms stored there. These weapons were apparently those whose redistribution to the counties was suspended at the emergence of the conspiracy, and possibly included some obtained the year before under external contracts. Perhaps glancing over his political shoulder, McRae posited that the "perfectly clear & conclusive" evidence "that the conspiracy among the blacks is of a most alarming intent & that many hundreds of them in various parts of the Commonwealth are concerned in it," justified that "no care or expense necessary to secure the public arms should be spared." His proposal did not carry much support, for the council instead chose to advise that a force of forty-five men, with "proper officers," be distributed among the penitentiary, jail, and capitol. Apparently, they thought the need to take these steps self-evident, for they did not include an explanatory preamble.[25]

On Friday, 19 September, the cart came again, and Ned, Laddis, and Isaac, all found guilty on Tuesday and ordered executed on that Friday, were loaded and sent off to the gallows, but it soon returned the men to the jail. In a petition dated 18 September, Andrew Dunscomb and twelve of Richmond's prominent citizens, including State Treasurer William Berkeley, had petitioned the Henrico Court to have the place of execution moved to the ground near the powder magazine. This may have been submitted simultaneously with a similar request to the executive. The petitioners explained that the executions had proven "extremely distressing to the view of our families—especially the female members." Monroe referred them to the Henrico Court, telling them the executive had no authority to move the gallows, but reassuring them that if he did, he would comply with their wishes. The order book is silent as to the court's response, if any, but according to Callender, the cart was stopped by an order of the council. He attributed their intercession to a petition from some women who lived near the gallows. "Perhaps you will suppose," he wrote Jefferson, "that the prayer of their petition was to save the lives of these wretches, but it was only that they might be hung *in some other place*, because the exhibition was offensive." The council stayed their execution until the following Monday, when it again reprieved the three men until 3 October, a delay that would ultimately save Ned's life. Monroe then asked the council whether the militiamen guarding the arsenal at Point of Fork should be discharged, and the council advised against their dismissal. Perhaps the new revelations of Woolfolk gave them pause.[26]

At the courthouse, Ben Woolfolk made his first appearance as a witness that Friday, when he joined Price's John to testify against George Smith. Woolfolk described Smith's efforts to recruit him—"the first time he ever heard any thing of a conspiracy and insurrection among the Blacks"—told of the colonel's recruiting about the Brook and in Manchester, and revealed his proposal to visit the "Outlandish people" at Pipeing Tree. Price's John again recounted the meeting at Young's spring and said George agreed "to fight the white people for their freedom" with Gabriel, "and gave him his hand." The court condemned him, and then put off more trials until Monday.[27]

If the executive hesitated in completely contracting the defensive measures which had reached their height around 13 September, it may have partly been due to the worries that began to be registered from elsewhere in the state. Across the river, George Markham reported that Burwell Gates, an enslaved "fellow of bad character," had been in contact with the conspirators in Henrico and had "seen some of the arms," presumably the federal arms stacked in Manchester. Up the James River, Colonel Mayo Carrington learned of evidence that the conspiracy had reached his neighborhood around Cartersville in Cumberland, so he hoped Monroe would approve of his ordering out men from Powhatan to Buckingham to watch the "Batteau men" gliding by on the river. He announced he was sending down under guard a man by the name of Stepney, a hired slave with a Goochland owner, who had been taken up as an alleged recruiter. The guard was later compensated, but no trial record survives of the captive's prosecution. Down the peninsula in Williamsburg, the city council instructed the mayor to request a loan of twenty-five "Stand of Arms with the proper Accoutrements," as a result of "Public Agitation" occasioned by the "meditated insurrection of Slaves." The mayor made the supplication the next day, and when Monroe placed the request before the council, the arms were ordered shipped to the former capital the following week. From Port Royal came a query from William Bernard, wondering if a man he had hired that year named Griffen had been implicated. Local scuttlebutt made him into a conspirator. If Monroe had evidence that he was in the plot, Bernard needed to know what to do. From Albemarle, a report soon arrived of four armed men asking a slave woman the direction to Columbia, near Point of Fork. These figures had subsequently disappeared, but Petersburg residents still wondered about the insurgents on their streets. The plot now framed white people's understanding of black people's behavior.[28]

Monroe was anxious too. His family had re-joined him in Richmond, and his hopes about his son's health were fading. He was also concerned about the number of men the state could be executing. "When to arrest the hand of the executioner is a question of great importance," he had observed to Jefferson after ten had been hanged, and with twice to perhaps four times that many men still to be tried. "A rebel who avows it was his intention to assassinate his master &c" was not likely to "ever become a useful servant" again if pardoned, and the council had no power to exile such men from Virginia as slaves; to "transport" them was the term commonly used. If doubts existed about guilt, he favored mercy over severity, but what number of executions would sufficiently terrorize the slaves and relieve the public's fears, he did not know. He invited Jefferson's advice.[29]

Jefferson agreed the question was significant. He noted that those close to the scene would naturally want many executed, but for those more distant, such as his neighbors in Albemarle, who understood the peril but had not felt the threat immediately, "there has been hanging enough." Jefferson warned of the condemnation of other American citizens, "and the world at large," if Virginia took "one step beyond absolute necessity." It would appear the state sought revenge, not justice. Still, Jefferson recognized the problem remained—what to do about the accused.

He wished the next session of the assembly would authorize transportation, but feared that incarcerating the guilty until then might invite an attempt to free them. He requested that Monroe keep these thoughts confidential and encouraged him to seek advice from many others, perhaps hoping some of them had arrived at similar conclusions and he would not be suspected as Monroe's sole confidant. When Monroe wrote again on 22 September, he noted that now fifteen men had been executed and that others had been reprieved for a fortnight. He thanked Jefferson for his advice and said "it wod. be unwise to make no provision agnst possibilities," apparently agreeing with Jefferson's assessment that holding the prisoners required special guards to keep them from being liberated. He hoped Jefferson would provide further advice if he had any before the next executions. Monroe reported his son "in the utmost danger," and feared for his life.[30]

On Monday, 22 September, the Henrico justices finally tried Gilbert, whose trial had been postponed several times over the previous week. Prosser's Ben, Price's John, and Ben Woolfolk each testified to his participation, and although Woolfolk recounted that Gilbert was unable to kill his master and mistress—"they having raised him"—he still revealed that Gilbert "was determined . . . [they] should be put to death by the men under him." The court found him guilty. At their verdict, Gilbert began making a statement, which the judges cut off, but John Foster collected one from him the next day. In his public outburst he apparently sputtered out the names of two Petersburg recruiters, the two uncles of Sam Byrd Jr. His revelations in court were quickly relayed by an observer to a friend in Petersburg, who apparently informed William Prentis that Jesse Byrd and Reuben Byrd had been named in the trial. Prentis quickly had the two men arrested and wrote Monroe asking if any evidence existed in his hands of their involvement, or of the mention of any others "this way." In Gilbert's private confession to John Foster, which was passed on to the executive but not made public, he identified the Frenchman Charles Quersey as a man who had encouraged the slaves in Caroline County to revolt three or four years before, but about whom he had not heard or seen since. Others, however, had said that Quersey was actively involved in "this late business." And he recounted the plot to set Richmond afire in 1798. The latter probably led to the arrest of Brutus, alias Julius, since Foster was a Richmond alderman. Perhaps Gilbert calculated that a further confession, beyond the naming of names he had done earlier, would lead to clemency. He did not know that the one man Gabriel would name when captured was him.[31]

With Gilbert subdued and sent off to jail, the court turned next to the case of Joe, a slave of Temperance Baker of Hanover. He avoided the gallows with the vote of one dissenting and unidentified justice. George, a slave of Izard Bacon of the Brook, was found not guilty, the testimony of Prosser's Ben apparently not considered sufficient. Prosser's Ben served as a more deadly state's witness in the next trial, that of Prosser's Tom. He swore that one morning as the two walked to Prosser's house, Tom confessed that he had joined and that he wished "this was the night appointed for the business." The judges found him guilty and ordered him hanged on 3 October at Prosser's Tavern, the same site of Gilbert's and George Smith's ordered executions. The court then put off any more trials until Saturday, vacating the courthouse for the use of the Richmond Hustings Court later in the week.[32]

On Tuesday, Gilbert gave his statement to John Foster. Its structure, for all of its shaping by Foster, appears as bursts of information, its revelations seeming to be those of a desperate man, or perhaps they are the way Foster made sense of Gilbert's stutterings. Gilbert named Matt Scott and told of the list he never saw; of James getting the key from Cowley's house and letting Gabriel into the capitol; of the disagreement between George Smith and Armistead over how much of the town to burn; of the fire at Purcell's in 1798 and the men involved; of Sam Byrd's claims to have enlisted men as far as Charlottesville; of men enlisted at or near Ross's ironworks and of the men around the Point of Fork; and finally of Charles Quersey's encouraging revolt three or four years before. The statement ended with the simple surrender of two more names: Moses, a slave of Samuel Parsons who was scheduled to become free, and Bob, a slave of Wilkinson. Foster provided the council with a copy, and probably started looking for Brutus, alias Julius, once hired to Dr. Foushee, and William Austin's Frank, the two men Gilbert alleged were conspirators in the fire of 1798.[33]

The authorities found Brutus and tried him for conspiracy and insurrection in the Richmond Court of Oyer and Terminer on Thursday, the 25th. He was found not guilty. The same court on the same day tried King, the slave of attorney general Philip Norborne Nicholas and found him guilty of the same charge. He was defended by "counsel assigned by his master," but to no avail. Ben Woolfolk swore of King's enlisting and of his willingness to kill the whites "like sheep." Mrs. Martin told of his coming to her shop the week after the plot was blown and speaking in cryptic phrases of "looking hard at the Bacon but can't get at it, and that we are doing all we can with our Guns and Bayonets, and what we can't do with our Guns we will do with our Bayonets." She described him touching his head and adding, "No person knew what was in there." Nicholas appealed to the court for mercy.[34]

While Gilbert gave his statement in Richmond on Tuesday, 23 September, the three-masted schooner *Mary*, captained by Richardson Taylor and crewed by Billy and Isham, and possibly more men, crept up the Elizabeth River and tied up at Norfolk. The ship had been boarded downstream just before pulling into Norfolk, perhaps to check for disease or for customs. It had pulled alongside a ship with a crew of twenty-five and then anchored by ten o'clock that morning. Billy was later sent on shore on some errand and saw a young man, a blacksmith's apprentice perhaps, named John Moss, most likely a relative of Sheldon Moss of Richmond, who held Billy's wife. Billy told Moss of his suspicions about a man who had boarded the *Mary* ten days before just below Richmond. He thought he was Gabriel, and said that he and Taylor "was then a going to secure him." But Moss, and perhaps another man, informed two constables, who boarded the vessel about 2 p.m., found an unrestrained Gabriel, and arrested him. Taylor tried to forbid them from doing so, "claiming him as his prisoner."[35]

Thomas Newton, the superintendent of quarantine, militia colonel, and state senator, could not believe that Taylor, leaving Richmond after the hangings had started and the conspiracy had become well known, had not suspected that his passenger was Gabriel. Nor could he fathom how Taylor had allowed a black man without papers to board his vessel, had foregone numerous opportunities while slipping down the river to gain help if he didn't trust his crew to assist him in taking Gabriel, and had even been boarded and passed other vessels while pulling into Norfolk, without mentioning the man's presence. He had even let Gabriel roam free on the ship. Taylor had once been an overseer, Newton observed, "an old inhabitant" who knew blacks, free or slave, could not travel without a pass or appropriate identification. For Taylor now to claim him as his prisoner, "when he never shewed the least disposition before of confining him," was beyond Newton's understanding.[36]

Newton's suspicions about Taylor grew after he interrogated Billy and Isham. They claimed they had tried to convince their captain that the man who admitted that some called him Gabriel but who claimed his name was actually Daniel, was in fact "the person for whom the reward was offered." But Newton had his suspicions about the crew as well as Taylor. He suggested examining Billy's wife, "at a Mr. Norris's on Shockoe hill" in Richmond, to discover if "Gabriel had concerted any measure to get on board this vessel with the hands." Billy belonged to Miles King of Hampton, and had actually been jailed for a time in Richmond "on suspicion," and his brother Ned incarcerated in Hampton for expressing approval of the conspiracy, or so Newton reported. Taylor told him he had freed Isham, but Newton learned from Isham that no manumission papers had ever been given him. The sailor said Taylor had "promised him to do it when he was a methodist, but as he was now turn'd again he was afraid he would not give him his freedom." Taylor, Isham feared, had either lost his faith or possibly his anti-slavery sentiments and had changed his mind. Newton then suggested that Taylor's character was probably best known by Mr. Hooper, the part-owner of the vessel, or Dr. Foushee, because Taylor had "lived at Rich Neck with Mr Hylton." Newton bound him over to appear before the mayor of Richmond by 25 October and enclosed his recognizance. He suggested the reward for taking up Gabriel should go to the two constables, who had "been very active and constantly looking out for him," with something to be given to Billy for revealing Gabriel's presence. Newton told Monroe that Gabriel "will give your Excy a full information," but no one else. The captive did tell Newton that "a negro Gilbert belong[in]g to a Billy Young, now with his master at the Springs, was chief in the consperation."[37]

Gabriel and the two constables boarded a vessel on Wednesday, 24 September, to return to Richmond. A large crowd of people, white and black, turned out to catch a glimpse of the man with "a mind capable of forming the daring project which he had conceived." *The Epitome of the Times*, a Republican paper, further reported something "a little singular": that "the exultation of his black brethern was not less apparent than that of the whites. If they truly felt all that was expressed by the countenance and the tongue, Gabriel could not deserve a greater punishment than to be delivered into their hands." The conspiracy, the paper explained, "in which he was concerned had drawn down on them greater rigour then formerly, and their resentment was naturally directed to him as the cause."[38]

The Federalist *Norfolk Herald* noted the vessel left under a wind, which if it lasted should give Gabriel "a short if not a *pleasant* passage." Indeed, the trip was much shorter than his earlier ride with the current, lasting just over three days. He was brought to the governor's house in Richmond about four o'clock in the afternoon of Saturday, 27 September, once again surrounded by a large crowd of blacks and whites. There seems to have been a short exchange of words between the governor and the general, which was apparently the only time the two men faced each other. Monroe then spotted Captain Giles among the throng and requested him to organize a guard out of the men in the group and to take Gabriel to the penitentiary. Monroe wanted him placed in a separate cell, and ordered that none of them should talk to him nor allow anyone else to do so. Monroe then retreated into his house and to his distraught family and dying son, who passed away at 10 p.m. the next night. Gabriel was marched to the penitentiary and would remain imprisoned until his trial nine days later. By then, the state had added more men to the executioner's list but also continued to cut its costs, as executive pardons began to replace trips to the gallows. For the man who was to lead the insurrection, there would be no mercy.[39]

5 } Putting a Period

With Gabriel in custody, a new phase in the public's response to the intended insurrection emerged. As the editor of the *Argus* expressed it from his vantage point in Richmond, "A period is put to the anxiety and perturbation which for several weeks past has convulsed the public mind by the capture and safe commitment of GABRIEL." The *Virginia Gazette* gave a brief description of the presentation of Gabriel to the governor, and reported that the captive "denied the charge of being first in exciting the insurrection" but admitted that "he was to have had the chief command." The paper also claimed that Gabriel had stated "that there were four or five persons more materially concerned in the conspiracy; and said he could mention several in Norfolk," but confessed nothing else. This paper, which had first published the news of the alleged Frenchmen, then relayed, "We have heard it slightly rumoured, that he has letters in his possession from white people, but do not pretend to set it forth as a report deserving of credit." But if any whites were involved in the plot, the editor hoped "that they may be bro't to justice."[1]

For the executive, however, the end of the affair seemed more distant. Men still awaited trial, Jack Bowler remained at large, and the forces of the state still patrolled the neighborhood of the Brook and guarded the public places in Richmond and the arsenal at Point of Fork. Pressures to reduce the associated costs and release militiamen were likely to increase, while the need to maintain vigilance remained. On the Saturday Gabriel stood before Monroe, 27 September, the governor gave notice to the council to meet in an extraordinary Sunday session. When they assembled, Monroe remained home with his anxious family, but sent them a letter describing Gabriel's arrival and listing a number of matters they should attend to, including those related to Gabriel's imprisonment. The council sent three of its members—Alexander McRae, William Foushee, and former governor James Wood—"to take his confession should he be inclined to make any." They soon returned to chambers, reporting that "Gabriel did not seem disposed at present to make any confession worth notice." With that, the council dismissed the men Monroe had appointed to guard him and ordered that the prisoner be kept in isolation, watched by a single sentinel drawn from the general guard at the penitentiary.[2]

The councilors reconvened the next day, again without Monroe, whose son Spence had died the night before, and allotted the $300 reward to the two Norfolk constables who physically seized Gabriel and were delegated to take him to Richmond. They were also reimbursed for the five dollars spent on the irons Gabriel wore, but the council did not yet reward Billy, whose information had triggered Gabriel's capture. They authorized the reenlistment of the permanent guard at Point of Fork, and agreed to allow some guns shipped to Richmond from Philadelphia under a contract with the state that sat at Rocketts to be placed in the penitentiary for safekeeping. They also ordered an examination of the weapons before formally accepting them as state property, but expressed "great anxiety that the law authorizing the executive to procure a supply of arms . . . should be carried into effect."[3]

When Monroe returned to meet with the council on Thursday, 2 October, the executive faced more cases of men condemned to death than had already been executed. The question of when to stop the executions, if one could, was more than an abstract consideration affecting the body politic. Just before Gabriel arrived in Richmond on Saturday, 27 September, the Henrico justices of the Court of Oyer and Terminer tried and found three more men guilty and condemned them to die on 3 October. Clarke's Sam Byrd Jr., Goode's Michael, and Young's William were crowded into the jail with Ned, Isaac, Laddis, George, Gilbert, Tom, and King, each awaiting their adjudicated fate at the gallows. On Monday, the court had acquitted Jim Allen and Moses, both slaves of James Price. But it had found guilty Sam Graham, the slave of Paul Graham of Hanover, and Abraham, a slave of Thomas Burton of Henrico, thus adding two more to the executioner's list. On Tuesday, they resumed with the trials of Jacob, a slave of Thomas Woodfin; Dick, belonging to Jesse Smith; James, the property of

Elisha Price; and Solomon, a slave from the estate of Joseph Lewis—all of Henrico. Each of these men was found guilty and ordered hanged on 10 October, except for Solomon, whose date of death was scheduled a week later. The court gathered again on Wednesday, 1 October, and condemned Peter, an enslaved man of Allen Williamson, as well as Lewis, a man held by Dabney Williamson, both of Henrico. Two men named Billy, one hired by Charles Sneed from Nathaniel Lipscombe of Hanover, the other in the estate of Ambrose Lipscombe, also of Hanover, left under sentence, all four marked for death on 17 October. Thus, as the council came to order on 2 October, twenty men awaited an appointment with the gallows, nine of them the next day. With a recommendation for mercy in hand for Jacob, the council pardoned him; his execution had been set for Friday, 10 October. The council then reprieved until the same Friday the nine men listed to die on the morrow.[4]

On Friday the 3rd, Monroe and council reduced the number of militiamen still in service. The two companies sent from Goochland and Fluvanna to the Point of Fork were finally dismissed and an express sent to inform them, the cost of the messenger probably less than the wages and sustenance of the fifty men for a day or two. The men who had been stationed at Priddy's or Gregory's Tavern north of the Brook were discharged too, but the guards in Richmond remained, as did those watching in Manchester, because the federal arms still sat there, never having been moved to the penitentiary. Monroe would quickly resume trying to get that done. Having cut the state's costs with these measures, the board now turned to what increasingly can be seen as another cost-savings measure—the pardoning of the condemned. The guilty verdicts of Abraham, the two Billys, Peter, and Dick had been accompanied with recommendations that each be considered "as an object of mercy." The council pardoned all five and granted a reprieve to Ned, the slave of William Young who had once been trundled toward the gallows. His stay was extended until the second Friday in November. Monroe then asked "whether any of the Negroes now under condemnation for Conspiracy and Insurrection should be reprieved until the meeting of the general assembly" so that their cases "might receive, in all lights in which it may be contemplated, a legislative consideration." The eight councilors in attendance split evenly on the vote, killing the proposal, Monroe not having a vote to break the tie. The decision left eleven men facing death sentences a week from that date, on Friday the 10th, three more the Friday following, and one with his sentence suspended and in limbo until November, but with others yet remaining to be tried.[5]

On Monday, 6 October, came the trials of Gabriel and four other men. Gabriel was docketed first, perhaps because disposing of his case early on would help dissipate any crowd that might continue to gather and prove threatening as the day passed. Prosser's Ben, Price's John, and Ben Woolfolk, the three men most consistently serving as the Commonwealth's witnesses, gave the testimony in the case. Ben described Gabriel's rise from captain "at first consultation" to general after "he had enlisted a number of men." He told of the intention to kill the masters along the Brook, to enter Richmond "where they would kill every body," to capture the treasury, and to divide up the money. He relayed that after taking the town, Gabriel intended to train his troops in anticipation of the force that would soon be upon them. But if the whites "agreed to their freedom," they would hoist a white flag and Gabriel "would dine and drink with the merchants of the City, on the day when it should be so agreed to." Prosser's Ben then said Gabriel made the handles for the swords Solomon pounded out, ran bullets with his brother Martin, and claimed under his command "nearly 10,000 men . . . 1000 in Richmond, about 600 in Caroline and nearly 500 at the coal pits besides others." He then testified that Gabriel "expected the poor white people would also join him and that 2 frenchmen had actually joined whom he said Jack Ditcher knew" but that Gabriel would not reveal to him. In the face of the storm, they agreed to meet the next night. Prosser's Ben added that his general claimed all the Negroes in Petersburg would join after the start of the uprising. Price's John repeated Gabriel's invitation to join him at the meeting at Young's spring, to meet in three weeks, and to work hard at recruiting until then. Ben Woolfolk also described the meeting at Young's, and then stated "that Bob Cooley and Mr Tinsley's Jim was to let them into the Capitol to get the arms out." He then told of what the expected events of the night of the revolt were to have been, of the sparing of "Quakers, Methodists and French people," of creating a flag with "death or liberty" emblazoned on it, and that "they would kill all except as before unless they agreed to the freedom of the Blacks in which case they would at least cut off one of their arms." Then he returned to Gabriel's claim of the cooperation of Cowley and how the Keeper of the Capitol had shown him "every room" in it. After the testimony, the judges pronounced Gabriel guilty, sentenced him to die the next day, and urged him to confess. Gabriel refused to do so, but requested a delay in his execution until Friday. The judges passed his plea on to the executive, where, in their only item of business the next day, he won the reprieve. The council then excused Alexander McRae and John Clopton, to see if Gabriel was "disposed to make confession," but they reported he was not. He remained, as Monroe had found when Gabriel had first been presented before him upon his arrival in Richmond, "resolved to say but little on the subject of the conspiracy."[6]

The repeated attempts to entice a direct statement from Gabriel suggest officials believed there was more to be learned of the plot. His general silence has left historians with only the trial testimony, news accounts, and rumors as to his motivation and ideology. James Sidbury has argued that the conspirators had "a sense that enslaved African Americans were God's chosen people and that he would lead them to the promised land," and there is good evidence to support his claim that Gabriel partly relied on this to build his plot. On less reliable ground is Douglas Egerton's assertion that Gabriel subscribed to an artisan republicanism. As Egerton partly expresses it, Gabriel "labored to gather together 'the most redoubtable democrats in the state' to destroy the economic hegemony of the 'merchants,' the only whites he ever identified as his enemies." Key to Egerton's argument is Ben's testimony at Gabriel's trial that he would sit and eat and drink with the merchants once Richmond had fallen, the only time merchants are mentioned in the record. As Sidbury has noted, this is not evidence that they were his enemies. Indeed, as Ford has observed, the whole scene appears more like "biblical notions of a 'Great Reversal' in which the last become first and the first become last." Egerton argues that Gabriel imbibed his artisan republicanism, and hence the hatred of merchants, from other white and black artisans while self-hired in Richmond. Nothing in the record indicates that Gabriel enjoyed that privilege from Prosser. Furthermore, if artisan republicans in and about Virginia towns were like those in the Mid-Atlantic cities explored by Alfred Young, they joined with merchants of a similar political outlook, transcending class to accomplish their goals, especially as the 1790s wore on. In Virginia, according to the statements of recruiters for Gabriel's plot, only the poor, some religious friends of freedom, and assumed French allies, not a shared artisan republicanism, set some whites apart from the butchery the conspirators thought they would have to employ to gain their freedom.[7]

In what probably seemed an anticlimactic atmosphere, since Gabriel gave them nothing to mull over, the court moved on to hear the evidence against three men each in the possession of Paul Thilman of Hanover: Dick, Bristol, and Randolph—a man he hired from Nancy Leftwich of King William. Dick and Randolph were both found guilty but recommended to the executive as worthy of mercy, while Bristol was declared not guilty. The fifth case of the day was unique.[8]

Thomas Jordan Martin stood before the court, a free man of color charged with conspiracy and insurrection. The state called two witnesses, Ben Woolfolk and Prosser's Ben, to make its case, but James Rind, the defense attorney, protested, "upon the principle of the prisoner being a free man and the witnesses thus introduced Slaves." After listening to arguments on the admissibility of the two Bens' testimony, the court ruled that they could testify "as legal evidence against the prisoner under the existing Laws of the Land." But, out of time, they adjourned the case until ten the next morning. At the continuation of his trial, Martin was found not guilty of the charge but was determined to have committed "a breach of the peace." The court ordered that he post a $100 bond for his good behavior for a period of six months, with good security "to be bound with him in the like sum." At this, his mother Macky, "a free mulatto," joined him in posting bond.[9]

Gabriel's reprieve from his immediate execution prolonged the problem of keeping him and the city secure until his hanging. Monroe requested Mayor James McClurg to have the town policed each night until the sentence had been carried out, and this by men who would serve in addition to the remaining guardsmen stationed at the penitentiary, capitol, and jail. McClurg revealed that Richmond had no watch in its employ to dispatch, but would apply to the commanders of the volunteer companies in the town for their assistance. As a civil officer, he held no authority to order a watch from among the militiamen. He also said he would take the request to the Hall the next day, seeking the creation of a watch, but this was apparently not done. Probably, the militiamen volunteered, reducing the immediate need for the watch.[10]

On Wednesday, the executive pardoned Solomon, the slave of the estate of Joseph Lewis. The Henrico judges had sent a statement declaring that after "taking all the Circumstances of the Case into our consideration," they believed him to be "a proper object of mercy." They also submitted a similar statement regarding Elisha Price's Jim, or James, but the council left his case open, granting a reprieve until the second Friday in November. And the executive pardoned Thilman's Dick and Leftwich's Randolph after reviewing the court's recommendation that accompanied their trial record. Even with these actions, eleven men still remained with death sentences scheduled to be imposed on Friday the 10th. The council also authorized the issuance of a warrant to pay the account of Robert Cowley the amount of £1.1.6 for express hire to Chesterfield, which may have opened a discussion of the council's doorkeeper.[11]

Due to its greater inherent significance and interest, it is likely the testimony presented at Gabriel's trial attracted closer scrutiny than other trial statements. It certainly brought Robert Cowley's peripheral place in the conspiracy to the attention of Monroe and others. At the trial of Jupiter on 15 September, Prosser's Ben had said that Jupiter told Gabriel he had a way of getting into the capitol, but did not specifically name Cowley as the means. In two narratives delivered by Gilbert to John Foster, Cowley was named but not accused of letting anyone into the capitol, or of personally handing the keys to Peter Tinsley's James, who opened the capitol door. Furthermore, these statements were not part of the public trial record. Woolfolk, however, had sworn at Gabriel's trial to a direct and more significant role for the capitol keeper. On 9 October, the governor wrote to Storrs and Selden, who, as Monroe pointed out, had "heard every thing," to ask if any evidence existed to indicate that the trust that had been "reposed on him" by the state had been misplaced. It was particularly troubling to the governor, because Cowley had always "acted in such manner as to inspire the Executive with high confidence of his fidelity." But if there was any reason to suspect him, this trust would end. Any written reply has apparently not survived, but in January, several weeks after submitting copies of trial records to the General Assembly, which contained Woolfolk's allegations against the Keeper of the Capitol, Monroe requested the legislature to provide better security for the building, and added that he owed a duty "to the character of the present Keeper to observe, that after the most strict scrutiny into his conduct, in reference to the late conspiracy, there does not appear to be any good cause to suspect his integrity." Robert Cowley continued as the main runner for the council and as its doorkeeper, but did end up surrendering the keys to the capitol in April 1801 to Captain Alexander Quarrier, after it became a major storehouse of the state arms. The sixty-year-old did not suffer any loss in his annual salary of $300 when his duties were reduced, nor does it appear that he was suspended from his work during the inquiry.[12]

On Friday the 10th, the council met early enough to grant a reprieve for a month to King, the slave of the attorney general, and save him for the time being from the gallows. But that day still became the deadliest single day of the conspiracy. Over the course of the trials, the court had ordered different men to be executed in two additional locations, perhaps out of some regard to the families of the petitioners. But it was as likely done to serve as a deterrent to any slaves still contemplating rebellion, not unlike what General Jones had suggested, and which had been a common practice when executing slave criminals in Virginia's past. To facilitate these dispersed hangings, the sheriff's office had requested the assistance of the state, "to attend them to the place of execution." Consequently, Monroe asked for two detachments from the Richmond Horse of four troopers each to assist at the two outlying places of execution, Watson's, that is, Prosser's Tavern at the Brook, and at the crossroads near Robertson's Tavern and the Four Mile Creek church in the lower part of the county. Backed by one contingent of mounted horsemen, Deputy Sheriff Samuel Mosby took Goode's Michael, Clarke's Sam Byrd Jr., Young's Gilbert, Prosser's Tom, and Smith's George up the Brook Road to Prosser's Tavern, where he later certified that he hanged the five men. The field that served as the site of execution was pointed out to a British visitor four years later from a stage that rolled down the road toward Richmond. Meanwhile, Deputy Sheriff Benjamin Sheppard and the second detachment headed east out of Richmond, following the river road to the site of the execution of Young's William and Graham's Sam Graham. He certified their deaths in the same manner. John M. Sheppard, the ranking deputy sheriff, took the quickest trip that day, carting Allen's Isaac and Williamson's Laddis, two men who had sat in jail under sentence of death since 16 September, and Prosser's Gabriel, the man who had been in jail the shortest time, to the usual place of execution in Richmond. No account exists to indicate that any of these men spoke from the gallows.[13]

Gabriel's execution brought another sigh of relief to the white population and the Virginia government, especially since Jack Bowler had surrendered to Gervas Storrs either Wednesday evening, according to the papers, or on Thursday, according to Storrs. Bowler simply walked in to Storrs's place accompanied by Peter Smith, a free black man. Smith probably lived near the magistrate at the lower end of the Brook, near the

Chickahominy. Storrs, who had examined each of the men taken up in the conspiracy in Henrico, mentioned the $300 reward to Monroe as if it were his to claim, but waived it in favor of $50 to be paid to Smith, for the "service he has rendered & the risk he has run & the odium he may incur from the blacks." He was convinced Smith had talked Bowler into surrendering, for Smith had given him "all the intelligence he could collect concerning him for some weeks past." Meanwhile, huge Jack Bowler sat awaiting his fate, which would be decided at a trial to be held on 29 October.[14]

The capture of Gabriel, however, had not ended the threat of the plot on those outside Richmond and Henrico. White residents within thirty or forty miles of the James River from Norfolk to Bedford County viewed any suspicious activity as being part of the plot, or believed themselves particularly vulnerable. In Louisa County's only recorded trial presumably connected to the conspiracy, its justices tried and acquitted a man named Ben, a slave of Charles Smith, for "deliberately conspiring to make rebellion, insurrection etc on the 16th day of June." On 1 October, the court examined several unidentified witnesses, and while a majority of the judges were convinced of his guilt, the lack of unanimity led to Ben's discharge. Apparently, his was the only trial in any county west of Henrico, although Sam Byrd Jr. had claimed to have recruited widely in Louisa, Albemarle, and about the Point of Fork, and Stepney had been sent down from Cumberland as a suspected recruiter. Watt was identified as a solicitor of troops in Goochland, but its records contain no evidence of prosecuting conspirators either, and the executive faced no decisions about men condemned in any of these counties for insurrection, another indication of the centrality of the Brook and the road that ran north through it in the conspiracy. But to the east, at the lower end of the Middle Peninsula in Gloucester County, authorities believed they had caught one conspirator and could identify another.[15]

Coincidentally, on the same day as Ben's Louisa County trial, William Morgain picked up a letter on a road connecting Gloucester County courthouse and Ware Neck. He took it the next day to Thomas Booth, a county magistrate and militia major. Written to "Mr. B. H.[,] Gloster" and dated 20 September 1800, it saluted its reader with "deer frind." It instructed B.H. to "Tel jacob at John Williams" that "Johny is taken up and wil be hanged i is afrade." Those in Gloucester "must keep still yet. brother X will come and prech a sermont to you soon, and then you may no more about the bissiness i must be killed if the white peple catch me and carry me to richmon." Under the closing, "i am your tru frind," it was initialed "A. W." Magistrate Booth thought he recognized the men mentioned in the scrap of paper. In a letter written to Alexander McCrae [*sic*] because he had not yet met Monroe, the major stated that Jacob was a "well known" and probably suspicious slave captain of a small boat that plied the waters of the Ware River and bay near John Williams's place. He immediately gathered a posse of five men and headed there, where he found a quantity of meal stashed in the quarters which the slaves said belonged to Jacob. With his boat emptied, Booth was convinced Jacob intended to spirit off to Norfolk or to some vessel "a parcel of negroes who had absconded from justice." He then received word that Jacob's vessel was in the Severn River to the south of the Ware, and hustled off three men to capture him. They arrived too late to prevent his departure, which Booth still believed was to Norfolk, loaded "full of negroes." He subsequently commissioned a party of fifteen men to guard the mouth of the river, hoping to catch him on his return. Booth claimed the man "A. W." called John was "a Feller sold by Col Thos Buckner of this county to a Mr Taloe of Richmond." He was seen about the time the news of the insurrection broke having talks with Gloucester slaves and in places where he was not known to have any acquaintances. This brought attention to his activities, which the major was convinced involved recruiting. When rumors came that he had been hanged in Richmond, it seemed to confirm Booth's suspicions, but word had arrived the day before that not only was John alive, he "was unsuspect'd." Booth thought he should relay the information, and asserted he would "use every exertion to secure such proof as will condemn the scoundrel." The electric atmosphere in which Booth wrote is revealed in another letter sent to Monroe from Gloucester at almost the same time. Word had arrived in the county, probably an inflation of a false report appearing in the newspapers, of eight thousand "Blacks being embodied in South Carolina, which . . . is well known to the People of Color & does not a little raise their spirits, which are much depressed by the failure of the intended explosion in your quarter."[16]

Elzy Burroughs caught Jacob about ten days later, assisted by a vessel commanded by Joel Thomas and manned with a deckhand and four militia men. Thomas had sailed about for ten days, the militia men serving between eight and ten. It is not known where they captured Jacob, but while sailing with him to be arraigned before a Gloucester magistrate, the captive was informed of the charges, and "whilst in the hole [*sic*] of the vessel . . . stabbed himself" and died. His owner, William Wilson, described him as a "valuable Waterman, & always supposed to be (until the late insurrection of the Slaves) an honest inoffensive Negro." To boost his chances of securing compensation from the state for his loss, Wilson pointed out that Jacob was in the custody of officially appointed pursuers when he died. He also observed that there was "little doubt that he would have suffered as a conspirator," that is, been hanged, and he may well have been. With twenty-five men executed in Richmond and Henrico, Jacob's suicide brought the toll to twenty-six.[17]

At the same time that Gloucester men scrambled to find Jacob, over fifty miles to the south and well up the Nansemond River in Suffolk, scared residents demanded military protection from an insurrection they were sure was about to explode in their midst. Colonel William Wilkinson ordered out "part of the Malitia . . . to suppress the business" by 1 October (the *Epitome of the Times* in Norfolk set the muster at two companies) and kept some of them together to guard the jail in which two unidentified individuals were held for trial. Joining them, it was reported, were numbers of blacks from North Carolina who had been passing as free people in Suffolk. The paper printed a letter from an anonymous source which revealed a gathering of about one hundred fifty slaves, including about twenty from Norfolk (probably the county, rather than the borough) toward the end of the first week in September. They had massed near the border between Norfolk and Nansemond Counties southeast of Suffolk. But none of those taken up weeks later would reveal anything about the gathering, which some said adjourned to find more men to join, while the correspondent thought it broke up after word arrived of the plot's failure at Richmond. The whole alarm was created, according to the *Norfolk Herald*, by the "discovery," or revelation, coming from two white women "that lived with some negroes," who were now being investigated. For a time, the residents of Suffolk patrolled their town nightly, and it appears the militia guard served for about two weeks, judging by the bill Wilkinson submitted to Richmond. The *Epitome's* correspondent, however, doubted that anyone's guilt would be proved, and the loss of Nansemond County records precludes any modern confirmation of his prediction. From Norfolk, on 9 October, Newton responded to an inquiry from Monroe, "if any symptom of a like spirit has been observed of late in Norfolk or the counties contiguous to it." He told Monroe that "some symptoms of impudence has prevailed among our negroes but it does not appear they had communications with those above," meaning the plotters in Henrico.[18]

In Petersburg, city authorities still waited on word from Monroe. On 11 October, in a belated reply to William Prentis's query following the arrest in Petersburg of Jesse and Reuben Byrd, the governor gave no confirmation of the charges against the Byrds, but pointed out a legal difficulty. He told of the arrest of Sam Byrd of Hanover Town, the free mulatto father of Sam Byrd Jr., one of the ten conspirators executed just the day before. After being taken up in Hanover and jailed in Richmond, the senior Byrd was released "for want of evidence, it being decided that people of his own colour, in Slavery, could not give testimony against him." He did not directly say so, but the implications were clear: it would be impossible to convict the two men arrested two-and-a-half weeks earlier without the testimony of a free person. Monroe told Prentis he had sent his letter on to Storrs and Selden, the "examining Magistrates," which he did the same day. He asked them to forward any information they possessed that involved Petersburg to Prentis or to himself. That seemed to bring an end to the issue, and presumably Jesse and Reuben Byrd were soon released, though probably with particular reluctance because in at least one previous instance Petersburg authorities had allowed a slave to testify against a free man of color accused of theft. Monroe's response is more interesting in light of the decision made in the Henrico Court just a few days before in the trial of Thomas Jordan Martin. Recall that there the court had ruled that the testimony of Woolfolk and Prosser's Ben was legally admissible. As it turned out, the evidence the justices admitted proved unconvincing of Martin's guilt as a conspirator. As Martin was a free man, even if they had found the evidence against him compelling, their decision would have served only as an indictment, requiring an actual trial to be held in the district court in Richmond. In the instance of Samuel Byrd Sr., it appears that the Henrico Court never faced the issue of evidence, because, as Monroe correctly stated, Byrd was not brought before the court, or at least there is no record of it in the order book. Thus, the decision that Byrd could not be tried on slave evidence was most likely made by Storrs and Selden, possibly after consultation with others. Indeed, there are many individuals who appear on lists, or are mentioned in the testimony of the trials or confessions, as "concerned," and who were never tried. Evidently, the examining magistrates concluded that there was insufficient evidence against them. With two different interpretations of the source of admissible testimony, it is not surprising that the next General Assembly clarified the 1792 law which had seemed to produce the confusion, by permitting slave testimony against free people of color. Still, the assemblymen did not entertain any suggestion, for none was forthcoming, that a black person could testify against whites, even in cases of insurrection.[19]

This fact may have determined the state's treatment of Richardson Taylor. On 30 September, the *Virginia Gazette* erroneously reported that Taylor had been jailed in Norfolk along with Billy and Isham, two of his crewmen. Based on "a letter which we have seen from Capt Taylor to the owner" of the *Mary*, the paper corrected itself on 3 October, stating that Taylor had been bound over on his own recognizance to appear before the mayor of Richmond by 25 October. Although Thomas Newton remained skeptical of Taylor's assertions in Norfolk, he suggested to Monroe that those who knew the man in Richmond could better evaluate his claims, and enclosed Taylor's recognizance. Contrary to some speculations, Taylor returned to Richmond, where he appeared before Mayor McClurg in fulfillment of his bond. With no one able to testify against him, such as Billy or Isham, any charges were most likely dismissed, or he was able to convince the mayor that he had been ill and unable to deal with Gabriel, perhaps only becoming satisfied of Gabriel's identity with the ship's arrival in Norfolk. But Taylor also faced a civil suit brought by Thomas Henry Prosser. Prosser had filed a complaint against Taylor in the Henrico Court at about the same time, claiming £1,000 damages "for harbouring" Gabriel "on board a vessel of which [Taylor] was Commander." Prosser's action forced Taylor to post a £2,000 bond for his appearance before the court to answer the charge. Prosser won an office judgment but dropped the case when Taylor appealed it to the county court in March 1802. Meanwhile, Taylor had found employment as a clerk with George Nicholson, one of whose enterprises was a rope walk in Rocketts. He remarried in the spring of 1802, and again in 1806, and remained in Henrico or Richmond until 1810, when he left for Lynchburg and, finally, Kentucky. Whether Isham ever received his manumission papers remains unknown, and one can only speculate whether some of Taylor's time would have been spent in the state penitentiary if Billy could have testified.[20]

The last individual to be executed, though not the last to be tried for conspiracy, was Peter, a slave prosecuted in the Dinwiddie County Court on 20 October. He belonged to the estate of William P. Claiborne and was charged with two counts of conspiracy. On 24 August, the justices were informed, Peter had conspired with others "to rebel and make insurrection . . . and on the same date plot and conspire with other slaves unknown the murder of Matt," who also belonged to the Claiborne estate. He was found guilty, and although the clerk did not record whether the judgment applied to both or only one of the charges, the fact that he was ordered executed at the county court house four days later indicates he was found guilty of the more serious charge of conspiracy to rebel. He was valued at $300. Interestingly, the executive does not appear to have reviewed Peter's case, as it did the others arising from Gabriel's plot. Noticeable too is the fact that this case was not filed with the other claims, receipts, reimbursements, and trial records that accompanied the cases associated with Gabriel's insurrection in the auditor's records. This may have been a simple clerical error, but it does raise the possibility that Peter's guilt arose from "loose talk" that may have been unconnected to Gabriel and his followers. If he was part of the plot of the brothers of the Brook, twenty-seven men died in the aftermath of the intended insurrection, all but one of them directly by the hands of the Commonwealth.[21]

The Claiborne estate did not collect their reimbursement for the price Peter paid until January. It is likely the executors simply waited until then to file their claim, but it was clear to Monroe and the council that they faced a fiscal, if not a legal problem long before then, having now depleted the fund for the compensation of owners of executed slaves appropriated in the budget for 1800. On 11 October, Monroe acknowledged to state treasurer William Berkeley that he had received Berkeley's notice of the empty fund and his request for directions for dealing with the claims that were still coming in, and which he expected would be for some time. Monroe had put the issue before the council, he assured Berkeley, but they had simply advised that he give the treasurer "no opinion on it." The treasurer was directed to the attorney general for guidance. In December, Monroe forwarded to the legislature the auditor's statement of the expenses created by the suppression of the conspiracy, along with "a letter from the Treasurer communicating an opinion of the Attorney General respecting payment for some of the slaves who were executed."[22]

With Gabriel executed and Jack Bowler in custody, Monroe decided that the services of the artillery men at the capitol were no longer needed. He soon responded to William Wilkinson's report of his actions taken in Nansemond and Suffolk, expressing his sorrow at the need to employ the militia, endorsing Wilkinson's actions, and urging him to keep the patrols active and searching for any arms that might be in the hands of slaves or free people of color, "not authorized by law to keep them." Then, with the press continuing to use the plot in its political war over the upcoming election, Monroe now turned to a different issue: the gathering of evidence to support his actions in the face of the crisis. He asked William Mosby and Roger Gregory to commit to writing the essence of what they had reported to Monroe, most likely on 1 September, it being "a principle ground of my conduct in that stage of the business." Mosby sent him a statement about a month later, but if Gregory replied, his statement does not seem to have survived. At the courthouse that day, the Richmond aldermen tried Ralph for conspiracy and insurrection but decided this slave of Elizabeth Page's was not guilty. He was the third and last man tried by Richmond City authorities that fall for conspiracy and insurrection.[23]

Lewis, the slave of Dabney Williamson, remained in jail, the only man still scheduled to die on the 17th. On 16 October, the executive reprieved him until 14 November. Then it acted favorably on Gervas Storrs's request that $50 be given to Peter Smith, who shepherded Jack Bowler's surrender, and also finally awarded $50 to Billy, who had revealed the presence of Gabriel on the *Mary*. It allowed Martin Mims his claim of $355.04 for "maintenance of sundry negroes" at the penitentiary, and it also ordered the reduction of the guard at the penitentiary and jail, leaving only about twenty men in place at the two sites. After nearly six weeks, Richmond was finally beginning to resume a more pacific posture. And the council approved payment of the bill submitted for hauling the federal arms in Manchester to the penitentiary, ordering the auditor to recover the cost from the national government in Washington, in spite of Monroe's earlier promise of state payment.[24]

But the expenses of the conspiracy continued to grow because more men remained to be tried. In Caroline County, militiamen guarded the county jail where several plotters recruited by the men on the Brook sat in chains. Caroline planter James Duvall traveled to Bowling Green on the 21st, a "fair & warm day," for the trials, but was disappointed. It is not clear if he returned the next day, which also broke "fair & warm"—"delightful for wheat," but not for the men who were finally prosecuted, especially the "two Negroes condemned for consperacy." Their trials began once Ben Woolfolk was sent under guard to testify, on the condition he be returned the next day. The court first tried two men belonging to Charles Carter of Shirley from his quarter at North Wales. John was a boatman who may have poled goods along the Pamunkey, and was probably among those Woolfolk recruited. But Woolfolk's testimony failed to convince the justices, and they declared John not guilty and discharged him from custody. Ben, however, faced both Woolfolk and Bristol's evidence, which was not recorded. The court found the one-eyed-man guilty and ordered him hanged on the next Wednesday, 29 October. The court then heard the cases of two of Paul Thilman's slaves, and again found one guilty and acquitted the other. Woolfolk's sole testimony condemned Scipio, an eighteen- or nineteen-year-old, whom the court ordered to the gallows with Ben. George, on the other hand, was discharged, the court ruling Woolfolk's testimony in his case "not sufficient to convict." Woolfolk was then escorted back to Richmond by a constable. Two days later, the executive reprieved both of the convicted men until 14 November. Monroe informed John Pendleton, the clerk of the Caroline Court, of the reprieves the next day and asked him to forward the trial testimony convicting Ben and Scipio. He needed it to evaluate any claim for the "interposition" of the executive on their behalf—seeming almost to invite it. He also sent Ben Woolfolk for the next round of cases scheduled for the upcoming Wednesday, as requested by Edmund Pendleton Jr., the Commonwealth's attorney for the county and father of the clerk.[25]

Planter James Duvall returned the next Wednesday, perhaps expecting to see a hanging, but found none, since the convicted had been reprieved. He stayed to see the trials of the three men brought to the bar on that overcast day. The court did not find the testimony from Woolfolk convincing in the case of Billy, a slave of William Penn, and the statement of Primus probably contributed nothing for the prosecution, since he later claimed he knew of no one involved in a conspiracy. The same two witnesses appeared in the next trial, that of Edward Garland's Humphrey. This time, four justices were persuaded of his guilt, but not the fifth judge, and he was acquitted. Up next was Jack Gabriel, another of Charles Carter's slaves from North Wales. This time, Humphrey joined Woolfolk and Primus in testifying, though his statement was not recorded and may have been given for the defense. Woolfolk revealed that he joined Jack Gabriel at a preaching near Littlepage's Bridge and afterwards at a spring when Jack claimed he had enlisted a company of men. Primus testified to seeing Jack Gabriel at the religious gathering, but he had left and could not swear to anything that happened afterwards. As noted above, Primus claimed he didn't know of any person engaging in a conspiracy. This time, the court thought Woolfolk's statement sufficient, pronouncing Jack guilty and ordering him hanged on 14 November.[26]

James Duvall did not return the next day, Thursday the 30th, but two more slaves faced the Caroline justices and both were found guilty. Woolfolk and Edmund, a slave of Paul Woolfolk, testified at both trials. Edmund's testimony confirmed the presence of Woolfolk, of his being seen with Paul Thilman's Thornton and Charles Carter's John Fells. But since he did not accompany them to the spring where the recruiting was alleged to have happened, like Primus the day before, Edmund claimed he knew nothing more. Woolfolk, however, told of the commitment of Fells to come to the Brook, even if his men would not, and of Thornton's making swords, of his recruiting, and of his instructing Woolfolk on how to make paper cartridges. The justices declared both men guilty and ordered them hanged, like Jack Gabriel, on the second Friday in November. With that, the Caroline trials came to an end.[27]

While Woolfolk testified on Wednesday, 29 October, in Bowling Green, the Henrico Court tried Jack Bowler. The Commonwealth's attorney really didn't need Woolfolk's testimony, having Prosser's Ben, Price's John, and Prosser's Sam available. Ben said Bowler was involved before Gabriel, had amassed gunpowder, recruited men, contended with Gabriel for command, and appeared at Prosser's on both the night of the storm and the next morning. As always, Price's John gave a reprise of the meeting at Young's spring and described the vote that anointed Gabriel the general rather than Bowler. Sam, a runaway who returned the week before the scheduled uprising, told of the huge man wrapping his arms around Lewis and saying, "We have as much right to fight for our Liberty as any Men and that on Saturday Night they would kill the White People." The judges set his execution for 14 November. The Henrico Court tried two more men the following Tuesday. Arraigned the day before, the judges heard the evidence, apparently provided by Ben Woolfolk, but acquitted Absolem and Emanuel. Their decision saved the men's lives and spared the executive from having to decide what to do with them.[28]

Some owners seized the time created by executive reprieves to make the case for the extension of mercy. The hanging of ten men on 10 October still left Elisha Price's James, and William Young's Ned, and Philip N. Nicholas's King in jail under reprieves, and Dabney Williamson's Lewis waiting to be executed on 17 October. But, as noted earlier, the council reprieved him the day before his scheduled hanging, until 14 November. The specific reasons for the Henrico Court's recommendation to the executive of mercy for Elisha Price's James are hidden in the legal boilerplate of their statement. But once obtained, owner Price moved to bolster the claim with concrete details. From Jesse Smith he received a sworn statement, dated 23 October, that when he had interrogated him, George had rejected the suggestion that James was a conspirator, essentially saying that James was never told about it because "he was afraid to let him know the secrets." From Thomas B. King, an overseer, came another sworn description of the day when Ben Woolfolk had come to a "feast" at Elisha Price's, and where he later claimed James spoke of being able "to kill white people stoutly." Overseer King said the two never spoke at all, and that James had asked, apparently with anger, who had invited Woolfolk? From James Rind, who served as the defense attorney for all the Henrico defendants, including George Smith, came another statement. He had impressed on George more than a dozen times that "the fuller his confession . . . the better chance he had of a pardon," but Smith still maintained that "James was totally ignorant that such a thing was intended." Rind revealed that "the substance at least in part of his declarations to this effect" had been passed on to Monroe "in his confession," and consequently the lawyer had anticipated "that as [James] was convicted on the uncorroborated testimony of the suspicious Mr. Ben Woolfolk alone, it would have been sufficient to have induced his pardon." How this statement sat with Monroe, who had wondered when the hand of the executioner should be stopped, is not known, but Smith's reputed confession has not survived in the files of the conspiracy. Perhaps Monroe never received it. Whatever the case, on 8 November, the executive pardoned James, an action that saved the state $500.[29]

Ned was left in suspense, reprieved again on 8 November until 12 December. But three days before his new date of execution, the council pardoned him after William Young applied for a pardon. Young submitted a signed statement of the justices who sat on the case indicating that a subsequent investigation had revealed Ned to be of a "verry weak mind" and that he was drunk when he supposedly enlisted. Scipio, reprieved from his Caroline sentence until 8 November, was also pardoned after the justices of Caroline pled he did not deserve the same fate as "the Generals and Colo[onel]s," especially since he was only eighteen or nineteen years old and had been enticed into joining by Thornton, who lived on the same plantation.[30]

Attorney General Nicholas had first initiated a plea for mercy for King before the Richmond alderman but failed. However, he found in Mayor James McClurg, Recorder George Nicholson, and the aldermen John Barret, William Richardson, and James Heron, who made up all of the men who sat on the case but one, a willingness "to do whatever with propriety" they could "to gratify the wish" of Nicholas. These men put together their recollections of the testimony offered in the case and submitted it to the executive in time to secure a reprieve for a week on 2 October, the day before King's scheduled execution. After that, King was again reprieved on 10 October until the second Friday in November. On 30 October, Larkin Stanard, a sometime delegate from Spotsylvania County, sent a testimonial about King's character. Stanard claimed he had long known the man, for he had been a slave of fellow Spotsylvanian Robert Brooke, once governor and then attorney general, until his death a few months earlier. He "always thought him much attach'd to his master and a verry honest man," he wrote, and then added, "tho subject to drink." He apparently knew him well enough to explain that King, "when in a state of Intoxication would say things which I do not believe he thought of when sober." With this, and the statement of the Richmond authorities, King continued in the ranks of the reprieved.[31]

It is not surprising that no effort was made to save Williamson's Lewis, who had said he would decapitate his master and mistress, or at least none has been found, but he benefited from a general reprieve issued on 8 November that lumped him with the rest of the men found guilty in Caroline, including King, Ned, and Jack Bowler. They all received reprieves until 12 December. By then, the legislature would be in session. These delays would thus buy time so that the legislature could do what the council would not do by direct vote—that is, address the issue of transportation. Indeed, on the day Ned was pardoned, all the rest were reprieved again until the fourth Friday in December, then again until the fourth Friday in January, and finally until the fourth Friday in March. By then, a transportation law had been passed and the state had moved quickly to sell these men for deportation.[32]

They were joined by Watt, the last man to stand trial for Gabriel's conspiracy. He had left Prosser's on the evening before the intended uprising to gather his sons and recruits in Goochland, and did not soon return. Although an older man, he managed to stay at large, possibly with the help of his sons, for perhaps two and a half months. He took a place in the penitentiary by 15 November, before being moved to the jail. He faced the judges of Henrico on the first day of December and was found guilty on the testimony of Prosser's Ben. They set his execution for the second Friday in January, valuing him at £55, or $184, the lowest of any of the condemned men. However, Watt also benefited from the delays and distaste for more executions, ultimately becoming one of the transported eight conspirators.[33]

Although no more men would be tried and no more evidence would be forthcoming about the plot, there remained questions about white involvement. In late September, Governor John Drayton of South Carolina had written to Monroe, "with much regret & anxiety," having heard "accounts of a Negroe insurrection, which has nearly taken place in some parts of Virginia." Drayton worried about the extent of the plot, and since no official account had emerged, he requested any information about the scheme which could prove useful to his state in "detecting a like conspiracy" or "guarding against any of its wicked effects should it be attempted" there. Monroe replied in late October, after twenty-five executions but with perhaps more still to come. He assured Drayton that although the plot "was a formidable one" to Virginia, there was no evidence it threatened any state south of the Old Dominion. He gave a brief account of it, of its centering near Richmond, the target of the planners, of its betrayal, and of the timely storm. With the original attack thwarted, his "Government had time to act with effect, which it did, for from that period it had the entire command of the affair," he reported with apparent pride. Any success the plotters might have expected could only have occurred in the initial attack and not from "any very extensive preconcerted combination." Monroe then added, "If whitemen were engaged in it, it is a fact of which we have no proof." Indeed, since no slave or free black could testify against a white, there would always be "no proof" without a white person's testimony or confession.[34]

Monroe may have included his observation denying white instiga-tion to Governor Drayton because rumors of white involvement clearly existed and the alleged role of two Frenchmen figured prominently in press reports of the plot. John Mayo had grilled the first men to go to the gallows about the rumored possibility, but to no avail. Michael's nam-ing of William Young, however, escaped the circle of troops surrounding the condemned, forcing a public statement from Young, an account from Mayo of his interrogation, and a testimonial signed by Republicans and Federalists alike as to Young's character. Someone named a man named Locust, or Lucas, who lived on the Brook, who said he would lead the men into Richmond. That offer could have been done in jest, the kind of ex-change that took place among working men. The jeweler Charles Purcell, who had lost his house to the flames in 1798, had to run an advertisement denouncing whoever dropped a letter addressed to him that implied he was involved. He offered a $200 reward for the discovery of the mali-cious hoaxer. An anonymous slave near Petersburg reportedly named two white men rumored to be plotters, but those names were never repeated publicly by anyone. Perhaps sober inquiries determined there was not much to his accusations.[35]

Still, there are the two Frenchmen mentioned by Prosser's Ben at the opening trial of Solomon, and by Gilbert in a confession gathered while he was incarcerated but never made public. And, of course, Gilbert iden-tified Charles Quersey as a Frenchman who had encouraged him and others in Caroline County to rebel in 1796, but again this was a revela-tion that never reached print. The names of the two white men accused in Prince George County, near Petersburg, were never reported; and the identities of the two Frenchmen, implicated but also never named, even once, in trial testimony, were apparently never pursued in the trial of Jack Bowler, the man reported specifically to have known them—wouldn't some effort have been made to find them out? If Bowler had names that could prove politically embarrassing, why would the man who claimed to know them be transported rather than executed, the only sure form of silence? Had he threatened to reveal their names if sent to the gallows? Perhaps their identities were known, but since the evidence was legally inadmissible, never entered into the record. Or perhaps few in Virginia really gave much credence to these statements.

These bits of enticing evidence led Douglas Egerton to level the se-rious charge that Monroe, with the aid of Gervas Storrs and Joseph

Selden, all Republicans, sifted out and suppressed evidence containing the names of white conspirators, apparently the two Frenchmen. Such a revelation would prove embarrassing to Jefferson and the Republicans in the election of 1800. Egerton bases his argument on the testimony of the two Frenchmen; on a letter from William Prentis that asked Monroe to check the names of Petersburg suspects against a list Prentis "heard" Monroe possessed; and on another, undated letter, but actually one of 1802, from Prentis, referring to a list of names of plotters. The absence in the archives of the conspirators' lists and of the letter reportedly carried by "General" John Scott and addressed to Alexander Beddenhurst, or Weddenhust, in Philadelphia, becomes confirming evidence of their intentional disappearance. The fact that Prentis's inquiry of a list in Monroe's hands was clearly based on rumor; that the list might not have been captured, but compiled from evidence; or the likelihood that the lists kept by the conspirators would have been the first things put on the coals in a blacksmith's forge or into the flames of a kitchen fire as the conspiracy collapsed, are not considered. To be sure, men's marks of their enlistment may not have been all that revealing, but it is also unlikely that any names of whites would have been entered with them. Furthermore, as noted elsewhere, there is no evidence of Beddenhurst's presence in Virginia, or of his involvement in the plot, or that John Scott possessed a list of recruits, all claims made by Egerton. There is nothing to corroborate Scott's status or place in the plot, leaving him as probably nothing more than a runaway slave caught at an especially inopportune time. The statement, as Egerton renders it, that "correspondence from Philadelphia, Norfolk and Petersburg had all been captured," most likely was a badly reflected facet of the rumored story of Scott's capture, his Petersburg origins, the letter to Beddenhurst in Philadelphia, and Scott's failed effort to reach Norfolk on his way to Philadelphia. Jefferson and the Republicans may well have been hurt politically if names could have been given of the two Frenchmen mentioned in trial testimony, but no one charged Monroe or the magistrates with suppressing evidence, something the Federalists would not have hesitated to do.[36]

As it turned out, the news report that emerged in the first day of the trials, of the allegation of the instigation and existence of the two Frenchmen, became the element that transformed Gabriel's Conspiracy into an event of national importance in the presidential campaign of 1800.

Since Federalists, especially outside of Virginia, were branding Jefferson with Jacobinism in an effort to associate him with all the excesses of the French Revolution, this was too good not to use.

The first notices of the conspiracy had appeared in Philadelphia and Boston newspapers on 10 and 13 September, respectively, and were then widely reprinted in regional papers thereafter. Based on letters received from Virginia written in early September, the reports were very brief and lacked any factual depth. As editors in Richmond began to create lengthier accounts, their counterparts inserted them in their columns, the earliest reports appearing in both Republican and Federalist papers. But the revelation of the *Virginia Gazette* of the alleged involvement of two Frenchmen, and the claim that no French people would be killed, transformed the news of the conspiracy from a missed massacre into a Federalist frontal assault on the candidacy of Jefferson and local Republicans, especially in Philadelphia, New York, and Boston.[37]

For over a month, columns and paragraphs about the plot, with charges of who had instigated or was responsible for it, frequently appeared in America's papers, though mostly those north of Virginia. Federalist editors, using the revelation of a French connection, lambasted Republicans for spreading the dangerous doctrines of the French Revolution encapsulated in "Liberty and Equality," and warned that the election of Jefferson and his followers would loose the violence of the Jacobins upon America as order and religion crumbled. Among Federalist newspapers, false claims circulated of handbills purportedly authored by the jailed Callender and spread about by "French people of colour, originally from Guadalupe." According to these editors, those convicted under the Richmond gallows blamed "our Jacobins and the friends of Jefferson" for "their *Political* errors," and they even asserted that Gabriel had reserved "two ladies of Richmond" for his "brutal purposes." Republican editors labeled the charges as lies, and Callender even laid the blame for the conspiracy on Alexander Hamilton, charging that he authored the revolt to create the chaos that would disrupt the presidential election in the South and deprive Jefferson of the region's electoral votes. The Republican *Epitome of the Times*, in Norfolk, more calmly pointed out that it was unlikely that any Frenchmen in Virginia were behind the plot, because most held slaves and a revolt was simply against their interests. It specifically ridiculed Federalist claims that Gabriel enjoyed the support of Virginia's "redoubtable democrats." By November, mention of Gabriel's Conspiracy swirled only in the eddies of papers far down the stream of reprints from the press centers of metropolitan America. But it was clear that the charge of French involvement had generated significant political attention and contributed to the mud-slinging of the campaign. It remained an allegation Monroe could neither suppress, nor completely ignore.[38]

6 } Politics and Policies

B etween 11 September 1800, when Solomon stood before the Henrico Court, and 1 December, when Watt appeared, the Commonwealth of Virginia had prosecuted seventy-two men for conspiracy and insurrection. The overwhelming number came from the neighborhood of the Brook and through the personal ties of the men residing there. Deputy sheriffs hanged twenty-five men in Richmond or Henrico, and one in Dinwiddie County. Another man committed suicide in Gloucester before he could be indicted or tried. Eight of the convicted men would be sold to slave traders to be transported from Virginia, forever banned from the state and facing execution if they returned. The courts condemned thirteen more whom the executive later pardoned; the rest, some twenty-five, were found not guilty of conspiracy and insurrection, including Thomas Jordan Martin, a free man of color. Of these, some gained acquittal only because a single judge dissented from the majority's declaration of guilt. In addition to these men, patrols and magistrates seized an unknown number of suspects who were later released because of insufficient evidence, or perhaps a misidentification, or, as in the cases of Sam Byrd Sr., Jesse Byrd, and Reuben Byrd, a decision or suggestion that slaves could not testify against a free person of color. Not one of those taken up or tried had actually shed the blood of master, mistress, or citizen in the conspiracy. As John Randolph noted, the only bloodshed was "that which streamed upon the scaffold."[1]

For an insurrection that had not occurred, the state had spent a significant amount of its resources, a fact that could create political grumbling and second-guessing, especially by those least endangered, and a problem that may have been anticipated by James Monroe and some of the council. As noted earlier, Alexander McRae had attempted to convince his fellow councilors to subscribe to a resolution justifying an open treasury to suppress the conspiracy, and Monroe had begun to marshal evidence to document why he had responded to the crisis in the manner he had, of course with the advice of the council. On 5 December, he sent a message addressed to the speakers of the two houses of the General Assembly, his second of the session, this one reporting on the conspiracy, "fully and accurately, in all its details," and on the measures taken to suppress it. He attached for the assemblymen's information "a copy of the documents which illustrate this transaction, with a report of the auditor of the expences attending to it." The latter was titled the "Amount of expence incurred in calling out the Militia to suppress the late insurrection of the Negroes," and was subtitled "Pay of the Militia, Rations, &c"; the sum totaled $8,829.66. What Monroe did not state was that significant claims against the state remained outstanding: costs like the nearly $900 yet to be billed for guarding the conspirators taken up and tried in Caroline County, or the payroll of the Richmond Horse he had requested to be made up in early October but had not yet received. When the unit finally submitted its claim in April, the state was charged $1,244.17 for pay, rations, forage, and even the use of their horses for the six weeks beginning 30 August. Even without these, by the time the legislators began constructing the state budget twelve days later, they figured that at least $9,139.67 in warrants had been issued for the costs of the insurrection.[2]

The amount the state reimbursed the owners of executed slaves, or of those who would later be transported, was not part of the sum Monroe reported to the assembly either. These payments would eventually reach over $11,000 for the twenty-six men found guilty and executed and the eight men who were finally transported. The state did recover $2,617.34 through the sale of the latter, a transaction completed just before the assembly adjourned. But the total outlay could have been much higher; pardoning thirteen men had saved the state around $4,572, no small sum compared to what was paid, but an amount never advertised, or perhaps even calculated. These reimbursements to the owners of the plotters may have loomed large in Monroe's mind, and likely helped shape his report to the General Assembly. Just the January before, in a vote that ignored party allegiances, the House of Delegates had passed by a vote of 69 to 62 a bill which would have eliminated the compensation paid by the public to owners of executed slaves. Although the measure had apparently failed in the Senate, to a majority of that session's delegates the $6,000 annually appropriated for this purpose was no longer supportable. A similar effort would be made when the sitting House of Delegates formed their budget, but this time the measure failed to pass in the lower house. Perhaps the newly adopted policy of transportation of convicted slaves was expected to reduce the number of executions and allow the recovery of most of the costs of reimbursing owners for any exiled slaves. But the policy of transportation had not yet been adopted when Monroe sent his message to the assembly, and with the fund for compensation exhausted by 1 October, with more claims yet to come, the governor attached the treasurer's letter explaining payments drawn from other funds and justified by the attorney general's opinion. Hence, it was not the Virginia Federalists, whose numbers were dwindling anyway, that concerned the governor in the face of these costs, but an already existing and lingering desire to shed the state of this century-old fiscal obligation.[3]

With these issues in mind, Monroe composed for the General Assembly his explanation of the conspiracy and his response to it. As such, it should be read as a defense of executive decisions, not just as a history of the event for the assembly's edification, although it was framed by Monroe to appear as one. In his recounting of the events beginning 30 August, Monroe confessed he initially did not believe there was anything much to the warning of Pharoah and Tom, but that prudence demanded some response. He told the assembly of his securing patrols from the Richmond Horse to watch the roads, and of the stationing of men from the Richmond militia to guard the penitentiary, magazine and capitol on Saturday and Sunday nights. He explained that the great Saturday night deluge washed out any evidence of any gathering, the only reported clue that anything was contemplated being the movement of some slaves from Richmond into the county to a possible rendezvous, but with whom was not discovered. Consequently, his skepticism continued through the weekend, until additional warnings from the gentlemen of the Brook on Monday convinced him something had been and perhaps was still afoot. By indicating his original doubts, he placed himself with those who questioned whether a conspiracy actually existed, while his limited response, with little initial cost to the state, testified to his careful husbandry of state resources. Then, by expanding the source for the existence of the plot from two slaves to include respected community members, Monroe began to build a foundation for the more extensive and significantly more costly responses he undertook on 2 September. Indeed, throughout the remainder of his report, Monroe balanced his account between stressing the size and seriousness of the conspiracy to justify his response, and asserting that only the minimum measures necessary for the public's safety had been undertaken.[4]

If the report of Major William Mosby and his allies on the Brook convinced the governor that the conspiracy existed, it was only Monroe's logic that first served as the basis for his conclusions about the size of the threat. To actually take Richmond, Monroe reasoned, would require more than the efforts of the slaves of the city and its neighborhood, and so he doubted that they would have launched "so bold an enterprize without support from the slaves in other quarters of the state. It was more reasonable to presume an extensive combination had been formed among them for that purpose." Therefore, he "advised"—he had no authority to order— county and city officials "to apprehend and commit to prison without delay all the slaves . . . whose guilt they had good cause to suspect."[5]

Monroe convinced the council of the reality of the plot, but lacking evidence of its extent, the councilors supported only guarding "those objects which it was understood were to be first assailed"—that is, the state properties within Richmond and the arsenal at Point of Fork. Monroe explained that "it was natural to conclude the attention of the insurgents would be directed in the outset to these objects," and that as additional information trickled in, they were confirmed in their "presentiment." The executive also ordered the commandant of every regiment in the state to send out patrols in every county. The first coffle of captives, along with some of their swords, spurred the governor and council to call up additional men to be stationed in the neighborhood of the Brook and to continue the patrolling by the Richmond Horse.[6]

Monroe explained that as more evidence of the plot accumulated, more men were mustered, additional measures taken to arm them, and the powder in the magazine removed to the penitentiary for safekeeping. The beginning of the trials increased information, Monroe noted, but interestingly and possibly intentionally, he did not remind the legislators of the date of the start of the trials as he provided them with a brief synopsis of the plot. He described the area of known involvement, but added, "There was good cause to believe that the knowledge of such a project pervaded other parts if not the whole of the state." In short, he had acted to protect even the neighborhoods of legislators far removed from the center of the conspiracy. Furthermore, since the ringleaders had not been caught and evidence existed that an effort could be expected to free the captured conspirators, it became necessary to keep the state's soldiers on station. To this danger, he added the threat that arose, almost as if he had not realized it before, from the concentration of slaves in and about Richmond who worked on the public buildings, on the canal, and in the mines west of the city, men who could gather quickly and "could be opposed only by a respectable force, which force if the city was surprized, could not be collected in a short time." But, in doing so, he abandoned any sense of chronology and cause and effect. Indeed, as he continued his account, he was actually describing conditions *before* the collapse of the plot, noting how the conspirators could have captured and torched the city, "its inhabitants butchered." He cogently observed that taking Richmond would have been easier than holding it. He claimed that as soon as a force was mustered, the "insurrection would be suppressed," since all the advantages of numbers, arms, training, and communication were on the side of the white population. Then Monroe skillfully used the rumor of the involvement of others, the issue that had dominated news accounts of the plot, to further justify the scale of his response. Calling it a "consideration which engaged the mind in the commencement of this affair from which it was not easy to withdraw," he wondered why, since in his estimation Virginia's slaves had been well treated since Independence, "they should embark in this novel and unexampled enterprize of their own accord." Discounting the conspirators' desires or abilities, Monroe claimed, "it was natural to suspect" that these slaves "were prompted to it by others who were invisible, but whose agency might be powerful," a sufficiently vague statement that could refer to the rumored Frenchmen, free people of color, men from Guadalupe, or perhaps even in some still politically inflamed Republican minds, Federalists. Monroe left it up to the predilections of his audience to fill in the blanks. If these instigators existed, and it was "natural" to think that they did, Monroe explained that this made it even more difficult to guess the extent of the plot, but more necessary to mount a response of appropriate scale. Thus began the massive mobilization of the 19th Regiment in Richmond, the 23rd in Chesterfield, and a portion of the 33rd in Henrico on 9 September. This, however, was two days before the opening of the trials on 11 September, trials which, according to Monroe, provided the additional information to support the expensive engagement of so many men. Rather than a strictly historical account, Monroe arranged and presented the evidence to justify the choices he and the council made.[7]

Although his mobilization of the militia proved expensive, Monroe argued, it was not money wasted, even though the forces of the conspiracy had not gathered and attacked their objectives. It "inspired the Citizens with confidence, and depressed the Spirits of the Slaves. The former saw in it a security from the danger which menaced them, the latter a defeat of their nefarious projects." Moreover, it gave officers the chance to train and discipline an important portion of the state's troops. Praising the activated men's progress in the martial arts, Monroe claimed their response provided "a useful lesson to our Country. It tends to confirm the favorable idea before entertained of their competence to every purpose of publick safety"—a conclusion that clearly swiped at the Federalists and their militaristic policies and warmed the hearts of the true republicans among the assemblymen. He fed their approbation by emphasizing how quickly he moved to reduce the size of the forces called up when no further efforts by the slaves to rise were forthcoming. He reported shrinking the overall forces to 650 men on 15 September, to 225 men on the 18th, followed by further reductions, until only two small groups of guards stood at the penitentiary and the jail, a gradual process that took until mid-October. Then, in good republican fashion, he left it to the legislature "to weigh with profound attention this unpleasant incident in our history." He warned it could happen again, for "while this class of people exists among us we can never count with certainty on its tranquil Submission." Escaping disaster this time should not lead to complacency, Monroe admonished, but it should "stimulate us to the adoption of a System, which if it does not prevent the like in future, may secure the Country from any calamitous consequences." However, he did not elaborate on what that "system" should be, leaving the legislators to set policy, again the mark of the real republican, but the source of some later frustration.[8]

Beyond the structure of his address, additional evidence of Monroe's purposeful rendering of the event exists in how he arranged the documents to support the account he sent the assembly. Like his address, the compilation appears to have a chronological structure, but key parts of the collection are reordered for his design. Not usually perceived as significant, the notations on the back of various documents that Monroe ordered copied to accompany his report actually reveal how he wanted the evidence of the conspiracy to be arranged and then read by the members of the General Assembly. On the back of Mosby Sheppard's statement to Monroe is written, "this 1st[,] Mosby's 2d[,] Solomon's confession 3d," with an additional "No. 1," an ordering that is followed in the documents copied for submission to the legislature by Leighton Wood, the chief clerk in the Register's Office. The arrangement of the sets of documents, one through ten, follows this numbering, but not necessarily the chronology of their creation. Nor did Monroe include all of the evidence produced at the trials or by the investigating magistrates, never reproducing for the public the two statements given by Gilbert, for example. On the other hand, the politically embarrassing allegation of the involvement of the two Frenchmen was not excluded from the trial testimony provided the legislature. By then, however, the election was over, or at least it was expected the Republican candidates had won, and there was no need to suppress the testimony already in the press accounts since mid-September. Indeed, given its key role in the newspaper wars of the preceding election, including the claims of the Frenchmen's alleged existence actually discounted them. Suppressing the testimony would have given the allegations additional credence and something else for an astute Federalist editor to carp about.[9]

As noted, Monroe opened his collection of supporting documents with Mosby Sheppard's first warning on 30 August, followed by William Mosby's recollection of his patrolling on the last two nights of August, an account he produced on 10 November at Monroe's request. By doing so, Monroe re-created the process of how he had come to conclude a conspiracy existed. But the third document, Solomon's confession, was not gathered until early 15 September, and the fourth, Ben Woolfolk's, did not emerge until the 17th. Although both documents are dated, to the uninformed delegate their placement could leave the impression that this information was at hand when the large numbers of troops were called up. If nothing else, they framed the reading of the remaining evidence. The compilation then reverts to the testimony given against Solomon and his co-defendants at the opening of the trials on 11 September, before proceeding in a generally chronological order until the evidence reported in the trial of George Smith. Although that trial was held on 19 September, it did not appear until late in the list, just before the report on Gabriel's trial of 6 October. Perhaps Monroe inserted it there because George was a colonel and Woolfolk's testimony at George's trial gave numbers to Smith's recruiting at Hungary Meeting House, revealed his activities in Manchester, and recounted his proposed journey to the Pipeing Tree in King William, thereby stretching the conspiracy toward the south and east. Or perhaps, sorting through so many statements, Monroe spotted it late in his assembling of the evidence and simply had it inserted once found. The exact reason for its peculiar place remains one of the unknowns in the compilation Monroe submitted of the event.

Included with the trial testimony of twenty-one of the twenty-five men executed in Richmond and Henrico were the testimonies against three who were pardoned and two who were acquitted. Perhaps this was an effort to demonstrate the fairness of the courts and executive, to portray a pursuit of justice, not revenge, if not also a subtle means to suggest that the funds spent for the executed slaves might have been much higher. But not submitted in the compendium were the trial records of two key individuals: Ben Woolfolk, who was pardoned, and Jack Bowler, who would be transported. Nor was the testimony included against any of the other men still confined in jail whose sentences had been reprieved and who would later join Bowler in being exiled. Did Monroe not want the executive to be second-guessed on their fate by not making the trial records of the reprieved conveniently available? Would the evidence given against Jack Bowler, for example, who from all accounts was as complicit as Gabriel, and more so than some who were executed, have undercut the effort to establish transportation as a legal alternative to execution? Although a close reading of the submitted trial records contained evidence against Bowler, the fact that he and the other convicted but not yet executed men were never individually identified or mentioned by Monroe may have reflected this concern, too. What is clear is that the promised full and accurate account, "in all its details," was not provided by Monroe. But the one he sent had the appearance of completeness and apparently satisfied those without access to all that was known. Like Gabriel and his recruiters, Monroe stated what in his judgment his audience, essentially the General Assembly, needed to hear.[10]

Another individual, whose identity was probably known to many but who used "A PRIVATE CITIZEN" as his nom de plume, also wanted to influence the assembly's response to the conspiracy. He submitted a lengthy column, which was published on 11 December in Augustine Davis's

Virginia Gazette & General Advertiser, the paper that first reported the allegations of the two Frenchmen. Addressed to Monroe, the writer praised the governor's firm response and claimed that without it and "the interposition of Providence," Virginia would look like the "dreadful scenes, which have been realized in the rich cities and fertile plains of St. Domingo." Monroe's actions, he predicted, would secure the governor's place in the state's history. He denounced those who thought little of the conspiracy, because they "hold the negroes (as an enemy) in contempt, alledge their inferiority in numbers, and want of courage, vaunt that one white man is equal to ten blacks," and consequently saw no real or persistent danger in their midst. He believed that "no person can repose in security and safety," and lamented that although he possessed "*the political power* of a common citizen," after the conspiracy, he felt "bereaved of the blessings of civil liberty, namely, 'security of property and safety of person and life.'" Knowing the effects of the threat, it was time to find a remedy. An end to slavery was one possibility, and he reported that he had found the proposal of "a learned judge"—he did not have to name him—to be most reasonable. He referred to St. George Tucker's 1796 proposal, which called for freeing all female slaves at birth, who would then under Virginia law pass freedom on to each of their children. According to Tucker's calculations, slavery would end in about a century, but his proposal excluded free blacks from any civil liberties or political rights. The denial of any rights would make the free people of color want to leave, or so he believed, and Virginia would be freed not only of slavery but of the former slave population. But the newspaper author complained that Tucker's dream for removal remained vague as to "where, how or at whose expence," and so he dismissed Tucker's plan. He then noted that most agreed that emancipation of the slaves, "*in their present state of ignorance,*" would lead to their "misfortune and ruin," but doubted that Virginia would ever go to the expense of providing appropriate schooling, since the state made little effort to educate its own poor white children. He dismissed the idea of a separate place in the United States as impractical, since no state would give up land to them, and the freedmen themselves would not likely want to migrate. He derided any scheme that relied on the federal government purchasing slaves to be sent abroad to places like Botany Bay or Sierra Leone, simply because it was politically and financially impossible. Unwilling to consider the possibility of living with blacks with any rights, or to believe that any program could really produce their removal, he concluded that emancipation under any scheme would prove too difficult and impossible. Hence, he found "the reproaches of our fellow citizens in the other states" to be "cruel and injurious," especially since in Virginia, "generally speaking, to call them slaves is a harsh term; they are in truth only black servants. In this condition we *must* keep them." Furthermore, emancipation meant perpetual struggles between the two classes of people until "Liberty and equality would be the order of the day," which he found unacceptable, or one group would exterminate the other. He offered no direct explanation for the conspiracy itself, not wondering why the well-treated "black servants" of Virginia would rise to destroy their servitude.

But if slavery continued, the threat of insurrection remained, and so he set forth a series of proposals to prevent any future uprisings, proposals he hoped the sitting assembly and Monroe would consider. By implication, he was revealing his sense of the origins of the aborted uprising. Briefly, he called for the government to have the power to crush any meditated insurrection through wide discretionary and summary powers, to give county lieutenants greater authority to order out the militia in emergencies, and to resurrect the law of outlawry, which he argued would reduce slave runaways because it would allow anyone to kill the outlawed fugitive without legal risk. He proposed that all urban householders produce monthly reports of the names and occupations of those who lived with them. Rural dwellers were to do the same every two months, and all "suspicious houses should be liable to search." Such a policy, he supposed, would rid communities of "the levy free negroes and mulattoes" he believed lived below the taxman's visage, and ferret out those who took stolen goods and had no honest sources of income. Under his multipoint approach, no expansion of any political rights should be granted to free people of color, no free black should be permitted to enter the state, no manumissions should be permitted unless the master provided for them, except for the truly meritorious, and no one should be freed without the final approval of the governor and state council. Finally, rejecting in advance the objections he knew would be raised against a standing army, he called for armed forces to be stationed in the four Southern states, presumably Virginia and those to the south, both infantry and cavalry, which apparently would be drawn from the federal establishment. They were to be stationed in "the principle cities and towns, as a rallying point for our militia."[11]

What the members of the assembly thought of the Private Citizen's proposals remains unknown, but they had already agreed to consider an anti-manumission petition that had been submitted on 2 December from King and Queen County when the House sat as a committee of the whole. It paralleled some of the Private Citizen's calls. Signed by thirty men, it claimed it was "notorious that the Law for Freeing Negroes hath tended to bring upon us our disturbed and distressed situation." Consequently, the petition called for the repeal of the 1782 law permitting private emancipations and wanted only "Meritorious Services" to be the criteria for any future manumissions, a throwback to pre-Revolutionary days. The petition's signers thought a "General Emancipation" was "impossible with our Safety, besides a commixture to our minds is abhorrent," but in the language of the supplicant, left it to "the Wisdom of y[ou]r Hon[ora]ble House." The submission also included a crossed-out line following their flattery, which read, "will devise ways and means to clear the State of all Free Negroes as Formenters of the late Disturbance." Obviously, these citizens would have found the expressions of the Private Citizen's letter welcome.[12]

When the delegates received the governor's message, they first tabled it. They subsequently scheduled a hearing on it when they met as a Committee of the Whole House. Apparently it was never taken up there, but it was finally committed to a special committee on 26 December, which the House had just named, to bring in a bill "To amend an act to reduce into one the several acts concerning slaves, free negroes, and mulattoes." It also directed the committee to address the petition from King and Queen County. With their threefold charge, the committee got to work and on New Year's Eve reported its recommendations arising from the governor's message to the General Assembly.[13]

The composition of the special committee probably helped shape the resolutions they constructed. Chaired by Edmund Harrison of Amelia, a county with one of the highest concentrations of slaves in the state, it was composed of seventeen delegates drawn from most sections of the Commonwealth, including Benjamin Dabney of King and Queen County, whose residents had submitted the anti-manumission petition, although he had not signed it. Also named were representatives from Dinwiddie and Prince George Counties, Peterson Goodwyn and Benjamin Harrison, who also spoke for Petersburg. Harrison, of course, was the delegate who informed General Jones of the local rumors of the plot there. Other urban voices were Robert B. Taylor, the delegate elected from Norfolk Borough, and Charles Copland, who sat for Richmond and who had served as Gabriel's attorney at the maiming trial a year earlier. Perhaps most significant for interpreting Monroe's message was the inclusion of Gervas Storrs of Henrico, one of the two examining magistrates who interrogated those arrested in the county and the man to whom Jack Bowler surrendered. No one other than Joseph Selden, not even Monroe, had as much firsthand knowledge of the full range of evidence of the core conspiracy than Storrs. His presence on the committee has been overlooked, and while the deliberations of the committee are unrecorded, his role must have been substantial.[14]

The committee, "to whom was referred the Governor's letter on . . . the late conspiracy" and the petition complaining "of the law for freeing negroes and praying a repeal thereof," made seven recommendations to their legislative colleagues, in the form of resolutions. One did not require legislation and was close to the scratched-out line in the King and Queen petition but broader in intent: it requested that the governor inquire of the president about the purchase of lands outside of Virginia, where "persons obnoxious to the laws, or dangerous to the peace of society may be removed." It was agreed to and sent to the Senate for its concurrence. Another resolution suggested that the state purchase, manumit, and grant a pension to both Pharoah and Tom, the two men who had first revealed the conspiracy to Mosby Sheppard. The committee also proposed that the executive be empowered "to transport certain slaves now under sentence of death, for conspiracy to be sold for the benefit of this commonwealth." They did not advise a general transportation bill, only one that applied to the eight men convicted for their part in Gabriel's plot. They called for a measure that would give civil magistrates the authority "to call out patrols, and subjecting the military in certain cases to the orders of the civil authority." The three remaining resolutions reflected the heightened awareness of the growth of Virginia's urban places and their emergence in Virginia's slave society as tempting targets, as storehouses of arms, and as homes to growing numbers of free people of color. One would request the executive to arm the citizens of Virginia's seven largest towns. The second sought to exclude free blacks from living in or near these towns unless licensed by town or county authority. The third would initiate the establishment of a publicly funded guard to be stationed in Richmond. In all likelihood, the key place of Richmond in the conspirators' plans, and the presence of the men who represented Richmond and Henrico, Norfolk Borough, and Petersburg, strongly influenced these latter proposals. Storrs, who probably knew them, may have pushed for the freeing of Pharoah and Tom, although Monroe had long before suggested some reward for them. Although the committeemen announced they were responding to the King and Queen petition, none of their resolutions proposed ending manumissions—but that would not stop a continuing effort to do so during that session of the assembly. Just a few days later, in the Committee of the Whole House, the delegates would face that issue, when the committee reported on its instructions to propose revisions to the basic law of slavery in the state, a law entitled "An Act to reduce into one the several acts concerning Slaves, free Negroes & Mulattoes." Perhaps the lack of an anti-manumission resolution at this juncture reflected the influence of men on the special committee who had manumitted slaves themselves, individuals like chairman Harrison and delegates Storrs and Copland. Each of them, and perhaps others, had freed slaves, and obviously saw some merit or justice in the practice, if only for individuals.[15]

The House endorsed all of the resolutions, but chose to amend the one calling for the establishment of the public guard in Richmond by having the guards, artisans, and military stores at the Point of Fork transferred to Richmond. The delegates then ordered that a bill or bills to implement the proposals be produced, but not all would survive to become law. And most would be amended in the House or Senate, or both.[16]

The first of the proposals to become a statute was an act purchasing and freeing Pharoah and Tom. However, the provision that they be pensioned was eliminated at the second reading of the bill. On 14 January 1801, the Senate agreed to the measure without further amendment, and on 27 January, Monroe wrote to Philip Sheppard wanting to know the price of the two men. This provoked an exchange in which the Sheppard owners demanded $500 for each of the two men, a price which shocked Monroe, since neither Pharoah nor Tom were as highly skilled as Gabriel or Thornton or Solomon, blacksmiths who had been valued at that level. In the end, he reluctantly met their demand. Interestingly, later in the year, a group from Richmond and Henrico contributed enough money to purchase $2,000 worth of United States bonds so as to provide a life annuity for each man. To increase each annual payment to $60, the bonds were held by Richard Adams of Richmond, who made up the shortfall in exchange for ownership of the bonds.[17]

On 2 January the Senate had requested the state auditor to report how much the state had paid owners of executed slaves over the previous decade. He responded three days later, and the Senate ordered on 7 January that the figure, $35,892.24, be entered into their journal. The statement summed all warrants issued between 1 January 1791 and 31 December 1800, which meant that some of the men convicted in Gabriel's Conspiracy were included. The Senate Journal is silent as to the origin of the request, but when the House passed its bill by 12 January authorizing the governor to transport slaves convicted of conspiracy, the Senate had obviously been thinking about the costs of executing slaves and perhaps making its own calculations of the monies to be saved by exiling them instead. In any case, it assigned the bill to a committee, heard its report with some proposed amendments, recommitted it to an enlarged committee which again amended it before the Senate passed the bill and returned it to the delegates on 15 January. The House then agreed to the Senate's amended version. The act, modified either in the Senate or the House (which body is not known), expanded the original resolution's provision for transportation from just the men found guilty in Gabriel's Conspiracy to include those who committed "other crimes" of a capital nature, a significant extension and one that specifically could apply retroactively to any convict not yet executed. This promised even greater future savings to the state even as it created a potential alternative punishment in some capital cases. The law also required that the trial records of all slaves found guilty of a capital offense in any court be submitted to the executive, a necessary stipulation to allow the governor and council to judge whether the convicted was an appropriate candidate for transportation. In practice, as it turns out, the executive's decision would usually depend on a recommendation to that effect from the justices sitting on the case or from respected members of the community where the crime occurred.[18]

But expanding executive mercy to include the option of transportation was more than just a financial measure. As Monroe had reported to Madison, some of the convicted "were less criminal in comparison to others." Being found guilty of conspiracy for some meant only talk; for others, it involved gathering arms, recruits, and providing leadership. Was the death penalty appropriate for all? In 1797, Virginia had moved to eliminate capital punishment for most crimes for free people, substituting prison sentences to be served in a penitentiary the state would then build. George Keith Taylor, a delegate from Prince George County had argued that the punishment should fit the crime, but had partly framed his point by noting that some criminals escaped any punishment. This was the case because some potential accusers failed to bring charges for lesser infractions, or juries refused to convict for serious crimes because, for humanitarian reasons, capital punishment was seen as too severe. Hence, Taylor argued, fitting the punishment to the crime would actually lead to more, but more appropriate, prosecutions and punishments of criminals currently escaping trial or guilty verdicts. The assembly agreed, but their efforts at penal reform applied only to free people, white and black, not to slaves. This was the dilemma county justices, city aldermen, and the executive faced. Indeed, the author of the letter first published in the New York *American Citizen* on 2 October claimed that at the trials, "the least doubt, the smallest suspicion, or contradiction on the part of the witnesses (who are kept in separate apartments) will often acquit Negroes who are really criminal." The executive found pardons not always appropriate either, for as Monroe wryly noted, "It was hardly to be presumed, a rebel who avows it was his intention to assassinate his master &ca if pardoned will ever become a useful servant." To Virginia authorities, the possibility of transportation reduced the sole reliance on pardons for mercy and resolved economic, humanitarian, and security concerns raised by the number of convictions under the conspiracy law. It is probable that recognizing these advantages led to expanding the original proposal to include other capital crimes committed by slaves as well. At the same time, the legislature did not consider eliminating the death penalty for conspiracy, or removing it as the punishment for actual insurrection.[19]

The next suggestion of the Harrison committee to pass the House of Delegates empowered justices of the peace to order patrols when they deemed it necessary and provided these patrollers with the same pay as those sent out by military officers. This provision echoes the Richmond mayor's statement to Monroe that he had no authority to order out a patrol from the militia following Gabriel's trial and the postponement of his execution. The second section of the act provided for the organization of the Petersburg militia in such a fashion as to create patrols for the town, and a third section gave the Fredericksburg Court the authority to tax the town's inhabitants to pay for watchmen. The House passed the measure without amendment, but the Senate had modified it in some unrecorded way, to which the delegates gave their assent. However, the bill to control where free people of color could live died. It had been committed to the Committee of the Whole House on the State of the Commonwealth, but on 16 January the body was discharged from considering it, and further debate was postponed until after the session adjourned, a procedural device to kill a bill.[20]

The two remaining committee proposals, to arm the militias of some of Virginia's towns and to establish a public guard in Richmond, finally passed on 21 and 22 January, respectively. In the final version of the specific order to the governor to arm urban militiamen, the list of towns was expanded from seven to fourteen, which likely helped its passage, and meant that even villages like Port Royal and Falmouth were to be separately armed. However, although the distribution was to take place "without delay," the governor was not to allocate more than two thousand arms beyond what had already been authorized by the militia act of January 1800. In a similar cost-conscious mode, the bill establishing the guard in Richmond had already been amended by forcing the closure of the arsenal at Point of Fork, with those men who wished to continue employment in Richmond being able to do so. This measure was the only one that referred "to the present crisis of affairs" when it authorized the establishment of the state-funded guard of sixty-eight men, who had to be citizens of the United States and were to be enlisted for a three-year term. The arms and supplies at Point of Fork were to be removed to Richmond, and the old arsenal property rented in a manner that would "provide for the safe-keeping thereof," a provision that suggests that this was seen as an experiment rather than as a final decision. The price the state expected to pay for the guard was set at $12,000 in the budget.[21]

As these measures moved through House and Senate, the two bodies also debated another bill which amended existing law concerning slaves and free blacks, the original purpose of the Harrison committee. Passed in the final days of the session, like the last two measures discussed above, it addressed a number of issues that Gabriel's Conspiracy had exposed, and early in the debate proposed an end to manumissions, one of the demands of the King and Queen petitioners. On 2 January, committee member Peter Johnston presented a proposed bill, which was read twice and then committed to the Committee of the Whole. In that form, on 8 January the House began discussing the measure. It then resumed its normal organization and formally heard a report of the actions it had just taken regarding the bill "To amend . . . the act concerning slaves, free negroes and mulattoes," which now included amendments. The bill and amendments were tabled. In a rare instance, the text of the proposed bill appeared the next day in the *Argus*. The tabled measure opened with a proposal that required any owner who freed a slave to post a performance bond that future emancipated persons leave the state within a yet to be determined number of days, "never more to return." If newly manumitted individuals were caught in the state after they were to have left, they could be imprisoned and put to hard labor to reimburse the state for their "apprehension, commitment and [ultimate] removal" from Virginia. In addition, anyone who transported a free black individual by ship or land into the state faced substantial fines. Here was the most direct response to the King and Queen petition, although whether this proposal came from the committee or was an amendment offered from the floor is not clear. Four days later, the House took up the bill, agreed to additional unrecorded amendments, and ordered the bill engrossed and read a third time. The next day, it passed the measure and sent it to the Senate, beginning a ping-ponging between the chambers of amendments and amendments to amendments, whose specific contents remain unknown. What did emerge as the act finally adopted on 21 January did not include the proposed exile of the freed. But a revision of existing law relating to how slaves illegally imported into Virginia were to be treated was included, having been added after the introduction of the measure.[22]

Other sections of the act grew more directly out of the challenges brought by Gabriel's insurgency, and were changed slightly from the bill as originally proposed. One attempted to tighten the existing law restricting owners from allowing self-hire, applying it as well to executors and administrators, guardians and trustees. Recall that Sam Byrd's recruiting followed his self-hiring from his widowed owner. Another section resolved the quandary of the admissibility of slave testimony against free persons of color by permitting it, whether in suits brought by the Commonwealth or in civil cases among free people of color. Gervas Storrs may have been involved in the decision to release Sam Byrd Sr., joining others in reading the 1792 law dealing with admissible slave testimony in a more restrictive manner than that of his fellow Henrico justices who sat on the case of Thomas Jordan Martin, or of Petersburg magistrates where it had earlier been allowed. Another section, perhaps one adopted in lieu of the measure to control where free blacks could live, required that the names, sex, location of residence, and occupation of all free persons of color be annually recorded by the district tax commissioners in each county or town and posted on the courthouse door. Another stated that if a free person of color moved from one location to another, to "intrude," in the language of the law, a warrant could be issued to determine whether the person had "honest employment," and if not, he or she could be treated as a vagrant under Virginia law. Perhaps in these provisions one can find a ghost of the Private Citizen's proposals.[23]

Taking these measures together, the General Assembly failed to produce what Monroe had hoped. Earlier, on 18 January, with knowledge of the resolutions but without knowing all of their final outcomes, Monroe had acknowledged the legislators' efforts "to unite in some measures to prevent or suppress future negro conspiracies," but judged them "without effect." In the end, harsher measures against free blacks had been contemplated but adjusted, and obstacles to manumissions considered but rejected. Free people of color lost the immunity from slave testimony enjoyed by whites, but this was a clarification of earlier legislation more than an innovation. Instituting transportation was more important to the state, as was the arming of its towns, creating a guard to protect the public property and arms in Richmond, and the tightening of slave mobility—of going at large—by attempting to eliminate self-hire. But these did not constitute a "system." At the same time, Monroe does not seem to have been able to come up with one either, or at least he publicly revealed none to his liking. In the end, the actions taken by the legislature, like the measures and institutions often adopted or created to prevent future wars, addressed this last conspiracy but would not prevent future ones.[24]

One important issue the state did not attempt was the proscription of all slave mobility, for that threatened an essential component of the slave system in place by 1800, although Monroe tried to come to grips with the issue late in December. The whispers among the slaves who continued to cluster and talk in Richmond and Norfolk still wafted down alleys and streets. On 26 December, while the Harrison committee began to deliberate their response to the governor's message, an alarmed Benjamin Duval warned Monroe of an overheard conversation on one of Richmond's cross streets. Hearing "Norfolk" and "cowards," he quietly crept back to listen to some men who talked of "the late alarm in Norfolk," who repeated words like "cowards" and "liberty," and who claimed "that the business only required a beginning & that there never was or would be a better time than the present." Monroe hastily informed local officers, including William Austin, whose Horse Patrol that night found all quiet, and who then inquired if another one was needed on the following evening. Monroe responded with a request to maintain the patrols for the rest of the holidays, which meant until the beginning of the year, when the annual hiring cycle resumed and slaves returned to work.[25]

The circle of men in Richmond may have been condemning the rumored gathering in early September south of Suffolk for not rising, or they may have heard of a recent incident in Norfolk. Thomas Newton, who served as the state senator for Norfolk and nearby counties took a leave of absence from the Senate on 22 December and learned of an alarm as he traveled home. From Norfolk he wrote to Monroe on the 29th that on his arrival he was informed that the uproar resulted from some "seditious speeches," but who had uttered them remained undiscovered. In reaction, the locals had mustered with speed and had been joined by "strangers" and seamen, who boosted the turnout and whose response suggested a solidarity among whites that ignored social distinctions in the face of a black uprising. But Newton also noted that their lack of arms left the men no better equipped than their slaves, and the "deranged" state of the militia, suffering as it did from an unwillingness of men to serve as officers, presented its own problems. He promised a fuller account when he returned to Richmond to resume his place in the Senate.[26]

Besides putting a patrol in the streets of Richmond, Duval's warning provoked Monroe to create a set of recommendations for the state's capital city which may have been partially influenced by the letter addressed to him from the Private Citizen in the *Virginia Gazette*. He sent Mayor McClurg a letter on 27 December informing him of his instructions for patrols to the militia officers of the capital, "to prevent a movement of the negroes and defeat its object should one take place." But Monroe wanted to eliminate the ongoing threat through measures only the city itself could take. Noting that "many negroes were yesterday and still are in town from the country," and guessing that many could be miners "who acting in a body at their ordinary labour, are more capable of forming and executing any plan" than slaves scattered on farms and plantations, he proposed new regulations on their movement. He suggested that none be allowed to come into Richmond before a particular hour. Moreover, all should be required to leave by a stipulated time. To accomplish this, Richmond would first have to register all city slaves and each owner would have to provide a pass or certificate of his residency in the capital, apparently in order to determine who was from the country and who lived in town. To enforce this, Richmond needed to instruct its constables or hire a watch employed both day and night to expel the non-residents. Monroe assumed that country slaves were only there for the market, and once it closed all should have to leave. He expected that the watchmen would be full-time employees of the city and felt confident that the municipality had the resources to pay for them. He assured the mayor he would continue to do all that he could to ensure the safety of the city, but his powers did not "extend to regulations of the kind above referred to." McClurg presented Monroe's memo to the common council two days later, and it resolved that "the safety of this city against fire and insurrection of free negroes and slaves" required the creation of a "constant watch." The Hall created the proposed body on 3 January, but it was to patrol only from late evening until dawn. Perhaps they expected that their constables and the presence of the new public guard whose existence was taking shape in the assembly would inspire order during the day.[27]

Once the assembly created its laws, the governor moved to implement them if his action was required. As noted, Monroe soon began the process that would lead to the purchase and freeing of Pharoah and Tom. William Morris Jr. and John Brown submitted a bid to purchase the eight men, plus another named Billy convicted of a different crime, who sat in jails awaiting their fates, which the council accepted on 23 January. The measure ended the ongoing costs to the public for guarding the four convicted men in Caroline, but the council did agree to pay for moving them to Richmond, where they were again jailed. On 28 January, the men to be transported were released from the control of jailor William Rose to Morris and Brown on Monroe's instruction. On the same day, the council authorized Monroe to gather statements from the appropriate regimental commanders of the number of militiamen in each of the fourteen towns so that the correct number of arms could be sent to them.[28]

The process of creating the public guard for Richmond and moving the arms and supplies from Point of Fork occupied the attention of Monroe and the council too. By 10 February, the executive had chosen Colonel Alexander Quarrier to captain the guard and he was instructed to begin enlisting the men. The commander at Point of Fork was ordered to begin packing up the materials there, and John Clarke was told to reinforce the capitol building to hold the arms to be used by the Richmond militia, having reported that was the best place to keep them. This decision later led to the keys of the capitol being turned over to Quarrier from Robert Cowley, who still kept the capitol and served at the council's door. In addition, the powder that had been moved to the penitentiary was returned to the magazine by the end of March.[29]

During and following the days of the legislative session, the executive continued to deal with the residuals of the conspiracy, some of them rather surprising. On 22 January, Paul Woolfolk submitted a bill of $23.66 for the "services of Ben, alias Ben Woolfolk," rendered between 1 September and 22 January 1801. Obviously, Ben Woolfolk had not testified for some time and was not likely to have been arrested by 1 September, but the council agreed to pay the claim, which was probably prorated at Woolfolk's normal rate of hire. In one of the anomalies in the record, Paul Woolfolk claimed Ben's wages, not owner Paul Graham or hirer William Young, without any noted authorization from either of them. Perhaps he had since purchased Ben, or perhaps, as Graham's stepfather, this was redundant. The end date of Ben's "services" probably indicates that the slave was released to Woolfolk on the same day. As he left confinement, the witness did sport a new suit of clothes and shoes provided by the state, but no effort appears to have been made by anyone to free him as a result of his multiple appearances in court, or for the names of the men he revealed. His pardon was his reward.[30]

Remaining in the penitentiary with Woolfolk over nearly this same period was Prosser's Ben, who also received the same clothing provision. No bill for his testimony, or lost time, appears from Prosser, but unlike Woolfolk, this Ben's service was thought worthy enough to be rewarded with manumission, though not by the state or Prosser. Five men of Richmond, including William Foushee of the state council, paid Prosser £110, or $366.66, to free him, which he did in September. Another frequent witness, Price's John, who often appeared with Ben, had revealed names under threat and testified against several who had been at a meeting at Young's spring. He was never tried, seems to have been sent home earlier than the two Bens, and like Woolfolk, appears to have remained enslaved, with no recorded public or private efforts undertaken to free him. His reward was to escape the possibility of facing trial and the hangman. Thus, as in the case of establishing annuities for Pharoah and Tom, it seems that some citizens who followed the trials made their own judgments about the relative contributions of the witnesses or the quality of their character, and took or supported what they considered appropriate action when the state did not.[31]

The council, on 6 April, issued a warrant on behalf of Elzy Burroughs and others for their services spent capturing Jacob, the enslaved waterman of William Wilson who committed suicide. It totaled $99.08. Interestingly, the council was willing to reimburse these men for their efforts in catching a suspected insurrectionist, even though the General Assembly had rejected Wilson's petition for compensation for Jacob, who had been in the custody of these same men when he stabbed himself. In a slightly different case, on 23 May the council authorized payment to Captain James Spears and thirteen men from Cumberland for services rendered the September before. Their bill included the expenses arising from renting a bateau used to transport a white man being sent to the new penitentiary, but more significantly, the warrant included expenses for the person of Stepney, a suspected conspirator who appears never to have faced trial either. Spears, however, had lost a public musket during the trip, most likely dropped into the James River, and the state deducted $6 from his share of the $63 bill submitted. At times, the executive must have wondered when the claims would stop.[32]

Having set in motion the process for freeing Pharoah and Tom, arming the towns, establishing the public guard, and transporting the convicted, Monroe wrote to the president, as instructed by the assembly, to inquire about lands for the unspecified dangerous and obnoxious in their midst. For whatever reason, even though the electoral tie between Jefferson and Burr was finally settled in the House of Representatives on 17 February and Jefferson inaugurated on 4 March, Monroe did not write him about the matter until 15 June. He enclosed the resolution, informed the president that the "obnoxious" they wished to deport were men like the conspirators, and tied the inquiry to the policy of transportation. He explained that his best understanding of the legislators' intent was to find a destination for them in the "vacant western territory" of the United States, but Monroe expanded the choice to include anyplace where they might be accepted outside of the country. The governor went further, though, in interpreting legislative intent, by suggesting that those described as "dangerous to the peace of society may be understood as comprizing many" who might not be insurrectionists, and if so, "an alternative of places" would be desirable. Then, meaning to make exile or transportation an option to those "beyond the contracted scale of providing a mode of punishment for offenders," Monroe seemed to be introducing the possibility of seeking a place to which freed people could be sent. At the next General Assembly, Monroe laid before the members Jefferson's lengthy response, which led to another resolution clarifying whom they meant by "obnoxious" and "dangerous." The first group were criminal slaves they wished to send to Africa or to Spanish or Portuguese regions of the Americas. "The second respects free negroes and mulattoes, including those who may hereafter be emancipated and sent, or chuse to remove to such a place as may be acquired." The assemblymen expressed no choice as to this location, Monroe explained, hoping only that by not stating a preference, it would leave open the largest possible number of places as a destination to speed them on their way. What they did not address, as the Private Citizen had complained of St. George Tucker's plan, was the "how and at whose expence." But it may have laid the groundwork for support in Virginia some years later for the American Colonization Society's efforts to create a place for free African Americans in Liberia. The freed former servant, the reliable craftsmen or nurse known in the local community, could be tolerated or even welcomed, but in the minds of many white Virginians, if slavery were not to exist at all, the safety and orderliness of Virginia society could only be preserved in racial separation through exile of its black residents.[33]

At the same session, the House of Delegates heard the petition of John G. Brown and William Morris requesting an extension of time on the bond they posted for the purchase of the slaves they had transported. They had started with their prizes and had reached Point Pleasant on the Ohio River when, "notwithstanding every precaution," two of the men bolted into the Northwest Territory. One could imagine that Jack Bowler, one of the most powerful men in Virginia, was one of the two, but the petitioners did not identify the escapees. Securing help, Brown and Morris recaptured the two men, but one of the guards had wounded one of the two escapees. Perhaps it was in Gallipolis, Ohio, that the guard was jailed and the slaves "discharged to the great delay & expense" of Brown and Morris. But after apparently settling accounts and securing their convicts again, they "continued their rout down the Ohio" to the "Territory of Spain." When they arrived there, they found the reputations of their prizes had preceded them, "particularly [among] those to whom application for sales would have been made." As self-proclaimed men of honor, they could not deny the truth of the "Crimes, Trials, & convictions of the sd Slaves," and so were forced to sell them on greatly extended credit and below their expected price. Now they faced paying the bond, but could not without the proceeds from the sale they could not yet collect. The delegates rejected the motion to submit it to a committee, killing the petition. The lesson would not be lost on future purchasers of slaves to be transported.[34]

Afterword

The suppression of the conspiracy disrupted and devastated lives along the Brook. For about five weeks, patrols regularly stalked the area. By mid-October, twenty-two men from the neighborhood had been executed; four of them, plus Michael from Chesterfield, were hanged near Prosser's Tavern to terrorize the inhabitants. The state kept records only of their deaths, taking no notice of the interment of the hanged men, no matter where they died. Last rites or proper burials by their families and friends may not have taken place; indeed, such gatherings might have been feared and dispersed. Perhaps the costs of interment were included in the $73.43 the sheriff collected for the executions, but no one otherwise submitted a bill for digging graves or making coffins. In addition to the executed, two more men from the Brook were among the eight plotters who were sold by the state and transported to Spanish territory west of the Mississippi. Together, these twenty-four men comprised approximately 5 percent of the adult slave men in the upper district of Henrico, perhaps 10 percent or more of the men of the Brook, and an even higher proportion of men in their prime who had lived in the neighborhood. Other souls were missing too. Michael, the Chesterfield slave noted above whose wife resided near the Brook, would never visit again; John would never trek up Brook Road between his hire at the penitentiary and his Hanover owner's place; nor would Sam Graham ever venture into the neighborhood from Hanover or Caroline, drawn on a visit, if not a funeral, at Young's spring. The death or removal of these sons, husbands, brothers, and acquaintances opened voids, destroyed connections, and made it necessary for kin, men and women, to assume new responsibilities for their grieving survivors, old and young, and to restring the cords of neighborhood.[1]

Other men did return to the Brook. Beginning with Martin's acquittal on 12 September, a total of eleven men came home after their trials, as did seven more who had received pardons. How many of them might have been seen as too troublesome or too dangerous to keep and were subsequently sold or removed from the locale cannot be counted, but it seems likely that some were. On the other hand, Frank and Daniel, or at least two men who shared names with the two acquitted slaves of Nathaniel Wilkinson, appeared on his estate inventory in 1808, a possible indication that some continuity remained. Even Peter, the pardoned slave of Allen Williamson, passed to his widow Lucy as part of her dower allotment in 1803. An unknowable number of other men, alleged to have been involved but not tried, also returned, as did a handful after serving as witnesses. Their whispers and banter were undoubtedly lowered for a while, but at the same time, these men had asserted themselves and shared a close encounter with death, an intense experience which may have strengthened the bonds among the survivors.[2]

Others returned to the Brook; whether they resumed a place in the fabric of the neighborhood cannot be readily determined. When requesting some reward for Peter Smith, the free man of color who fostered Jack Bowler's surrender, Gervas Storrs noted the "odium he may incur from the blacks." It is not possible to know whether he suffered any, but considering Bowler's physical prowess, most observers would have believed it was Bowler's decision to submit, not Smith's ability to seize him, that put him in irons. Until at least 1803, Smith remained in the neighborhood, and was even listed with a tithable slave in 1802. He then moved to Richmond and was again listed with a taxable slave. That person may have been a black man named Jerry Smith, perhaps a son, whom he freed in the fall of 1804. The following year, he bought from an estate and then manumitted a woman named Nanny, along with her infant daughter Mary. In 1811 and in 1812, he paid taxes on yet another slave aged at least twelve years. He then dropped from Richmond's tax records.[3]

The Commonwealth's witnesses had played a different role, and as the plot broke, Monroe had believed that they needed to be taken up, in part, to secure their own safety, too. Three of them would seem particularly vulnerable in the aftermath of the trials. Prosser's Ben had testified at thirty-six prosecutions. As noted earlier, by the following fall, a group of Richmond men would pay Thomas Henry Prosser to emancipate the young man. How was his testimony and subsequent freedom viewed? He seems to have disappeared, or at least none of the local free black men has yet been identified as a man formerly known as Prosser's Ben. Price's John, whose dozen appearances at the trials helped send ten men to the gallows and another into exile in the West, was not freed. He may have resumed his hired position in Richmond. Did he ever venture back to Price's quarters on his own? Perhaps these men initially displayed the bruises, swellings, or stripes of a "close examination." Even if not, both these men's actions were likely understandable to their neighbors, given the violence that pervaded the system of slavery. The third was Ben Woolfolk, who Price's John had also testified against. Brought into the Brook neighborhood on hire, he had given sworn testimony against more than thirty men, including all nine of those tried in Caroline County. He did so only after being found guilty. Would he have been given the same consideration? Perhaps Paul Woolfolk quickly returned him from prison to Paul Graham in Hanover, rather than hiring him in Henrico again, but there he would have been close to the courthouse and Littlepage's Bridge, the home grounds of the conspirators there. Even Graham's subsequent move into Caroline would not have placed Woolfolk beyond the reach of men against whom he had given evidence. He may have been sold at the death of Graham in 1802, or even earlier. In 1807, Woolfolk appeared in Richmond as one of four slave witnesses against a free man of color who had been charged with burglary. He now belonged to Wilson Miles Cary, presumably the large slaveholding planter, then of Williamsburg but with substantial slave holdings at his ultimate residence in Fluvanna County. What placed Woolfolk in Richmond to witness the crime is unknown. Perhaps he was hired there. Beyond this incident, the rest of his life seems to have escaped the record.[4]

More evidence exists about Tom and Pharoah, the two men who revealed the plot on the morning of 30 August. Unlike the heavily used witnesses—Ben, John, and Ben Woolfolk—they made their decision to provide information before the plot had collapsed. Monroe wanted them apprehended so that "they will be secure against the suspicion of being" informers. Just as Storrs expressed his concern over Smith, and as he had over the witnesses, the governor also believed that Tom and Pharoah were at risk. But the deed of the two men could not be kept secret long and their subsequent manumission would have exposed their role too. In fact, the two men stayed in the general neighborhood, Tom more than Pharoah, and both apparently collected the $60 annuity each had been provided through private subscription. Tom assumed the surname of Sheppard, became a farmer, rented land, and worked seasonally for the Sheppard family until at least the mid-1820s. Pharoah also took the Sheppard name, soon moved to Hanover County, but remained close enough to work in the spring harvest for the Sheppards for nearly a decade and a half, sometimes as an overseer, before resuming residence in Henrico by 1818. When he returned, he drove a gig. In 1803, he obtained a loan from Mosby Sheppard, not his former owner Philip, to buy his son. He could not free him until he had repaid the sum five years later, at a time when newly manumitted slaves were required to leave the state within a year. This drove him to petition the legislature in 1810 to allow Pharoah Jr. to remain in Virginia, a plea which was granted. He manumitted his son in 1815, probably as the young man was coming of age. Interestingly, Mosby Sheppard did not permit Pharoah's son's manumission to take effect before the 1 May 1806 deadline, as other masters sometimes did, to avoid the threat of deportation. But again, there is no evidence that any reprisals were meted out to the two informers from their black neighbors of the Brook. In all likelihood, the two men were not alone in their appraisal of the potential outcome of the uprising. Neither man appears to have been intimately involved, and thus neither was caught up in the surge of excitement and bravado that helped sustain the hopes of other men. Perhaps, after a cold-eyed appraisal, and one that could not be made until the last moment, they concluded that an insufficient number of men would actually rally on that Saturday night, that the plot's leadership was lacking, or that the scheme itself was flawed. If so, exposing the conspiracy may have been done to cut the fearful losses to a minimum. But if their rationale is unknown, so too is their sense of what reward they might expect. Since they were subsequently emancipated, historians have assumed they betrayed the plot to secure their own freedom. However, it had been decades since Virginia had freed any slave for revealing a conspiracy, or for any other serious threat to the public, such as counterfeiting, so they had no direct knowledge of the potential for freedom their revelation might produce. Indeed, the woman who revealed the decision to reassemble after the storm would receive no public reward, and Prosser's Ben would only later be freed through private sources. The two men may have gambled on personal rewards, even manumission from the Sheppards, but with the state committed to their purchase for emancipation, the Sheppard owners certainly held out for the highest price they could get. But if any anticipated rewards were unknown, one thing was certain: slavery rested on violence, and when resisted, wantonly applied. Thus, preventing the bloody reprisals that could be expected to be launched against their neighborhood may have been paramount in their thinking. As James Sidbury postulated, if the reaction to Nat Turner's uprising is any indication, the response would have been brutal. The Brook would have flowed with blood, and it would have been mostly the blood of the slaves.[5]

But for all the hangings, the whispers still continued. In 1802, the Henrico Court tried two men for conspiracy and insurrection in the midst of a larger conspiracy scare. One was acquitted, the other found guilty and ordered executed, but his sentence was commuted to transportation by the executive. In the same year, Glasgow and Tom, two slaves held by Paul Thilman in Hanover, were convicted of conspiracy, apparently on the testimony of a man described by Paul Woolfolk as "a bad character," a "liar," and a sometime runaway who provoked more complaints from his owner than any other servant in Woolfolk's experience. Thilman had either just died or very soon would, and his financial circumstances were so shaky that his slaves were being sold off. Tom served as his widow's cook at the tavern, and Glasgow was described "as a mere boy." After their conviction, two groups of Hanover citizens pled for executive mercy, with the first simply supporting the court's recommendation for transportation. A belated second effort sought full pardons, and explained why. Referring to a series of arrests that led to trials but no convictions in adjacent King William County, the latter petitioners claimed they were "well convinced from recent circumstances, that when a meeting happens among this description of people, that they hold conversation relative to what hath not only already happened, but what may hereafter come to pass, without having any real intention of puting [sic] the same into Execution." While they admitted the men had conversed on "something about an insurrection," they complained that the single witness against the two was "perhaps" the one to initiate the talk. They proposed pardons, for they averred that transportation "to another part of the World make but little, if any impression on others." By the time they submitted their plea, however, the executive had already received and granted the first petition calling for transportation.[6]

If Thilman's slaves allegedly still talked insurrection, so did Thomas Henry Prosser's. In May 1806, three of his slave men, Ben, Ned, and Isaac, were each tried for conspiracy but found not guilty. None of them had been charged in 1800. About three weeks later, two more men stood before the Henrico bar for the same reason. Harrison, likely a hired slave, and Richard Key, a free black man from the upper half of the county, were each acquitted. Several whites from the upper district testified at Harrison's trial, but the Commonwealth could produce no witness against Key. Since none of these trials ended with a guilty verdict, no testimony was recorded or forwarded and nothing further is known of their plans or of any connections which may have existed among the five men.[7]

Other changes came to the Brook and to Virginia that unsettled life and became marks of the new century. In a rare instance of a large emancipation after the 1806 deadline, the slaves of Izard Bacon were freed by his will, apparently including the acquitted George. In 1819, after some legal and political maneuvering, the group of fifty-five freed men, women, and children moved en masse to Pennsylvania. Their migration, however, left behind slave family members and connections who lived on neighboring farms and plantations. After living for a year in Pennsylvania, John Winston petitioned the legislature for permission to return. Forced, along with the others, to leave the state under the 1806 law, his "love of liberty" had led him to "sacrifice . . . his domestic happiness." He revealed he had left his wife and two children behind but now found it impossible to be happy without them. He pled for the legislature's indulgence. Several testified that Winston had been Bacon's best slave, and urged that he be allowed once again to reside in Virginia, but the pleas apparently fell on deaf ears.[8]

As the chances of private emancipations declined, especially after 1806, the future of many of the enslaved turned away from the prospects of freedom. Looming larger was the threat of being sold and transported out of state, as the interstate slave trade increased in volume and intensity and as Virginians abandoned the Old Dominion for new lands to the south and west. It was a market and a migration even more destructive of families and neighborhoods than the sales and scatterings among kin that had always marked slavery. Consequently, as slavery was carried south and west through what Ira Berlin calls "The Passage to the Interior," the threat of sale or removal to distant places became an owner's most effective means of controlling his slaves in the antebellum era. The out-of-state slave trade was also seen as a way to reduce the numbers and proportions of Virginia's slaves and make the New Dominion a safer place for whites.[9]

Interestingly, Thomas Henry Prosser resorted to both sales and migration. In 1801, he married Lucy Bolling Hylton, a daughter of Daniel L. Hylton, one of the justices who sat on several of the conspiracy trials and known to history as the man who challenged the constitutionality of a federal tax on carriages in 1796. In 1803, Prosser himself became a county justice; in 1806, Thomas Sully painted the couple's portraits; and in 1814-15, Prosser served as sheriff of Henrico. But even as his political and social standing seemed to rise, his fortune was shifting. When Daniel Hylton wrote his will in September 1808, he prevented any property that would go to his two daughters from being used to pay the debts of their husbands. Such a specific proviso suggests the Prossers may not have been doing well and that Hylton questioned or doubted his daughters' husbands' abilities or judgment or, perhaps, their habits. Indeed, Prosser was borrowing against his lands and slaves. His three thousand acres in the neighborhood of the Brook backed a $10,000 bond in 1808, and two years later he advertised the lands for sale. Eventually, Brookfield passed into the hands of Benjamin Sheppard, while Prosser subdivided the rest of his lands into small parcels, probably to make them more attractive to a broader range of purchasers. In 1811, his labor force in the county shrank substantially, from forty-nine to nineteen taxable slaves, but as he moved his family into Richmond he brought only six taxable slaves. The rest may have been sold or hired out. In 1818, to indemnify Thomas Ritchie for endorsing more than $25,000 in notes, the Prossers put up a Richmond lot and thirty-six slaves as security, and in 1819 they moved to Wilkinson County, Mississippi. The next year, Prosser reported twenty-one slaves to the census taker, presumably the remnant of his Virginia slave holdings carried with them to the West. Five of the unnamed individuals were below the age of fourteen, while the others reflected his reshaping of his labor force to meet the demands of a new frontier: among them, males outnumbered females ten to six. None of the men, and only one of the women, was older than forty-five. In 1823, Prosser again relied on his movable capital, in this case, seven men between the ages of twenty-one and thirty-five, to obtain a loan of over $3,000. He apparently then used the money to pay for a 245-acre tract he had contracted for and on which they already lived. Two years later, he proffered six adults, one man and five women, four of the latter each with an infant about a year old, along with two boys between twelve and sixteen, as collateral in a further effort to secure notes due to Thomas Ritchie in Richmond. Thus his human capital secured and underwrote Prosser's move and reestablishment. Like other migrating slave owners, indeed even rooted ones, his most important source of wealth primarily existed in his slaves. For whites, new or head starts in life, staying afloat in bad times, or overcoming bad judgments often depended on accumulated slave holdings. It is no small wonder, then, when slaves proved so portable, disposable, and valuable, that efforts to eliminate the threat of slave insurrection through voluntary emancipation or removal were doomed. Slavery was worth fighting for, as the events a half-century later would prove.[10]

But, of course, a lot would happen before then. When Monroe left the governorship in December 1802, some Virginians, like the "Private Citizen," were resigned to a society perpetually based on slavery. Others, like George Tucker, St. George Tucker, and apparently Monroe himself, were committed to slowly eliminating the institution, whether through a state-mandated system of disincentives to induce gradual emancipation and removal, or through voluntary manumissions coupled to exile. As Monroe expressed his feelings to Jefferson in 1802 about a possible colony in Africa for those who "are or may hereafter become free," he floated the idea that the expense of their transportation might be defrayed by sending them as indentured servants, soon to be free, with freedom for their children. He judged his scheme, in contrast to the slave trade that originally brought their ancestors to Virginia and the slavery they endured, to be "mild and benevolent." He recognized the unlikely adoption of the proposal, but grasped for a policy "that would make these people instrumental to their own emancipation, by a process gradual and certain, on principles consistent with humanity, without expence or inconvenience to ourselves." Although pushed by Gabriel's threat to look to a future

Virginia without slaves, in 1802 Monroe could not envision obtaining it without "expence and inconvenience." With these caveats in place, Virginia would remain a slave society, just as the Private Citizen expected. It would take a war, one that involved the largest slave uprising in America's history, one where "these people [were] instrumental to their own emancipation," to end the peculiar institution and the whispers of rebellion.[11]

Appendix A

The Geography of Conspiracy

Gabriel's Conspiracy was both more and less than a Henrico County plot. Measured by who was accused or prosecuted, there is little evidence that its organization had spread much beyond the capital into the eastern or lower half of the county, though accusations do not encompass all who were party to the plot. It seeped into northern Chesterfield, partly though connections with the Brook, and leapfrogged, probably through the efforts of the Byrd family, into the environs of Petersburg. But with one possible exception, no evidence was collected that led to any prosecutions or revelations about the extent of the plot in those locations. It was carried north along the stage road from its base along the waters of the Brook in Henrico across Hanover and into Caroline County and the adjacent corner of King William. And it apparently stretched west into Louisa County. Significantly, in the counties to the north of Henrico, the men who were tried mostly worked close to the Brook Road or stage route and between the Meadow Bridges and Hanover Court House. Even along these routes, few of the recruits worked very far north of Littlepage's Bridge on the Pamunkey River, the boundary between Hanover and Caroline Counties. It is instructive that the arrest of men in Hanover and Caroline at the behest of Monroe came from information obtained from Ben Woolfolk, not from evidence gathered by local county officials. The geographical centering and reach of the conspiracy, however, only become apparent by plotting the locations of the plantations or farms of the owners or employers of the conspirators, and the connections among them.

In 1800, Gabriel, Solomon, Ben, Martin, and others at the core of the conspiracy lived in and about Brookfield, the plantation of Thomas Henry Prosser which sat on the north side of the Brook roughly three miles upstream from the Chickahominy. He paid taxes on a total of 2,474 acres, but they were actually distributed among six parcels, ranging between a 2-acre mill site and one of 1,540 acres. His father, Thomas Prosser, began acquiring the tracts in 1764 while a resident of Cumberland County and just before his permanent expulsion from the

House of Burgesses because of fraudulent practices involving some of his business transactions in Cumberland. Thomas Prosser's next acquisition of Henrico land seemed to come with the death of his father-in-law, Henry Stokes, who left his home plantation on the Brook, of unstated acreage, to his daughter Ann at the death of her mother. The Prossers apparently moved to Henrico with their daughter Elizabeth close to the time of Stokes's death in 1766. Henry Stokes's land sat near the tracts of John Watson, portions of whose estate Prosser started purchasing in 1771. Two decades later, Watson's grandson transferred 354 acres of his inheritance, which included two grist mills, to Thomas Henry Prosser, who would have been only about fourteen years old, unless the clerk had inserted the middle name by mistake. Thomas Prosser's last recorded purchase was for 200 acres and was obtained within a year of his death. These lands passed to Thomas Henry Prosser in 1798 at the death of his father, his mother having died two years before. To work them, he had to deploy his slaves among the different tracts, which touched on Beachem's Run on the east, the North Run on the west, and up near the Rocky Branch, or Creek, to the north. The slaves' movement between the main house, fields, and outlying quarters created opportunities to interact with others working about the Brook and its tributaries. Similarly, the proximity of the Prosser tracts to the Brook Road made contacts easier with other mobile men who traveled the road from points farther north and south. In 1800, Prosser was taxed for thirty-seven slave tithables and eleven more between the ages of twelve and sixteen, and he employed two overseers. Six Prosser slaves were executed as conspirators and one was transported. None were acquitted. An eighth slave, Ben, served as a key Commonwealth witness.[1]

Downstream from Brookfield sat most of the lands of Nathaniel Wilkinson. He and Prosser shared Beachem's Run as a boundary, which flowed into the Brook from the north, with the bulk of Wilkinson's lands abutting the Chickahominy River. In an 1800 petition, he claimed his land ran for about three miles up the swampy river beginning near the Meadow Bridges, or where the Brook emptied its waters. But these acres, some 1,686 of them, were in six parcels, the largest containing 910 acres, the smallest with 42½ acres. In 1799, the elderly Wilkinson had leased three of his tracts, called Owen's, Thomas Wilkinson's, and Bacon's—clues to past owners of the land—containing about 1,300 acres, to Absalom Johnson. The term was for five years and included twenty-one slaves, four of them identified as children. Johnson paid taxes on thirteen slaves above the age of twelve in 1800. Wilkinson retained for his own use the house that sat on the former Bacon tract and paid taxes on twelve slaves. His other parcels of land appear to have been located farther west and north within the drainage of the Brook, one perhaps not far from Young's. Four of Nathaniel Wilkinson's slaves were tried for conspiracy, two of them executed and two acquitted. A fifth man was implicated but not prosecuted.[2]

Both Prosser and Wilkinson shared boundary lines to the north with Roger Gregory Jr., whose tavern stored some of the arms of the Henrico militia. Gregory was likely a migrant from King William County and had married the daughter of Fendall Southerland of that county, from whom he had purchased at least 272 acres. In 1785, he sold the tract to Samuel Parsons, of Goochland County, partly as a land exchange in which Gregory obtained what proved to be around 586 acres. This holding was made up of three probably close tracts called Level Green, Oranges, and Laws. Gregory also paid taxes in 1800 on an additional 100 acres, and reported holding ten slaves, nine of them above the age of sixteen. Two of them, Billy and Charles, were executed as conspirators; another man, Martin, was acquitted.[3]

Upstream on the main course of the Brook, a couple of miles above the mouth of the North Run of the Brook and the lands of Prosser and the Bacon family, were the fields and mills of William Young. The conspirators gathered at one of his springs to recruit and select their officers. Young initially acquired a tract of just over 100 acres in 1792, and added a 2-acre mill site to it two years later through purchase from Robert Price of Bedford County. In 1798, he purchased a larger tract of 418 acres, which probably included the gathering site at the spring and which adjoined a small plot containing a schoolhouse. He obtained it from John and Mary Young of Caroline County, a property that had also once been in the hands of Robert Price. In his house, fields, and mills Young reported he worked nine slaves. Whether Ben Woolfolk and Sawney, both hired men, were counted among them cannot be determined, but Gilbert, William, and Ned probably were. Five of his men, owned or hired, were prosecuted and condemned. Two were pardoned; three were hanged.[4]

Collectively, nineteen of the fifty-eight men prosecuted in Henrico were held by Prosser, Wilkinson, Gregory, and Young. The rest were scattered among many of the individuals who lived in the spaces between or adjacent to these four. Near to Young, for example, was the estate of Elisha Price, the owner of James, and that of Ann Smith, the holder of George, and of lands which adjoined those of Sally Price. The latter's man John, though hired in Richmond, returned to the Brook, most likely for the funeral on 10 August of the unidentified infant child, and later testified of those who attended that meeting at Young's spring, with deadly consequences. Jane Clarke lived nearby and apparently let Sam Byrd Jr. hire his time, while a bit farther downstream, near the Trumpet Branch, was the 400-acre tract of Dabney Williamson, who held Lewis and Billy Chicken. Nearer to the plantations of Gregory, Wilkinson, and Prosser on the north side of the Brook were Judith Owen and the slave Michael, Anne Lipscombe Parsons and Ned, and Charles Sneed, who hired Billy from Nathaniel Lipscomb of Hanover. Joseph Mosby also had lands there, and he held the wife of Goode's Michael, who visited her from Chesterfield, the only man prosecuted from that county. Mosby also leased lands and hired slaves from the estate of William Lewis, to which Sawney belonged. On the south side of the Brook sat the holdings of John Brooke, including the accused Daniel, those of Drury Wood with Emanuel, and those of Thomas Burton, who held Abraham. William Burton was located there too, but Isaac, George, and Isham may have been scattered among his eight tracts that spread upwards from near the mouth of the Brook.[5]

Like Sally Price, several residents of the Brook hired slaves in Richmond who journeyed between home and town on the weekends or holidays or when work was more pressing at home. No evidence indicates that the blacksmiths Gabriel or Solomon ever hired their time in Richmond, though Gabriel journeyed in on the weekends of the summer of 1800 to secure powder and spy out arms. But an important set of links between Richmond and the Brook may have been built through the connections that emerged through the public positions held by several Brook families in the tobacco industry, assuming they are the same men. Dabney Williamson, Thomas Burton, John Mosby, and William Price, all of whom had men accused in the plot, were tobacco inspectors at the Shockoe warehouse. Similarly, James Price, Jesse Smith, and Elisha Price, tobacco inspectors at Byrd's warehouse, also owned or held men charged with conspiracy. So did John Williamson, the head inspector at Rocketts's warehouse, a man with Brook connections, but not so for Elijah Franklin, Richard Allen, or Mathew Hobson, the remaining inspectors at Rocketts's, who were not from the Brook. These men moved frequently between the Brook and their warehouse responsibilities and likely used their slaves in both pursuits. Indeed, one of the reported Richmond recruiting fields was among "the warehouse boys," and men like Bob and Stephen at Rocketts's were allegedly involved in the plot, though never tried. Perhaps they were held by the other inspectors, but that remains unknown.[6]

The conspiracy stretched north through Hanover and into Caroline Counties along the Brook Road as it took the form of the stage road stretching between Richmond and Fredericksburg, and to some extent along the road between the Meadow Bridges and Hanover Court House. The slaves of Paul Thilman, county jailer, tavern owner, and entrepreneur, led by the blacksmith Thornton, appeared as prominent participants. Thilman was taxed on twenty-six slaves in 1800; some, like Randolph, may have been hired from others. Three of them were tried in Henrico, because of their attendance there, while three more were prosecuted in Caroline Court for their activities around Littlepage's Bridge. One was pardoned; one was transported; and the rest were acquitted. Another man, Simon, was reported carrying a message from Gabriel to Thornton, but avoided prosecution, while Holmes was accused but also escaped a trial.[7]

Thornton, the blacksmith who worked near the Court House and the lone Thilman slave to be transported, claimed to another plotter that he had found recruits among the men of "Mr Toler or Gist's Estate" and in Thomas Nelson's, William Penn's, and Charles Carter's workforces. Samuel Gist, an absentee Loyalist in England, whose affairs had been looked after in part by members of the Toler family, was listed with sixty-four taxable slaves in 1800, but none were prosecuted. Some of his lands were strung between Hanover Court House and Hanover Town to the east. William Penn had twelve slaves in Hanover, and a man with the same name had thirty in King William in 1800. A man named Billy, identified as one of the slaves of a man named Penn of King William, was acquitted in a Caroline trial. I have not found the specific location of Penn's holdings, but they may have been near Horn Quarter, a short distance from Hanover Court

House along the Pamunkey. Thomas Nelson's slaves, given the concentration of the plotters around Littlepage's Bridge, were most likely the forty-three not far from Hanover Court House across the Pamunkey River in King William, rather than those of another, or perhaps the same, Thomas Nelson, located about twenty miles to the west. However, none of the Nelson slaves were prosecuted. Charles Carter of Charles City County had the most slaves in the area, some forty-six in Hanover and one hundred and seven in Caroline, besides younger children. His quarters, and especially North Wales in Caroline, adjacent to Littlepage's Bridge, contained four accused plotters, three of whom were transported, while one was acquitted.[8]

Other conspirators in Hanover lived between the Brook and Hanover Court House. Stephen, though tried in Henrico and acquitted, belonged to Thomas Wingfield, who had a place just west of the Court House and five tithable, or older, slaves. Perhaps Stephen had been enticed to attend one of the meetings on the Brook, and hence his trial was in Henrico. Sam Graham was tried and executed in Henrico, although he came from Hanover. He had the misfortune of being recognized at a meeting at Young's spring. He was held by Paul Graham, who was also the owner of Ben Woolfolk. Paul Graham may have been residing on land of his Thilman relatives that year, along with seven of his slaves, but that is not clear. He would soon move on up the road into Caroline, apparently to lands his grandfather, Duncan Graham, once held. Closer to the Brook itself, but on the Hanover side of the Chickahominy, were other men thought complicit in the plot. John, the executed slave of Mary Jones, who hired him in Richmond, came from the reaches of Totopotomoy Creek south of the Court House. Farther south, George, a slave of Martha Whitlock, who was named but never tried, worked in the same drainage but even closer to the Chickahominy. Three more men who were tried but acquitted in Henrico Court seem to have been within shouting distance of the Brook. Their master, Thomas Austin, held nineteen slaves, apparently on lands on the Hanover side of the Meadow Bridges close to where the Brook emptied into the Chickahominy. They may represent the lowest extension of the plot.[9]

Instead of a scattered collection of plotters, it appears that the conspiracy clustered in neighborhoods. The two most prominent clusters were the one along the Brook and its tributaries, and one near Hanover Court House that extended and spread up and down the Pamunkey for a few miles on either side of Littlepage's Bridge, penetrating a short distance into Caroline County. A third cluster probably existed in Richmond, but it contained men of the Brook too. Other men with connections to the Brook, or who could have been contacted on the road or roads that led to Richmond through that area, also became interested and perhaps joined. But the outreach clearly originated from the Brook and followed the corridors of connections men had to family and acquaintances elsewhere. In the eyes of scared whites, such as those in Suffolk, Williamsburg, Cumberland, New London, and perhaps in and about Petersburg, all suspicious activities of slaves and free black men in their area were seen as signs of the presence of plotters in their midst. Whether their fears were justified remains an open question.

Appendix B

Men Tried for Conspiracy and Insurrection

Name	Owner	Residence	Disposition of case
HENRICO COUNTY TRIALS (58)			
11 September 1800			
Solomon	T. H. Prosser	Henrico	Executed 15 September
Will	John Mosby Sr.	Henrico	Executed 12 September
John[1]	Mary Jones	Hanover	Executed 12 September
Isaac	William Burton	Henrico	Executed 12 September
Michael	Judith Owen	Henrico	Executed 12 September
Ned	Anne Parsons	Henrico	Executed 12 September
12 September 1800			
Billy	Roger Gregory	Henrico	Executed 15 September
Martin	T. H. Prosser	Henrico	Executed 15 September
Charles	Roger Gregory	Henrico	Executed 15 September
Frank	T. H. Prosser	Henrico	Executed 15 September
Martin	Roger Gregory	Henrico	Acquitted
13 September 1800			
George	William Burton	Henrico	Acquitted
Frank	Nathaniel Wilkinson	Henrico	Acquitted
Sawney[2]	William Lewis estate	Henrico	Executed 18 September
15 September 1800			
Daniel	John Brooke	Henrico	Acquitted
Peter	T. H. Prosser	Henrico	Executed 18 September
Jupiter	Nathaniel Wilkinson	Henrico	Executed 18 September
Sam	Nathaniel Wilkinson	Henrico	Executed 18 September
Daniel	Nathaniel Wilkinson	Henrico	Acquitted
Isham	William Burton	Henrico	Executed 18 September
16 September 1800			
Ned	William Young	Henrico	Pardoned 9 December
Isaac	James Allen	Henrico	Executed 10 October

Name	Owner	Residence	Disposition of case
Harry[3]	Thomas Austin	Hanover	Acquitted
Ned	Thomas Austin	Hanover	Acquitted
Joe	Thomas Austin	Hanover	Acquitted
Laddis	John Williamson	Henrico	Executed 10 October
Billy Chicken	Dabney Williamson	Henrico	Acquitted
Ben Woolfolk[4]	Paul Graham	Hanover	Pardoned 18 September
17 September 1800			
Stephen[5]	Thomas Wingfield	Hanover	Acquitted
19 September 1800			
George[6]	Jacob Smith estate	Henrico	Executed 10 October
22 September 1800			
Gilbert	William Young	Henrico	Executed 10 October
Joe	Temperance Baker	Hanover	Acquitted
George	Izard Bacon	Henrico	Acquitted
Tom	T. H. Prosser	Henrico	Executed 10 October
27 September 1800			
Sam Byrd Jr.	Jane Clarke	Henrico	Executed 10 October
Michael[7]	Thomas Goode	Chesterfield	Executed 10 October
William	William Young	Henrico	Executed 10 October
29 September 1800			
Sam Graham[8]	Paul Graham	Hanover	Executed 10 October
Jim/James Allen	James Price	Henrico	Acquitted
Moses	James Price	Henrico	Acquitted
Abraham	Thomas Burton	Henrico	Pardoned 3 October
30 September 1800			
Jacob	Thomas Woodfin	Henrico	Pardoned 2 October
Dick	Jesse Smith	Henrico	Pardoned 3 October
James	Elisha Price	Henrico	Pardoned 8 November
Solomon	Joseph Lewis estate	Henrico	Pardoned 8 October
1 October 1800			
Peter	Allen Williamson	Henrico	Pardoned 3 October
Billy	Ambrose Lipscombe estate	Hanover	Pardoned 3 October
Billy[9]	Nathaniel Lipscombe	Hanover	Pardoned 3 October
Lewis	Dabney Williamson	Henrico	Transported
6 October 1800			
Gabriel	T. H. Prosser	Henrico	Executed 10 October
Dick[10]	Paul Thilman	Hanover	Pardoned 8 October
Randolph[11]	Nancy Leftwich	King William	Pardoned 8 October
Bristol	Paul Thilman	Hanover	Acquitted
7 October 1800			
Thomas J. Martin[12]	Free man	Henrico	Acquitted
29 October 1800			
Jack Bowler/ Ditcher	Wm. Bowler estate	Caroline	Transported

Name	Owner	Residence	Disposition of case
4 November 1800			
Absolem	William Price	Henrico	Acquitted
Emanuel	Drury Wood	Henrico	Acquitted
1 December 1800			
Watt	T. H. Prosser	Henrico	Transported

RICHMOND CITY TRIALS (3)

Name	Owner	Residence	Disposition of case
25 September 1800			
Brutus/Julius[13]	William Anderson	Caroline	Acquitted
King	Philip N. Nicholas	Richmond	Transported
13 October 1800			
Ralph	Elizabeth Page	Richmond	Acquitted

LOUISA COUNTY TRIAL

Name	Owner	Residence	Disposition of case
1 October 1800			
Ben	Charles Smith	Louisa	Acquitted

DINWIDDIE COUNTY TRIAL

Name	Owner	Residence	Disposition of case
20 October 1800			
Peter	W. P. Claiborne estate	Dinwiddie	Executed 24 October

CAROLINE COUNTY TRIALS (9)

Name	Owner	Residence	Disposition of case
22 October 1800			
John[14]	Charles Carter	Charles City	Acquitted
Ben	Charles Carter	Charles City	Transported
Scipio[15]	Paul Thilman	Hanover	Pardoned 8 November
George	Paul Thilman	Hanover	Acquitted
29 October 1800			
Billy[16]	William Penn	King William	Acquitted
Humphrey[17]	Edward Garland	Hanover	Acquitted
Jack Gabriel	Charles Carter	Charles City	Transported
30 October 1800			
John Fells	Charles Carter	Charles City	Transported
Thornton	Paul Thilman	Hanover	Transported

Sources: With respect to the disposition of the cases, the dates of pardons can be found in the Journals of the Council of State, 1799–1801 (microfilm), at the Library of Virginia, as well as the dates of reprieves which led to either a delay in execution or, in the cases of eight men, to their transportation. The trials were recorded in skeletal form in the respective Order Books of Henrico, Louisa, and Caroline Counties, and Richmond City. The lone Dinwiddie trial record is included among Auditor's Item 756 and is a copy of what would have appeared in the Dinwiddie County Order Book, which is no longer extant. Trial testimony from Henrico, Richmond, and Caroline resides in the ExP II, box 8.

Notes: The "Date of Trial" column heading refers to the date of trial judgment. "Residence" refers to the place of residence of the listed owner of the slave. "Disposition of Case" refers, in the case of capital punishment, to the actual date of execution, not to the date set by the court, since some executions were delayed by executive order. For defendants who received a pardon, the date listed under "Disposition of Case" refers to the actual date of pardon by the executive. The numbers in parentheses indicate the number of recorded trials for conspiracy and insurrection in that court.

[1] John was hired to Henrico sheriff John Harvie, who contracted to build the penitentiary in Richmond.

[2] Sawney was hired to William Young.

[3] Austin paid taxes on nineteen slaves in Hanover in 1800.

[4] Ben Woolfolk was hired to William Young along the Brook. Paul Graham held seven taxable slaves in Hanover in 1800.

[5] A man otherwise identified only as "Stephen at Rockets," probably the warehouse, appears on an undated list of unknown authorship which contains the names of others involved. This is the only Stephen tried, and the list contains the only mention of a Stephen otherwise appearing in the record.

[6] George was in the hands of Ann Smith, the relict of Jacob.

[7] Michael's wife was held by Joseph Mosby in the Brook neighborhood. His master, Thomas Goode, was the brother-in-law of Thomas H. Prosser.

[8] Sam Graham was one of the men from Hanover who attended a meeting at Young's spring and was part of the group who gathered at Littlepage's Bridge in Caroline County. The testimony against him concerned his presence in Henrico. His attendance in Caroline came from his own statement.

[9] Billy was hired to Charles Sneed, whose land appears to have been close to William Young's and an upstream tract of Nathaniel Wilkinson's near the Brook.

[10] Dick, Randolph, and Bristol all attended a meeting at Young's spring.

[11] Randolph was hired to Paul Thilman. No Nancy Leftwich appears on King William personal property tax lists in 1800, but the estate of Elijah Leftwich, with five slaves, is listed, as are the holdings of James H. and John Leftwich.

[12] Martin, acquitted of conspiracy and insurrection, was found guilty of a misdemeanor.

[13] Brutus had been and perhaps was still hired to Dr. Foushee in Richmond.

[14] John, Ben, and Jack Gabriel resided on Carter's North Wales quarter in Caroline, close to Littlepage's Bridge, where he was taxed for thirty-seven slaves and apparently one overseer. The location of John Fells was not stated. He could have been at the same quarter, or at one of Carter's four other Caroline quarters with seventy other slaves, or he could have worked in Hanover at Carter's South Wales quarter, and perhaps at others, where forty-six more taxable slaves toiled.

[15] Scipio, George, and Thornton were tried in Caroline because of their meeting on the Caroline side of Littlepage's Bridge.

[16] William Penn is taxed for thirty slaves in King William in 1800, and a William Penn is also taxed on twelve slaves in Hanover. One cannot tell from the tax lists if the white male listed is Penn, an overseer, or if there are two men of the same name.

[17] Edward Garland held twenty-five taxable slaves in Hanover in 1800. Unlike the other owners of Hanover slaves allegedly involved, Garland's holding appears to have been west of the Court House some distance.

Appendix C

Alleged Participants Not Prosecuted

Name	Owner	Accuser	Source
Bob[1]	Unknown	Unknown	Undated list
Stephen[2]	Unknown	Unknown	Undated list
Nathan[3]	William Price	Unknown	Undated list
slaves of[4]	Dick Bowler	Unknown	Undated list
Ned[5]	Col. [John] Harvie	Unknown	Undated list
John	Col. [John] Harvie	Unknown	Undated list
Jack	Col. [John] Harvie	Unknown	Undated list
Billy	Buchanan	Unknown	Undated list
Ballard	Buchanan	Unknown	Undated list
Jack[6]	Stras (Southall)	Unknown	Undated list
David	Stras (Southall)	Unknown	Undated list
Lucas or Locust[7]	White man	Unknown	Undated list
George[8]	John Mayo	Unknown	Undated list
George	Hatcher	Unknown	Undated list
Roger	John Price	Unknown	Undated list
John[9]	Quarles	Unknown	Undated list
Peter	Quarles	Unknown	Undated list
Bob[10]	Mrs. Sutton	Unknown	Storrs & Selden
Humphrey[11]	Mrs. Sutton(?)	Unknown	Storrs & Selden
Linkin[12]	Giles Raines	Unknown	Storrs & Selden
Moses[13]	Mrs. Mathews	Unknown	Storrs & Selden
Moses Brooke	John Graham	Unknown	Storrs & Selden
John[14]	George Nicholson	Unknown	Storrs & Selden
Simon[15]	Paul Thilman	Sam Graham	Graham statement
Charles[16]	Mrs. [Ann] Smith	Gilbert	Foster list
Moses[17]	Unknown	Gilbert	Foster list
Armistead[18]	William Galt	Gilbert	Foster list

Name	Owner	Accuser	Source
Bob [19]	Sally Price	Not clear	Foster list
Billy [20]	William Lewis estate	Gilbert	Gilbert undated
Backus [Bacchus] [21]	Dick Bridges	Gilbert	Gilbert undated
Peter [22]	John Fox	Gilbert	Gilbert undated
Jimmy Wilkes [23]	Not given	Gilbert	Gilbert undated
Matt Scott [24]	Free man	Gilbert	Gilbert undated
Frank [25]	Unstated	Gilbert	Gilbert undated
Billy [26]	Richard Gaufney	Gilbert	Gilbert undated
Davy [27]	Unstated	Gilbert	Gilbert undated
Bob [28]	John Gunn	Gilbert	Gilbert undated
Billy Chicken [29]	Free man	Gilbert	Gilbert undated
Robin [30]	[John] Adams	Gilbert	Gilbert undated
James [31]	Peter Tinsley	Gilbert	Gilbert undated
George [32]	Mrs. David Whitlock	Gilbert	Gilbert undated
Frank [33]	William Austin	Gilbert	Dated statement
Bob [34]	Nathaniel Wilkinson	Gilbert	Dated statement
Charles Quersey [35]	White man	Gilbert	Dated statement
Edmund [36]	Paul Woolfolk	Ben Woolfolk	Monroe list
Holmes [37]	Paul Thilman	Ben Woolfolk	Monroe list
Jim [38]	Mr. Mason	Ben Woolfolk	Monroe list
Lewis Barret [39]	Not given	Prosser's Ben	Ben's testimony
Stepney [40]	James Salmons	Unknown	Carrington letter
John [41]	Mr. Taloe	Unknown	Booth letter
Jacob [42]	William Wilson	Unknown	Booth letter
Jacob Brandum [43]	Free man	Unknown	Prentis letter
Jos./Jas Bartlett [44]	Unknown	Unknown	Prentis letter
Martin Bartlett	Unknown	Unknown	Prentis letter
John Pidgeon [45]	Unknown	Unknown	Prentis letter
James Vaughan [46]	Free man	Unknown	Prentis list
Cyrus Skinner [47]	Unknown	Unknown	Prentis list
David White [48]	William Davies	Unknown	Prentis list
Dick White [49]	James Murray estate	Unknown	Prentis list
Charles Timberlake [50]	John Bell(?)	Unknown	Prentis list
Jonathan [51]	Unknown	Unknown	Prentis list
Jesse Byrd [52]	Free man	Gilbert	Prentis inquiry
Reuben Byrd [53]	Free man	Gilbert	Prentis inquiry
Burwell Gates [54]	George Brown	George Markham	Markham information
Griffen [55]	Benjamin Hurt	Unknown	Bernard letter
Robert Cowley [56]	Free man	Gilbert and Woolfolk	Trial testimony

Sources: "Undated list": undated document beginning "Bob at Rocketts," ExP II, box 8, folder 5; "Storrs & Selden": Gervas Storrs and Joseph Selden to Monroe, 13 September 1800, ibid., folder 1; "Graham statement": undated document that begins "Sam, alias Sam Graham says," ibid., folder 5; "Foster list": "Information respecting insurrection received of John Foster," 9 September 1800, ibid., folder 1; "Gilbert undated": "Communications made by Gilbert," undated, ibid., folder 5; "Dated statement": "Information from Mr. Foster [from Gilbert] respecting the intended Insurrection Sepr 23d 1800," 23 September 1800, ibid., folder 2; "Monroe list": undated document beginning, "The following Negroes living in Hanover and Caroline," and ending, "The foregoing Negroes are implicated by the discovery of Ben alias Ben Woolfolk," ibid., folder 5; "Ben's testimony": testimony of Prosser's Ben at the trial of Solomon, 11 September 1800, ibid., folder 1; "Carrington letter": Mayo Carrington to Monroe, 17 September 1800, ibid., folder 2; "Booth letter": Thomas Booth to Alexander McCrae, 5 October 1800, ibid., folder 3; "Prentis letter": William Prentis to James Monroe, 6 September 1800, ibid., folder 1; "Prentis list": undated document endorsed "Information of some supposed to be acquainted with the intended insurrection," ibid., folder 5; "Prentis inquiry": William Prentis to James Monroe, 24 September 1800, ibid., folder 2; "Markham information": "Information from Mr. Markham," 15 September 1800, ibid., and James Monroe to Matthew Cheatham, 15 September 1800, ExLB, 1794–1800, 415; "Bernard letter": William Bernard to James Monroe, 20 September 1800, ExP II, box 8, folder 2; "trial testimony": testimony of Ben Woolfolk at trial of Gabriel, 6 October 1800, ibid., folder 3, and Gilbert undated and dated statement, noted above. Information in the footnotes is derived from the sources cited elsewhere in the book.

Notes: "Name" refers to an individual identified as somehow involved in the plot. "Owner" refers to his ascribed owner. "Accuser" is the person who identified the man. "Source" is the document wherein the person is named.

[1] He is identified as "at Rockets—big Man—to own warehouse." He may be one of the men of the same name appearing in this appendix who were otherwise not prosecuted.

[2] "at Rockets." He may be the Stephen, tried and acquitted on 17 September in Henrico (see Appendix B: Men Tried for Conspiracy and Insurrection).

[3] "Cooks in town has a wife at Mrs Singleton." Anthony Singleton's estate sat not far from the Brook, but he also had a residence in Richmond. His widow, Lucy Harrison Randolph Singleton, reported nine taxable slaves in town in 1800.

[4] "Bowlers Jack said all Dick Bowler's negro's are in it, to be light horse. Jack wanted him to take them." Richard Bowler ran a Richmond tavern and supplied the description of Jack Bowler for Monroe's advertisement for his capture.

[5] John Harvie, the sheriff of Henrico, had also been mayor of Richmond and a register in the Land Office. The man named John who was tried and executed may have been the one hired by Harvie from Mary Jones of Hanover. However, in his 1806 will, Harvie left "John" and "Jack" among the house servants placed into the hands of his wife. He had scattered lots in Richmond and land in Henrico, including a tract near those of Philip N. Nicholas and John Pendleton, not far from the Brook above William Young's. For Harvie's will, see Barbara Wright, comp., *Green County, Kentucky: Abstracts of Circuit Court Records*, vol. 6 (Utica, Ky., n.d.), 43–44.

[6] George F. Stras married Martha Wood Southall, the widow of Stephen Southall, in 1799. Jack and David may have been her slaves. Stras reported taxable slaves in both the upper district of Henrico and Richmond in 1800.

[7]"Lucas or locust a white man lives on the brook told Geo he'd lead them & his object was to get money."

[8]George was a frequent runaway and the object of Mayo's interrogation of the condemned at the gallows.

[9]John and Peter were both listed as working at the foundry. They may have been in the employ of Maj. Robert Quarles at the state armory at Point of Fork, perhaps contacted by Sam Byrd Jr.

[10]Possibly the Bob on the undated list above. Sutton lived in Caroline. One of six incarcerated men Storrs and Selden sought evidence about from Monroe. All appear to have been released.

[11]A man named Humphrey was tried in Caroline but was identified as belonging to Edward Garland. The name of the owner is not clear, but appears to be "ditto." In 1800, a Salley Sutton reported eighteen slaves above twelve years of age to the Caroline County tax man. Elizabeth Sutton reported twelve such slaves.

[12]Giles Raines owned seven slaves in Caroline in 1800, the year after he married Dorothy Austin. In 1815, Dolley Raines's estate was listed as being nineteen miles south of Bowling Green, which would be not far from Littlepage's Bridge.

[13]Moses was hired by John Graham of Richmond, who reported three slaves above twelve to be taxed in 1800. Mrs. Mathews remains unidentified.

[14]Nicholson was the recorder for the Richmond Hustings Court and proprietor of a rope walk, among his other enterprises. He employed Richardson Taylor after his return from Norfolk.

[15]Sam Graham said Simon first brought word from Gabriel to Thornton to rendezvous on the night of 30 August. If he were not hired out, Simon was among twenty-six slaves Thilman was taxed for in Hanover in 1800.

[16]Charles appears with George on the list John Foster gathered from Gilbert by 9 September.

[17]A man named Moses is named three times by Gilbert, though never prosecuted. On the Foster list of 9 September he appears as "living at the Coal Pitts at Tuckahoe," and is probably the man Monroe ordered to be sent to Richmond from Goochland after Foster presented his list. On a different, undated statement of Gilbert, a "Moses" is identified as the brother of Billy, a slave of the estate of William Lewis. Moses was initially described as belonging to Samuel Parsons, but that was corrected to Joseph Woodson in Goochland, which could be at the mines. In a third statement, dated 23 September, Gilbert reasserted the ownership of Samuel Parsons and said Moses was to become free "at a certain age." It is possible these are all the same man.

[18]Armistead appears in all three of Gilbert's reported statements. William Galt was listed with one slave above the age of twelve in Richmond in 1800.

[19]It is not clear who identified Mrs. Price's Bob to John Foster, but it was probably Gilbert. Bob was said to be with her. Ben Woolfolk named a Sally Price's Bob in his confession, who was most likely the same man.

[20]Billy, brother of Moses, identified by Gilbert in his undated statement, was said to be hired to Joseph Mosby. Mosby's holdings were in the neighborhood of the Brook, and he reported eighteen taxable slaves in 1800. He leased the land and hired some of the slaves of the Lewis estate.

[21]Backus also appears on the list of men to be arrested that Monroe sent to Caroline based on information from Ben Woolfolk. It notes that Woolfolk had no direct knowledge

of Backus's involvement. Richard Bridges held ten taxable slaves in 1800; he was listed as living "adjacent" to White Chimneys in 1815.

[22] Like Backus, Peter appears on both Gilbert's and Woolfolk's lists, with the latter admitting no direct knowledge. He is identified as a Caroline slave by Woolfolk, but was owned by John Fox of King William, according to Gilbert. Fox, of a prominent local family, was a King William planter with ten taxable slaves in 1800.

[23] Wilkes is simply stated to be "at work up the country among the canal negroes, he went up with Matt Scott a free negro . . ." Wilkes appears to have been recruited by Scott.

[24] Scott, as noted, was upcountry with Wilkes and a recruiter. In his statement of 23 September, Gilbert stated that Sam Byrd Jr. sent him into Richmond to check his list of recruits. Gilbert found Scott, but never saw his list. Scott may have told Gilbert of Wilkes's enlistment.

[25] Frank, a blacksmith and a son of Martin, though which one is not clear, was an alleged plotter in Goochland.

[26] "Billy" and "owner of King William" were crossed out. Gaufney is likely Gwathmey, who does appear in King William tax records with eleven slaves in 1800.

[27] "Davy the brother of Jack Bowler" is crossed out.

[28] Identified as being in Henrico, John Gunn reported a single slave on the Henrico Upper District tax list.

[29] Gilbert identified Chicken as a free man in Richmond. A man of the same name, a slave of Dabney Williamson, was prosecuted but found not guilty. He was named by Price's John on the Foster list of 9 September, but with no listed owner. Prosser's Ben was the named witness on the information at the trial, not John. Perhaps Chicken was acquitted because of confusion over his status. Or there could have been two men of the same name.

[30] Robin is placed at the Eagle Tavern, then run by John Adams. In 1800, Adams listed nine taxable slaves at the tavern and reported two more, apparently at his home.

[31] Gilbert said James obtained the keys to the capitol from Robert Cowley to let in Gabriel. Tinsley, who reported four taxable slaves in Richmond in 1800, was the clerk of the High Court of Chancery.

[32] George was described as a "yellow fellow" by his owner, Martha Whitlock, who was identified as a Hanover resident. She was widowed in 1798, and reported ten taxable slaves in 1800. She held a life interest in land listed on Totopotomoy Creek, ten miles south of the Hanover Court House in 1815, not far from the Brook neighborhood across the Chickahominy.

[33] Described as "one of the boys with several others the names of whom" Gilbert could not recall, Frank was held by the captain of the Richmond Horse, who listed only one taxable slave in 1800. Since Frank's alleged involvement is contained within Gilbert's account of the 1798 Richmond fire related to Brutus, it may mean Frank was not engaged in Gabriel's plot, only the arson two years earlier. The same may be true for Brutus.

[34] If Bob had been charged, he would have been the fifth Wilkinson slave tried. Gilbert provided no other information beyond the name of his owner.

[35] Named by Gilbert after his trial, Quersey was a Frenchman, probably the man who appeared as Dequasay (various spellings) on Caroline tax lists between 1784 and 1796, and who moved to Hanover only to disappear after 1799. Gilbert reported that the Frenchman had encouraged slaves to rebel "three or four years" earlier.

[36] Edmund appears on the list of men Monroe sent to Caroline to have arrested. Although ordered to be brought to trial in Henrico, he was not. It is noted on the back of this list that all those ordered to Richmond had been apprehended, except for Edmund. However, he did

serve as a witness at the Caroline trials of Thornton and John Fells just over a month later. Paul Woolfolk held twelve taxable slaves in Caroline in 1800.

[37] Although ordered taken up by Monroe for trial in Caroline, Holmes was not among those tried in Bowling Green. Since he was identified with Paul Thilman of Hanover, he was probably alleged to have been at the meeting at Littlepage's Bridge. This is the only mention of him in the records. Perhaps he was never arrested, or died in jail before a trial could be held.

[38] One of the three individuals about whose involvement Woolfolk stated he did not have any direct knowledge, he was attributed to a Caroline owner named Mr. Mason. There are several Masons in the county, some, it would appear from the 1815 land tax list, within a radius of a few miles of Littlepage's Bridge.

[39] Named during the trial of Solomon as one of the "Town Negroes concerned," it seems Barret is otherwise unmentioned in the record.

[40] Stepney's stated owner, James Salmons of Goochland, had died in 1799, but apparently his widow Martha hired out Stepney as a waterman to James and Samuel Boyd of Cartersville in Cumberland County. James Boyd worked four tithable slaves, according to the Cumberland tax list for 1800. Stepney was sent to Richmond under guard after being accused of being a recruiter. Mayo Carrington, who dispatched him, said, "There is a positive proof of his guilt here, but I have been advised to send him to Richmond where he is well known." Other than the bill for his escort, he does not reappear in the records.

[41] Thomas Booth informed the executive that John, once the property of Thomas Buckner of Gloucester but sold to a Richmond owner, had been in the county allegedly recruiting for the plot. They had thought he had been hanged. A Bennett Tayloe appears on the 1800 Richmond tax list with one slave.

[42] Jacob, a boat captain, committed suicide after being captured and while being taken to Gloucester jail for trial. His name had appeared in a letter written by a plotter which had been dropped and discovered on a Gloucester road.

[43] Named by William Prentis as one of those first suspected in Petersburg, Brandum, or Brandon, appears as a forty-year-old carpenter on an 1803 Petersburg census of "People of Color." While he is listed on Petersburg tax records by 1799, he does not appear as a registrant in the Petersburg Free Black Register. His wife Cloe, listed next on the 1803 census as a forty-year-old washer, or laundress, does register in 1810. At that time, she is identified as his wife and as being one of the individuals emancipated by Robert Pleasants in Henrico.

[44] Also named by William Prentis among the first Petersburg suspects, neither he nor a man named Maclin or Martin Bartlett can be identified, though since Prentis wanted Monroe to check these names against "a list of a number of blacks" he had heard Monroe possessed, they were likely men of color—but whether free or enslaved remains unknown.

[45] Like the Bartletts, Pidgeon remains unidentified but was probably a black man.

[46] A James Vaughan appears as early as 1795 on the Prince George portion of the Petersburg tax lists, along with a William and Sarah Vaughan. In his 1807 will, he left a life estate in his house and lot in New Blandford to his mother, Sarah—probably the woman, aged eighty, a washer, or laundress, according to the 1803 census—and noted his brother William held a bond of his. William had actually registered in 1794, claiming to be forty-one years old and freeborn. A daughter named Sarah was to get part of his estate, and was probably the sixteen-year-old who appeared on the 1803 census just after her ancient namesake. A son John was to inherit the rest. Vaughan also appears to have held a woman named Fanny and her three children. In 1806, James Vaughan, identified as a barber and claiming

to be fifty-one years old, was examined for murdering his "supposed wife Milly Johnston" by slitting her throat. His mother Sarah had sent for the authorities. According to an 1810 list of inmates at the state penitentiary, Vaughan entered the prison on 28 April 1807 to begin serving an eighteen-year sentence for second-degree murder.

[47] Cyrus Skinner remains unidentified. A Ned Skinner does appear in Petersburg records.

[48] David White may have been the shoemaker Davy White held by William Robertson in 1788. In 1800, he belonged to the estate of a Mrs. Murray, probably the widow of James Murray. His wife, Polly Spruce, hired him from the estate and allowed him to work on his own, contrary to law. He may have been soon sold, for by 1803 he had passed into the hands of William Davies, once a resident of Petersburg but then of Norfolk. Davies manumitted White that year. Three years later, White was dead, leaving an estate worth $855.25, of which $350 represented the value of a slave named Kitt, who may have been his brother. Graham Bell, a prominent free black shoemaker, became the administrator of White's estate, and in 1809 White's three children—Kit, aged about nine; John, seven; and Polly, five—were bound out. Polly Spruce, listed on the 1803 personal property list as responsible for "D and Kitt," both above sixteen, also appears that year on the census of free people of color with four-year-old Kit; Bitty, or Billy, sixteen; and Jack, aged two. Spruce had earlier given birth to a daughter, Elizabeth, in 1791, who was baptized the following year in Bristol Parish.

[49] Polly Spruce purchased Richard White from William Murray, administrator of the estate of James Murray, for $300 in January 1801, and freed him in March. He appears to have been the brother of David and Kit, and the son of Richard. White left a will in 1807 where he named Polly White—his slave wife—and his brother Kit, and also asked that his late brother's two sons, presumably David's, be bound out. He requested that his executor attempt to free his wife Polly and his own two sons, Richard and Thomas, and if his brother Kit could become free in two years, then a $30 contribution would be made toward his emancipation.

[50] In 1805, John Bell of Petersburg advertised in the Petersburg *Intelligencer* for help in capturing his "mulatto Charles," promising a reward of $100 for his capture. "Mulatto Charles" was described as "known here by the name of Charles Timberlake." Bell had shipped him off to Norfolk for sale in the West Indies, "for sundry malpractices committed here," but he had escaped ten days before, while in Norfolk, before he could be exiled. He had been seen over the weekend back in Blandford. He was between thirty-five and forty years in age, "artful, insinuating," and still missing.

[51] Jonathan remains unidentified.

[52] Jesse Byrd was arrested in Petersburg following Gilbert's trial. Alleged to be an "uncle" of Sam Byrd Jr., he registered on 29 August 1800 in Petersburg as a man of about thirty-four years of age, born free in Essex County. A Jesse Bird had been listed on Dinwiddie tax lists for most years between 1792 and 1798. He began appearing on the Petersburg 1801 personal property lists, and in 1803 was described on the census of free people of color as a thirty-six-year-old tobacco manufacturer. Listed just below him were Betsey Byrd, also thirty-six, a spinner, and three children: Polly, aged eleven; John, eight; and Samuel, four.

[53] Reuben Byrd was also arrested following Gilbert's trial statement, as an "uncle" of Sam Byrd Jr. In 1800, there were two Reuben Byrds in Petersburg. One had been there since at least 1795. When he finally registered in 1810, he claimed to be forty-seven years old, a stonemason, and to have been born free in Essex County. In 1803, he listed himself as a forty-six-year-old stonemason. Judith Byrd, also forty-six that year and a washer, along

with four-year-old Archer, followed him on the list. The other Reuben Byrd had registered along with Jesse Byrd on 29 August 1800, and presented a certificate obtained in 1799 from the Essex County clerk describing him as free born and just over twenty-two years of age. In 1803, he appears on the personal property list as a carpenter, the same occupation he is credited with on the census of free people of color that year. His age is given as twenty-six. Sally Byrd, aged twenty-four and likely his wife, follows him on the page, along with Betty Moore, aged seven. Her relationship to them is unknown.

[54]George Markham of Chesterfield informed the executive that Burwell Gates had been in Henrico, had had contact with the conspirators, and had seen "some of the Arms." Markham described Gates as "a fellow of bad character." Monroe ordered Cheatham to have him arrested, but any subsequent actions do not seem to be recorded.

[55]Local sources suggested to William Bernard of Port Royal in northern Caroline County that Griffen might be involved. Bernard had hired Griffen from Benjamin Hurt, another Caroline resident. Monroe replied he had no information of Griffen's involvement.

[56]In both of Gilbert's narratives to John Foster, Cowley, the keeper of the capitol and doorman to the council was mentioned. Woolfolk claimed Cowley actually took Gabriel through the building. He was allegedly ready to hand out arms when the men made their way into Richmond. After Woolfolk's testimony at Gabriel's trial, Monroe asked Storrs and Selden what they knew of Cowley's involvement, and Monroe informed the General Assembly that Cowley had been exonerated. He continued to serve the state and council throughout the crisis. Cowley, once a slave of Peter Randolph, convinced Edmund Randolph in 1785 to purchase him at an estate auction, providing the sum for his own purchase. Randolph quickly freed Cowley, who was then approximately forty-five years old.

Appendix D

Slave Witnesses at Trials

Name	Owner	Court	Prosecution/ Defense
Ben[1] (36)	T. H. Prosser	Henrico	Prosecution
John[2] (12)	Sally Price	Henrico	Prosecution
Pharoah Sheppard (2)	Philip Sheppard	Henrico	Prosecution
Toby	John Holeman	Henrico	Prosecution
Daniel	John Williamson Jr.	Henrico	Prosecution
Charles	William Winston	Henrico	Prosecution
Daniel (2)	William Burton	Henrico	Prosecution
Ned	Judith Owen	Henrico	Prosecution
Wilshire	Benjamin Mosby	Henrico	Defense
Patrick	Unknown	Henrico	Prosecution
Billy	Unknown	Henrico	Prosecution
Moses	Unknown	Henrico	Defense
Davey	Unknown	Henrico	Not clear
Bristoe	Unknown	Henrico	Not clear
Frank	William Burton	Henrico	Defense
Nutty	Izard Bacon	Henrico	Defense
Ben Woolfolk[3] (ca. 32)	Paul Graham	Henrico/Caroline	Prosecution
Unnamed man	Parke Goodall	Henrico	Defense
Jack[4]	Mrs. Riddle	Henrico	Defense
David	Anderson Barrett	Henrico	Prosecution
Arch	Hezekiah Ford	Henrico	Prosecution
Sam	T. H. Prosser	Henrico	Prosecution
Edmund[5] (2)	Paul Woolfolk	Caroline	Prosecution
Primus[6] (3)	William Overton(?)	Caroline	Prosecution
Bristol	Charles Carter(?)	Caroline	Prosecution
Humphrey[7]	Edward Garland	Caroline	Not clear

Sources: This list is based on the trial testimony in ExP II, and in the case of the Henrico trials, on the Criminal Informations in Henrico Judgements and Ended Causes. No slave witnesses were identified by name in the single trials in Louisa and Dinwiddie Counties.

Notes: "Name" refers to that of the slave who served as a witness. The number in parentheses refers to the number of times they appeared. "Owner" is the name of a slave witness's owner, while "Court" refers to the place of trial. "Prosecution/Defense" indicates for whom they appeared.

[1] Ben testified at thirty-six trials, all heard in Henrico. Of the twenty-five men executed on the order of that court, he had testified against twenty-one of them, against two who were transported, and against two who were pardoned. The court acquitted eleven defendants he had provided evidence against.

[2] John testified only in Henrico. All of the men he testified against were found guilty, and all were executed, except for Ben Woolfolk, who was pardoned, and Jack Bowler, who was transported.

[3] Ben Woolfolk testified between approximately thirty-one and thirty-three times in the Henrico, Richmond, and Caroline Courts. He testified in each of the nine trials in Caroline. He gave testimony against five men who were executed and six who were transported. Eleven men found guilty solely on his testimony were later pardoned. The court acquitted ten, perhaps eleven, men after Woolfolk presented evidence against them. His was apparently the only evidence in seven of these acquittals.

[4] Jack was deemed by the court to have committed perjury in his statement for defendant James and was given thirty-nine lashes. James was later pardoned after questions were raised about Ben Woolfolk's testimony. Jack may not have been the perjurer in this case.

[5] Edmund testified at the Caroline trials of John Fells and Thornton. He said that he saw the accused with Ben Woolfolk and even walked with Woolfolk and Thornton to the preaching near Littlepage's Bridge, but afterwards left. At the trial of Fells, he stated, "He does not know or ever heard of any Negroes undertaking or engaging to join in the intended insurrection."

[6] Primus was identified by Sam Graham as held by William Overton, who appears on a Hanover tax list in 1800 with seven slaves from St. Martin's Parish, the area west of the courthouse. He and Bristol, who Graham said was a slave of Charles Carter's, warned Thornton "to desist" or they would "inform the white people." The two were threatened and they promised silence. Primus's testimony was only recorded at the trial of Jack Gabriel, where he said that he left "the preaching" near Littlepage's Bridge and that he "knew not of any person's engaging directly or indirectly to join in the conspiracy." This may have been perjury. Bristol testified at the trial of Ben, who was found guilty and transported, but the testimony at this trial does not seem to exist.

[7] Humphrey had been found not guilty before he testified at Jack Gabriel's trial. Since his testimony was not recorded, though the statements of Ben Woolfolk and Primus were, it may have been given for the defense.

Notes

Introduction

1. This sketch of William Palmer is compiled from several sources: his obituary, which appeared in the *Virginia Magazine of History and Biography* 4 (January 1897): 320; the account compiled by Samuel Bassett French available on the Library of Virginia website at http://image.lva.virginia.gov/cgi-bin/GetBF.pl ?dir=0067/P0119&card=11; the article "History of the Virginia Historical Society," *Virginia Magazine of History* 39 (October 1931): 308; the article "Preservation of Historical Papers, 19 January 1872," reproduced as part of the *On This Day: Legislative Moments in Virginia History* page of the Virginia Historical Society, http://www.vahistorical.org/onthisday/11972.htm; and the William Price Palmer Scrapbook, ca. 1890–95, Mss5: 7 P1828: 5, at the VHS. The scrapbook clippings of the columns on slavery are undated and unidentified as to their place of publication, but are signed with a "P." They were published in the *Richmond Times* from 7 December 1890 through at least 8 February 1891. No installment appeared on 14 December 1890. I am grateful to Frances Pollard at the Virginia Historical Society for first pointing me to the *Richmond Times*, and to the essay of Bernard Henley, "Dr. William Price Palmer: 'A Man . . . with Antiquarian Propensities,'" which appeared in the *Richmond Quarterly* 4 (Fall 1981). That Palmer seemed to use the published version of the documents appearing in the *Calendar of Virginia State Papers* rather than the originals is suggested from his reproduction of Thomas Newton's letter to Monroe of 24 September 1800 in his column of 4 January 1891. It replicates the letter in H. W. Flournoy, ed., *Calendar of Virginia State Papers* (Richmond, 1890), 9:154–55, rather than the original. Published before the advent of modern documentary editing standards and intended as a calendar, this work did not indicate where documents were modified or shortened. In the case of Newton's letter, the printed document omits approximately the last fifth of the original text.

2. *Richmond Times,* 7 and 21 December 1890.

3. *Richmond Times,* 21 December 1890.

4. *Richmond Times,* 28 December 1890, 4 January 1891.

5. *Richmond Times,* 4 January 1891.

6. *Richmond Times,* 11 January 1891.

7. Ulrich Bonnell Phillips, *American Negro Slavery* (1918; repr., Baton Rouge: Louisiana State University Press, 1966), 474–75. The short accounts in the two monographs cited were in James Curtis Ballagh, *History of Slavery in Virginia* (1902), and John H. Russell, *The Free Negro in Virginia, 1619–1865* (1913). Phillips counted twenty-five men executed and ten transported, a more-nearly-accurate count than Aptheker's later account cited below.

8. Herbert Aptheker, *American Negro Slave Revolts* (1943; repr., New York: International Publishers, 1983), 219–26.

9. Winthrop Jordan, *White Over Black: American Attitudes toward the Negro, 1550–1812* (Chapel Hill: University of North Carolina Press, 1968), xi–xii, 393–96. See, too, Robert McColley, *Slavery and Jeffersonian Virginia* (Urbana: University of Illinois Press, 1964), 107–13.

10. Gerald W. Mullin, *Flight and Rebellion: Slave Resistance in Eighteenth-Century Virginia* (New York: Oxford University Press, 1972), 140–63, 197–204.

11. Douglas R. Egerton, *Gabriel's Rebellion: The Virginia Slave Conspiracies of 1800 and 1802* (Chapel Hill: University of North Carolina Press, 1993), ix–x, 17, 179–81, 192n46. (All subsequent citations or discussion of Egerton's *Gabriel's Rebellion* will refer to this edition.) The first scholarly citation to Palmer's scrapbook columns on slavery appears to be that of Philip J. Schwarz in "Gabriel's Challenge: Slaves and Crime in Late Eighteenth-Century Virginia," *Virginia Magazine of History and Biography* 90 (July 1982): 283n1, where he identifies the columns as appearing in the *Richmond Times* in "1890 or 1891." Egerton cites the columns in the scrapbook as an "unidentified newspaper clipping," but with no indication that they might not be contemporary to the event, or that Palmer was the author.

12. James Sidbury, *Ploughshares into Swords: Race, Rebellion, and Identity in Gabriel's Virginia, 1730–1810* (New York: Cambridge University Press, 1997), 1. See, too, Sidbury, "Thomas Jefferson in Gabriel's Virginia," in *The Revolution of 1800: Democracy, Race, and the New Republic,* ed. James Horn, Jan Ellen Lewis, and Peter S. Onuf (Charlottesville: University of Virginia Press, 2002), 199–219.

13. Walter C. Rucker, *The River Flows On: Black Resistance, Culture, and Identity Formation in Early America* (Baton Rouge: Louisiana State University Press, 2006), 123–51; William G. Merkel, "To See Oneself as a Target of a Justified Revolution: Thomas Jefferson and Gabriel's Uprising," *American Nineteenth Century History* 4, no. 2 (Summer 2003): 1–31; Robert A. Ferguson, *Reading the Early Republic* (Cambridge, Mass.: Harvard University Press, 2004), 198–217, a revision of an earlier essay, "Untold Stories in the Law," in *Law's Stories: Narrative and Rhetoric in the Law,* ed. Peter Brooks and Paul Gewirtz (New Haven, Conn.: Yale University Press, 1996), 84–98; Lacy K. Ford, *Deliver Us from*

Evil: The Slavery Question in the Old South (New York: Oxford University Press, 2009), 49–80.

14. Thomas J. Davis, "Conspiracy and Credibility: Look Who's Talking, about What—Law Talk and Loose Talk," *WMQ*, 3rd ser., 59 (January 2002): 168; Sidbury, *Ploughshares into Swords*, 75, 99–100.

15. Peter Kolchin, *Unfree Labor: American Slavery and Russian Serfdom* (Cambridge, Mass.: Harvard University Press, 1987), 257; Winthrop D. Jordan, *Tumult and Silence at Second Creek: An Inquiry into a Civil War Slave Conspiracy*, rev. ed. (Baton Rouge: Louisiana State University Press, 1995), 184, 199, 100; David Brion Davis, "The Culmination of Racial Polarities and Prejudice," *Journal of the Early Republic* 19 (Winter 1999): 760. Both Kolchin and Jordan have questioned the necessity of rebels having to possess ideologies of rebellion.

16. Walter Johnson, "On Agency," *Journal of Social History* 37 (Fall 2003): 118; Anthony E. Kaye, *Joining Places: Slave Neighborhoods in the Old South* (Chapel Hill: University of North Carolina Press, 2007).

17. Jordan, *Tumult and Silence at Second Creek*, 7.

1. The Brook and the Road

1. The evidence for the location of the key slave conspirators and the white families who held them is built from the Henrico Processioners Returns, No. 1, 1795–1824 (microfilm), especially those conducted in 1799–1800 (pp. 37–84). Also helpful, if used with care, are the 1815 land tax lists, which indicate how far tracts sat from the courthouse or their proximity to other topographical or prominent markers, such as streams, like the Brook, or taverns. Unless otherwise cited, the microfilmed county and municipal records (including processioners returns, land and personal property tax lists, order books, plat books, deed books, will books, marriage bonds, records of the common council, etc.), as well as all legislative petitions cited in this study, are available at the Library of Virginia in Richmond. Copies are also available at the Family History Library, Salt Lake City, with the exception of Richmond Common Council minutes, marriage bonds, personal property and land tax lists, and the Henrico land tax lists for the era. The Family History Library does contain microfilm of the Richmond legislative petitions, but it is incomplete. No contemporary maps of Henrico exist, but the earliest two, the Wood-Böye maps dating from 1819–20, are useful. Online images of them can be found at the Library of Virginia website under county and state maps within the Board of Public Works. Also useful are Civil War–era maps, such as "Hanover, Henrico, and part of Chesterfield Counties, southeast to Williamsburg and east to York River," drawn by Jeremy Francis Gilmer, in the Gilmer Civil War Maps Collection, with an online image from the University of North Carolina Southern Historical Collection available at http://dc.lib.unc.edu/cdm4/item_viewer.php ?CISOROOT=/gilmer&CISOPTR=163&CISOBOX=1&REC=14; and the "Map of Henrico County . . . [1864]," in the Hotchkiss Map Collection at the Library of Congress, with images available online in the American Memory Collection,

http://hdl.loc.gov/loc.gmd/g3883h.cwh00041. For the Brook being seen as a distinct area, see Henrico Order Book 9, 1799–1801, p. 273, where its drainage served as the boundaries of an election district for the overseers of the poor. For Young's property, see Henrico County Plat Book, 1815–38, 1; Deed Book 4, 1792–96, 182–84, 555–56; and Deed Book 5, 1796–1800, 408, 613. Young's ownership of a share of the schoolhouse lot is noted in Henrico Processioners Returns, No. 1, 75. See also Appendix A: The Geography of Conspiracy.

2. See Processioners Returns, 70–84; and Henrico County Order Book 8, 1798–99, 372. Joseph Selden, who served with Storrs in the investigation of the plot, was recommended by the county court to the executive to be added to the Henrico slate of justices at the same time.

3. For Prosser's lands and mills, see Henrico Deed Book 1, 1781–85, 217; Deed Book 2, 1785–88, 436; and Deed Book 3, 1789–92, 178, 463. In 1800, T. H. Prosser paid taxes on six tracts totaling 2,475 acres (see Henrico Land Tax List, Upper District, 1800). For Prosser's Tavern, see Order Book 3, 1787–89, 168; Order Book 8, 1798–99, 373–74, 451–52; and Order Book 9, 1799–1801, 5, 7, 237, 298, 302, 389. For Thomas Prosser's repairs to Brook Bridge, see Order Book 8, 329; and Order Book 9, 223; and for Prosser's Tavern as an election site, see Order Book 9, 273. Egerton (19) states that Thomas Prosser employed Patrick Henry to help him regain his seat in the House of Burgesses and out of gratitude named his son after the patriot. In fact, Prosser was permanently expelled (see Appendix A: The Geography of Conspiracy). Egerton (22–23) portrays Thomas Henry Prosser as an aggressive young man on the make, and claims in support of his portrayal that Prosser bought the tavern within months after his father's death, as well as joining one "V. M. Moncure" in an auction and real estate firm. The tavern had been in family hands for years, and the Prosser of the firm Prosser and Moncure was John Prosser, who created with William Moncure an auction and commission firm in 1798. The "V. M." following the firm's name stood for "vendue merchant[s]" or "vendue master[s]" (see *Virginia Gazette and General Advertiser,* 26 June 1798; and Richmond City Hustings Deeds 2, 1792–99, 424). For Gregory's Tavern, see the *Virginia Argus,* 1 May 1802, and "Memoranda Made by Thomas R. Joynes on a Journey to the States of Ohio and Kentucky," *WMQ,* 1st ser., 10 (January 1902): 147. For Priddy's connections and relocation, see Order Book 7, 1796–98, 554; Order Book 8, 347; Order Book 9, 454; Order Book 10, 1801–3, 87; Deed Book 5, 604; Deed Book 6, 1800–1803, 85; and Samuel Shepard, *Statutes at Large of Virginia* (1835; facsimile repr., New York: AMS Press, 1970), 3:96. For Nathaniel Wilkinson as county treasurer, see Order Book 9, 137, 535. Three taverns figure importantly in the evidence, and establishing their location helps gauge the physical extent of the plot and the state's response to it. It appears that Prosser's Tavern was run by George Watson in 1800 and hence was referred to both as Prosser's and Watson's Tavern. Similarly, Gregory's Tavern was also known as Priddy's, since Thomas Priddy still operated it in 1800, although he would soon leave to run his own establishment in the western portion of the county near Short Pump, which then became the new Priddy's Tavern. Finally, Goodall's Tavern was the

same as the Indian Queen in Richmond, built by Andrew Dunscomb but then known as Parke Goodall's, and should not be confused—as Palmer apparently did in his column in the *Richmond Times* of 4 January 1891—with Goodall's Tavern in Hanover, which is about a dozen miles from Gregory's up the left-hand fork of the road toward Louisa. Establishing tavern locations, important geographical markers, clarifies the movement of men and patrols and puts Pharoah and Tom in Richmond on 30 August, before the storm, where they revealed the plot to Mosby Sheppard, rather than at Elizabeth or at Philip Sheppard's north of the Brook, part of the story discussed below.

4. For the location of the Caroline taverns and the distances to Bowling Green, see Marshall Wingfield, *A History of Caroline County, Virginia, From Its Formation in 1727 to 1924* (1924; repr., Baltimore: Regional Publishing Co., 1975), 33; and John H. Gwathmey, *Twelve Virginia Counties Where the Western Migration Began* (1937; repr., Baltimore: Genealogical Publishing Co., 1981), 180–81.

5. See "Extract of a Letter from Richmond, dated September 11," *Washington Federalist*, 25 September 1800; and testimony of Prosser's Ben at the trial of Solomon, September 11, box 8, folder 1, 1–15 September 1800, in the Executive Papers of James Monroe, Series II: Subject Files—Gabriel's Insurrection, Acc. no. 40936, LVA [hereafter cited as ExP II].

6. See Order Book 3, 1787–89, 59, 231; and Personal Property Tax List, Upper District 1800. In the fall of 1786, the General Assembly had directed that some counties, including Henrico, have two tax districts, others one; see William Waller Hening, *The Statutes at Large* (1823; facsimile repr., Charlottesville, University Press of Virginia, 1969), 12:244 (subsequent citations to Hening are to the facsimile edition).

7. For the growing sense of place and neighborhood over time among slaves, see Allan Kulikoff, *Tobacco and Slaves: The Development of Southern Cultures in the Chesapeake, 1680–1800* (Chapel Hill: University of North Carolina Press, 1986), 340–45; Philip D. Morgan, *Slave Counterpoint: Black Culture in the Eighteenth-Century Chesapeake & Lowcountry* (Chapel Hill: University of North Carolina Press, 1998), 476; Kaye, *Joining Places*, 1–50; and Kaye, "Neighborhoods and Nat Turner: The Making of a Slave Rebel and the Unmaking of a Slave Rebellion," *Journal of the Early Republic* 27 (Winter 2007): 705–20. For an important appraisal of nineteenth-century slave society that calls for "viewing black people's lives on their own terms" in all their complexities, see Dylan C. Penningroth, *The Claims of Kinfolk: African American Property and Community in the Nineteenth-Century South* (Chapel Hill: University of North Carolina Press, 2003).

8. See Ira Berlin, *Many Thousands Gone: The First Two Centuries of Slavery in North America* (Cambridge, Mass.: Harvard University Press, 1998), 7–9; Philip J. Schwarz, *Twice Condemned: Slaves and the Criminal Laws of Virginia, 1705–1865* (Baton Rouge: Louisiana State University Press, 1988), 17–34; Sally E. Haddon, *Slave Patrols: Law and Violence in Virginia and the Carolinas* (Cambridge, Mass.: Harvard University Press, 2001); Eva Sheppard Wolf, *Race and Liberty in the New Nation: Emancipation in Virginia from the Revolution to Nat Turner's*

Rebellion (Baton Rouge: Louisiana State University Press, 2006); Alex Lichten-stein, "'That Disposition to Theft, with Which They Have Been Branded': Moral Economy, Slave Management, and the Law," *Journal of Social History* 21 (Spring 1988): 413–40; and Loren Schweninger, "The Underside of Slavery: The Internal Economy, Self-Hire, and Quasi-Freedom in Virginia, 1780-1865," *Slavery and Abolition* 12 (September 1991): 1–22.

9. See Robert P. Sutton, *Revolution to Secession: Constitution Making in the Old Dominion* (Charlottesville: University of Virginia Press, 1989), 21–51; Willi Paul Adams, *The First American Constitutions: Republican Ideology and the Making of the State Constitutions in the Revolutionary Era*, trans. Rita and Rob-ert Kimber (Chapel Hill: University of North Carolina Press, 1980); Norman K. Risjord, *Chesapeake Politics, 1781-1800* (New York: Columbia University Press, 1978), 552–63; Edward J. Larson, *A Magnificent Catastrophe: The Tumultuous Election of 1800, America's First Presidential Campaign* (New York: Free Press, 2007); and Michael Durey, *"With the Hammer of Truth": James Thomson Cal-lender and America's Early National Heroes* (Charlottesville: University Press of Virginia, 1990). For a discussion of the newspaper war and the use of Gabriel's Conspiracy in the national election of 1800, see Michael L. Nicholls, "'Holy Insur-rection!': Spinning the News of Gabriel's Conspiracy," *Journal of Southern His-tory* (forthcoming).

10. See James Morton Smith, *Freedom's Fetters: The Alien and Sedition Laws and American Civil Liberties* (Ithaca, N.Y.: Cornell University Press, 1956); Du-rey, *"Hammer of Truth,"* 116–36; John Minor to Mrs. Minor, Hazel Hill near Fred-ericksburg, 25 May 1800, Minor Family Papers, box 4, James Monroe Museum and Memorial Library, Fredericksburg; Richard H. Kohn, *Eagle and Sword: The Federalists and the Creation of the Military Establishment in America, 1783-1802* (New York: Free Press, 1975), 193–273; *The Papers of Alexander Hamilton*, ed. Harold C. Syrett (New York: Columbia University Press, 1975), 22:383–88; William J. Murphy Jr., "John Adams: The Politics of the Additional Army, 1798-1800," *New England Quarterly* 52 (June 1979): 234–49; Kohn, *Eagle and Sword*, 262, citing St. George Tucker to James Monroe, 29 December 1799; and *The Pa-pers of James Madison*, ed. David B. Mattern et al. (Charlottesville: University of Virginia Press, 1991), 17:388–89. Notices regarding the 7th Regiment appear in the *Virginia Argus*, 14 June 1799, and in the *Virginia Gazette and General Adver-tiser*, 25 January 1799 and 7 February 1800.

11. Virginia Council of State, *Journals*, Acc. no. 35356 (microfilm), 1799–1801, 177–87, LVA [hereafter cited as *Council Journals* with date range and page num-ber]; Edward Carrington to Monroe, 10 and 11 June 1800, box 2, folder 1, in Executive Papers of James Monroe, Series I: Chronological Files, Acc. no. 40936, LVA [hereafter cited as ExP I]; William Berkeley to Monroe, 14 June 1800, ibid.

12. *Council Journals*, 1799–1801, 201; Executive Letter Book, 4 October 1794–5 October 1800, 379ff., LVA [hereafter cited as ExLB, 1794–1800]; Thomas Newton Jr. to Monroe, 12 July, 13 July, 30 July, 22 August, and 29 August 1800, ExP I, box 2, folders 3–6.

13. Monroe to Dr. John Foushee, 11 August 1800, ExLB, 1794–1800, 379; Monroe to Mr. Mulford, 11 August 1800, ibid.; Monroe to Newton, 25 August 1800, ibid.; James Allan to Monroe, 13 August 1800, ExP I, box 2, folder 5; Newton to Monroe, 29 August 1800, ibid., folder 6; resolution of the Richmond Common Hall, 28 August 1800, ibid.; *Council Journals*, 1799–1801, 221. For the proclamation in print, see the *Virginia Argus*, 29 August 1800, and the Alexandria *Times and District of Columbia Daily Advertiser*, 1 September 1800. For Norfolk accounts of deaths and the frustration with the town's unhealthy reputation, see the *Norfolk Herald*, 30 August 1800, and 2 and 6 September 1800.

14. Testimony of Ben Woolfolk at trial of Sam Byrd, 27 September 1800, ExP II, box 8, folder 2; "Communications made by Gilbert," undated, ibid., folder 5; "Information from Mr Foster [from Gilbert] respecting the intended Insurrection Sepr 23d 1800," 23 September 1800, ibid., folder 2. Gabriel reportedly admitted being head of the plot but denied being its author, which, if true, could bolster Byrd's claim to being the originator (see *Virginia Gazette*, 30 September 1800). While the mention of the Catawbas seems far-fetched, men from the tribe, as well as Chickasaws, occasionally passed through Richmond on their way to the nation's capital during this period. Interestingly, their stay in Richmond was usually hosted, at the direction of the executive, by Robert Cowley, a free black man and doorkeeper to the council, who was implicated in the conspiracy (see *Council Journals*, 1797–98, 187, and *Council Journals*, 1799–1801, 10, 45, 286). Egerton (25) states that Byrd was hired to William Young of Richmond, and locates Joseph Mosby in town, too. I find no evidence that Mosby or Young lived in Richmond in 1800, or that Byrd was hired to Young. As noted, Clarke was a near neighbor of Young's on the Brook. Joseph Mosby rented the lands and hired some of the slaves of the estate of William Lewis from 1798 through 1803 (see Henrico Order Book 14, 1808–9, 123–31). Slaves from the Lewis estate were involved.

15. Henrico County Will Book 2 with Inventories and Accounts, 1787–1802, 183; testimony of Ben Woolfolk at trial of George Smith, 19 September 1800, ExP II, box 8, folder 2. In *Flight and Rebellion* (159), Mullin appears to imply that the name "Pipeing Tree" was associated with the presence of the "outlandish" people Smith referred to, when in fact it was the name of a public tobacco warehouse created in 1748 in King William County (see Hening, *Statutes at Large*, 6:174). Besides the public warehouse, a storehouse and granary of Miles King sat there in 1798 (see *Virginia Gazette and General Advertiser*, 21 August 1798). In the late nineteenth century, William Price Palmer thought that "outlandish" referred to the Native Americans along the Pamunkey (see *Richmond Times*, 28 December 1890). Egerton (52) reports that Gabriel refused to listen to Smith's proposal to seek the help of the "outlandish," but the record is silent as to any reaction.

16. Thomas Newton to Monroe, 24 September 1800, ExP II, box 8, folder 2; testimony of Prosser's Ben at trial of Gilbert and testimony of Ben Woolfolk at same, 22 September 1800, ibid.; "Comunications of Ben alias Ben Woolfolk," 17 September 1800, ibid.; "Information from Mr Foster [from Gilbert] respecting the intended Insurrection Sepr 23d 1800," 23 September 1800, ibid.;

"Communications made by Gilbert," undated, ibid., folder 5. Newton's report of Gabriel's accusation against Gilbert has been overlooked by historians, the emphasis instead being placed on Gabriel's refusal to reveal anything of significance to officials in either Norfolk or Richmond. By the time Gabriel reached Richmond, Gilbert had already been convicted, so if he repeated his charge then, it did not add anything new to their knowledge other than an ascribed importance. Although Gilbert provided nearly as many names as Ben Woolfolk, the court made no recommendation for executive mercy, his revelations to John Foster never becoming part of the court record. Interestingly, he never appeared as a sworn witness. Perhaps he refused to testify, although he revealed names, and one wonders if his speech impediment may have deterred him or the prosecution from using him.

17. An article entitled "Extract of a Letter from a Gentleman at Richmond, Virginia to his Friend in This City, dated September 20th, 1800," in the New York *American Citizen and General Advertiser* for 2 October 1800 identifies Ben Woolfolk as a mulatto and Prosser's Ben as being eighteen years old. See also the testimony of Price's John, and that of Prosser's Ben at the trial of Ben Woolfolk, 16 September 1800, ExP II, box 8, folder 2; the testimony of Ben Woolfolk at the trial of Abraham, 29 September 1800, ibid.; and James Rind to Elisha Price, undated, ibid., folder 3. Woolfolk gave evidence in more than thirty trials in Henrico, Richmond City, and Caroline. The article in the *American Citizen* was reprinted in Virginia in the *Virginia Argus* for 14 October, and in the *Norfolk Herald* on 18 October. Citing the Norfolk reprinting, Egerton incorrectly reports that Ben Woolfolk was the one who was eighteen, and by frequently mentioning his ascribed youth, implies that it explains his ultimate cooperation with the state (see Egerton, 54, 62, 67, 91, 95, 101, 109, 173). Woolfolk does not appear to have revealed anything, nor did he serve as a state's witness until after he had been convicted and sentenced to hang. His owner, Paul Graham, is listed as owning a two-wheel carriage, seven slaves above the age of twelve, and three horses (see the Hanover personal property tax list in 1800), but he does not appear on the Caroline rolls for that year. He died in 1802, identifying himself in his will as being from Caroline (see Caroline County Wills, 1742–1830, 69). He left one tract to be sold, which was on the stage road—that is, the one that connected Bowling Green with the Brook and Richmond. In 1815, the Caroline County land tax list located his estate as being nineteen miles south of the courthouse, which would place it about three or four miles above Littlepage's Bridge. Paul Graham was the son of Robert Graham, deceased, and became the stepson of his second cousin Paul Woolfolk when the latter married his mother, Sarah Thilman Graham. She and Paul Woolfolk were first cousins, or so it appears. This may explain why it was Paul Woolfolk who collected Ben Woolfolk's lost-hire wages from the state in January 1801, and not hirer William Young or the slave's reported owner, Paul Graham.

18. A scrap of paper over Richard Bowler's signature, dated 17 September 1800, in ExP II, box 8, folder 2 (apparently cited by Egerton [125n29] as "Wil-

liam Bowler [Jr.] to James Monroe, September 27, 1800") contains the description which was used for Monroe's proclamation published in the newspapers (see *Richmond Examiner*, 19 September 1800). In the one part of the original description not reproduced in the proclamation, Richard Bowler had listed Jack Bowler, in a nearly unreadable, interlined scrawl, as being "the property of William Bowler's wife of Caroline," a location misread by Mullin as Urbanna, a small port in the more distant Middlesex County (*Flight and Rebellion*, 142). Her Caroline residence places Jack Bowler closer to the reach of the Brook conspiracy. For the appointment of guardians for William Bowler's two sons, John and William, see the file "Condemned Slaves, Transported, Gabriel's Insurrection," in Auditor of Public Accounts, Item 756: "Condemned Blacks, Executed or Transported" (microfilm), FHL [hereafter cited as Auditor's Item 756], which includes a copy of a Caroline County Order Book entry for 12 February 1799. For Jack Bowler's other activities, see the testimony of Prosser's Ben, Price's John, and Prosser's Sam at Bowler's trial, 29 October 1800, ExP II, box 8, folder 3 [misfiled as 9 October]; and "Confession of Solomon read Sept. 15th 1800," 15 September 1800, ibid., folder 1.

19. "Certificate of Gervas Storrs and Joseph Selden," 8 September 1800, ExP II, box 8, folder 1; *Council Journals*, 1799–1801, 233; *Richmond Examiner*, 12 September 1800; Henrico County Deed Book 5, 1796–1800, 556–58; Philip J. Schwarz, "Gabriel's Challenge: Slaves and Crime in Late Eighteenth-Century Virginia," *Virginia Magazine of History and Biography* 90 (July 1982): 283–309; Henrico County Order Book 9, 1799–1801, 94–95, 102, 105. There is no evidence that Gabriel was directly involved with Jupiter in the hog stealing, but he was probably indirectly connected to it. His brother Solomon was found not guilty of posing a threat to Johnson and his property, but Gabriel had actually bitten off part of Johnson's ear in the fight. Presumably, Gabriel's plotting would have violated Prosser's bond for his good behavior posted in November 1799, but I have found no record of any attempt by the court to prosecute Prosser's bond. For the descriptions of Gabriel in the press, see chapter 3, note 24 below.

20. For Martin, see the testimony of Prosser's Ben at the trial of Martin, 12 September 1800, ExP II, box 8, folder 1; "Communications of Ben alias Ben Woolfolk," 17 September, ibid., folder 2; and "Communications made by Gilbert," undated, ibid., folder 5. For Solomon, see testimony of Prosser's Ben at the trial of Solomon, 11 September, ibid., folder 1; "Confession of Solomon . . . ," 15 September, ibid.; and the testimony of Prosser's Ben at the trial of Gabriel, 6 October, ibid., folder 3. I believe Egerton (51–52, 179, and passim) correctly downplays Gabriel as a messianic figure, though he incorrectly states that Gabriel's claiming the benefit of clergy "indicated the capacity to recite a passage from the Bible." Although Gabriel was literate, according to the description in the proclamation seeking his capture, the law no longer required a demonstration of literacy to claim the privilege, let alone the ability "to recite" a passage from scripture. More to the point, as part of his interpretive effort to downplay the significance of religion in the plotting, Egerton also claims, "There is not a *single* extant document that supports the contention that . . . Martin was a slave

preacher" [Egerton's emphasis]. He acknowledges that both Gabriel and Martin were familiar with scripture, but assumes that the latter was illiterate, probably a field slave, and not part of the inner circle of leaders. Ben Woolfolk, however, testified at Gabriel's trial that Martin said, "I read in my bible . . . ," which suggests he asserted his literacy. It seems hard to believe that Gabriel would turn to him to declare when the uprising was to begin if he were not part of the inner circle or without some standing as a spiritual leader. The "Extract of a Letter written . . . from Richmond," in the New York *American Citizen* for 2 October identified Martin as "a preacher, brother to Gabriel." At the same time, it should be pointed out, the newspaper also identified Solomon as a mulatto, as it did Ben Woolfolk, although Solomon was described as a Negro in his petition, as were both men in other court documents. Obviously, in 1800 lineage was in the eye of the beholder, or the mouth of the gossiper if one lacked genealogical knowledge. Perhaps the title of preacher was misapplied as well. Martin's use of scripture, however, does suggest that religion resonated with others in the conspiracy, if not Gabriel. Gabriel, however, apparently recognized the importance of religion or spirituality in the lives of his followers in turning to Martin for support, especially in opposing a proposal to delay the day of attack. Callender also mentioned to Jefferson that the black convicts who remained in the jail in late October were "singing psalms" and contributing to the general din of the place (see *The Papers of Thomas Jefferson*, ed. Barbara B. Oberg et al. (Princeton, N.J.: Princeton University Press, 2005), 32:236. These facts offer support for the argument of Sidbury (*Plowshares into Swords*, 74–79) for a more important place for Christianity in the Virginia slave culture of the period, and to Sidbury's thus taking exception to Egerton's conclusions about the relative insignificance of religion in the conspiracy. Peter P. Hinks, in *To Awaken My Afflicted Brethren: David Walker and the Problem of Antebellum Slave Resistance* (University Park: Pennsylvania State University Press, 1997), 56–57, also sees Christianity as more significant, but otherwise relies heavily on Egerton's account for his brief discussion of the plot. See, too, Sidbury, "Reading, Revelation, and Rebellion: The Textual Communities of Gabriel, Denmark Vesey, and Nat Turner," in *Nat Turner: A Slave Rebellion in History and Memory*, ed. Kenneth S. Greenberg (New York: Oxford University Press, 2003), 119–33.

21. Testimony of Prosser's Ben at the trial of Nat [Ned], 11 September 1800, ExP II, box 8, folder 1; testimony of Prosser's Ben and Ben Woolfolk at the trial of Gilbert, 22 September, ibid., folder 2; testimony of Prosser's Ben at the trial of Michael, 27 September, ibid.; testimony of Prosser's Ben at the trial of William, 27 September, ibid.; *American Citizen*, 2 October 1800; Henrico County Deed Book 6, 1800–1803, 227. For the role of Prosser's Ben as a witness, see chapters 4 and 5. He gave evidence at thirty-six of the fifty-eight Henrico trials. Sidbury incorrectly states that Ben was pardoned in exchange for his testimony (*Ploughshares into Swords*, 103). Like Price's John, who also provided many trial statements, a deal to testify to avoid prosecution was apparently made with him.

22. Sidbury, *Ploughshares into Swords*, 160–67; Sidbury, "Saint Domingue in Virginia: Ideology, Local Meanings, and Resistance to Slavery, 1790–1800," *Journal of Southern History* 63 (August 1997): 531–52. Besides the accounts of the St. Domingue revolution, there are accounts appearing in Virginia newspapers which highlight the urban focus of revolts. For example, one account in 1797 discusses rumors of uprisings in Charleston, S.C. (see the article in the *Virginia Chronicle and Norfolk and Portsmouth General Advertiser* for 19 October 1797; and one in the *Virginia Gazette and Petersburg Intelligencer* for 1 December 1797, which was reprinted in the *Virginia Gazette and General Advertiser* of 6 December 1797. Egerton (59) states, "Until the last moment Gabriel's conspiracy was completely urban, the only plot of its kind in southern history." The evidence indicates that the plotters hoped to engage urban slaves, but that the core of the plot and the bulk of the recruits for an attack on the town were to be found in the countryside, a small but important distinction.

23. "Communications of Ben alias Ben Woolfolk," 17 September 1800, ExP II, box 8, folder 2; "Information from Mr Foster [from Gilbert] respecting the intended Insurrection Sepr 23d 1800," 23 September, ibid.; *Virginia Gazette and Weekly Advertiser*, 11 January 1787; *Federal Gazette & Baltimore Daily Advertiser*, 30 November 1798; *Claypoole's American Daily Advertiser*, 30 November 1798; entry for 22 November 1798, John Boyce Journal, 1798–1808 (microfilm), LVA; Richmond Hustings Court Order Book 4, 1797–1801, 473; James Thomson Callender to Thomas Jefferson, 29 September 1800, in *Papers of Thomas Jefferson*, 32:174. A Charles Purcell was also identified as a bricklayer who contracted for work on the construction of the public buildings in Richmond in 1793 (see Sherwin McRae, ed., *Calendar of Virginia State Papers* [Richmond, 1886], 6:649–50).

24. James C. Scott, *Weapons of the Weak: Everyday Forms of Peasant Resistance* (New Haven, Conn.: Yale University Press, 1985), 29; "Communications made by Gilbert," undated, ExP II, box 8, folder 5.

25. "Confession of Solomon . . . ," 15 September 1800, ExP II, box 8, folder 1; "Communications of Ben alias Ben Woolfolk," 17 September, ibid., folder 2; testimony of Prosser's Ben at the trial of Solomon, 11 September, ibid., folder 1; testimony of Daniel at the trial of Isaac, 11 September, ibid.; testimony of Prosser's Ben at trial of Michael, 27 September, ibid., folder 2; testimony of Prosser's Ben at the trial of Gabriel, 6 October, ibid., folder 3. Solomon listed the governor as one of the objects to be attacked, not indicating whether Monroe was to be held hostage or killed. He is the only conspirator to identify Monroe as a target.

2. Are You a True Man?

1. I am indebted to Philip Schwarz, who first provided me with transcriptions of the criminal informations filed by George William Smith against the defendants, which I then compared to the originals in the Henrico Court Records; see County

Court Judgements and Ended Causes 1800, box 70, Commonwealth Causes: September–October, 1800 (Gabriel's Rebellion), LVA [hereafter cited as Henrico Judgements and Ended Causes]. These served the same purpose as an indictment of a grand jury would for free people accused of crimes. Each of the surviving informations claimed that criminal conversations had occurred between 1 July and 1 September, except for those of Gabriel, tried 6 October, Jack Bowler tried 29 October, and Emanuel and Absolem, both tried 4 November. In these cases, the date range was between 1 June and 1 September. The different opening date may have been a prosecutorial or clerical slip since all of these men were taken up sometime after the others and the initial date misremembered by the time of their trials (see testimony of Ben Woolfolk at trial of Samuel Byrd, 27 September 1800, ExP II, box 8, folder 2; testimony of Woolfolk at trial of George Smith, 19 September, ibid.; New York *American Citizen and General Advertiser*, 2 October 1800; Louisa County Order Book 1799–1802, 284 [the evidence recorded in the Louisa trial does not reveal a link to Gabriel's plot; the case could be coincidental, but I have included it in my tally of trials discussed here]. Herbert Aptheker, in *American Negro Slave Revolts*, 220, cited a letter from Monroe to Jefferson dated 22 April 1800, but noted that it could not be found in the Library of Congress. From the few facts listed in the abstract, it appears it is the letter Monroe wrote to Jefferson on 22 September. Hence, the state did not have the evidence as early as Aptheker stated, though he warned his evidence was based on a "missing" letter. Egerton (49) cites Aptheker, and builds his story and Monroe's response to the conspiracy using the erroneous April date. Cf. *Calendar of the Correspondence of Thomas Jefferson*, pt. 2 (1895; repr., New York: Burt Franklin, 1970), 405, with the *Papers of Thomas Jefferson*, 32:161–62. See p. 136 of the latter volume for Callender's quote from a letter to Jefferson of 13 September 1800. Callender had sent almost the same exact letter, dated 12 September, to James Duane, which the editor published in the *Philadelphia Aurora* on 23 September.

2. In 1783 and 1784, magistrates appointed to list an individual's taxable property in Henrico included the names of individual slaves. It was common to list slaves of tithable age, or those sixteen and older, ahead of the younger ones. Keeping in mind the difficulties of knowing that individuals listed in 1783 or 1784 were the same as those present in 1800, a search of men tried in Henrico for conspiracy indicates that of the handful or two that were found, most were non-tithables in those years. Hence, the men charged would generally have been under thirty-two or so in age—men in their physical prime. There were exceptions.

3. Sidbury, *Ploughshares into Swords*, 75, 99–100; Shepard, *Statutes at Large of Virginia*, 1:125; Jordan, *Tumult and Silence at Second Creek*, 100. For a discussion of Egerton's claims about Gabriel's political ideology, see chapter 5 and Nicholls, "'Holy Insurrection!'"

4. "Confession of Solomon . . . ," 15 September 1800, ExP II, box 8, folder 1.

5. Testimony of Ben Woolfolk at the trial of George Smith, 19 September 1800, ExP II, box 8, folder 2; testimony of Woolfolk at the trial of Sam Byrd, 22 September, ibid.; "Communications of Ben alias Ben Woolfolk," 17 September, ibid.;

testimony of Woolfolk at the trial of Abraham, 29 September, ibid.; testimony of Ned, Pharoah, Prosser's Ben, and William Gentry at trial of Michael, 11 September, ibid., folder 1. Contrary to Egerton's claim (54), nothing in the sources he cites substantiates that Woolfolk volunteered to make cutlasses. His error arises from confusing which Ben is being referred to in the news article at the time. No trial testimony states that he was taken to Gabriel's, where he enlisted; instead, it was at Smith's and Byrd's and again back at Woolfolk's where the intense discussions were held, with no record of Gabriel's involvement in his recruitment. However, the claim that he was taken to Gabriel's is made in the account that originally appeared in the New York *American Citizen* of 2 October 1800, wherein it is reported that Ben—that is, Prosser's Ben—had "assisted in making cutlasses." Egerton cites the *Norfolk Herald*'s reprinting of this account, but adds a citation to the *Kentucky Gazette* of 3 November, as if it were an additional report of the conspiracy, when it is simply a reprinting of the same column. Other reprints of the few newspaper accounts of the conspiracy are similarly handled, creating an inflated sense of the actual number of accounts emerging from Virginia. For a discussion of the spread of the few reports that were created, often for political purposes, see Nicholls, "'Holy Insurrection!.'"

6. Testimony of Ben Woolfolk at trial of Jacob, 30 September 1800, ExP II, box 8, folder 2; testimony of Billy at the trial of Martin, 12 September, ibid., folder 1; testimony of Prosser's Ben at the trial of Watt, 1 December, ibid., folder 4.

7. For slave hiring, see Sarah S. Hughes, "Slaves for Hire: The Allocation of Black Labor in Elizabeth City County, Virginia, 1782–1810," *WMQ*, 3rd ser., 35 (April 1978): 260–86; Sidbury, *Ploughshares into Swords*, 187–201; Jonathan D. Martin, *Divided Mastery: Slave Hiring in the American South* (Cambridge, Mass.: Harvard University Press, 2004); and John Joseph Zaborney, "Slaves for Rent: Slave Hiring in Virginia" (PhD diss., University of Maine, 1997).

8. "Communications made by Gilbert," undated, ExP II, box 8, folder 5; "Information from Mr Foster [from Gilbert] respecting the intended Insurrection Sepr 23d 1800," 23 September 1800, ibid., folder 2; testimony of Prosser's Ben at the trial of Watt, 1 December, ibid., folder 4; testimony of Prosser's Ben at the trial of Michael, 27 September, ibid., folder 2; testimony of Ben Woolfolk at the trial of George Smith, 19 September, ibid.; testimony of Ben Woolfolk at trial of William, 27 September, ibid., folder 2; Henrico County Deed Book 5, 1796–1800, 408. Michael's master, Thomas Goode, was the brother-in-law of Thomas Henry Prosser (see Egerton [19]). Joseph Mosby also rented the plantation and some of the slaves of the estate of William Lewis (see Henrico County Order Book 14, 1808–9, 123–32). For some of the interconnections of the Woolfolk, Graham, and Thilman families, see Caroline County Chancery Cause: Paul Woolfolk and wife v. Infant[s] of Robert Graham (1814-012), and Hanover County Chancery Cause: Benjamin Pollard, admr. of John Thilman v. Henry Hill and wife, admr. of Paul Thilman (1845-014), images online through the Library of Virginia Chancery Records Index at http://www.virginiamemory.com/collections/chancery. Michael's location, and that of his wife, however, is misstated by Egerton (25, 54),

who places him as a hired slave in Richmond, where Egerton claims Michael's wife lived.

9. "[Sam, alias Sam Graham's] Information respecting the Insurrection," undated, ExP II, box 8, folder 5; testimony of Ben Woolfolk at trial of Thornton, 30 October 1800, ibid., folder 3; testimony of Woolfolk at trials of Dick and Randolph, 6 October, ibid.; testimony of Woolfolk at the trial of William, 27 September, ibid., folder 2; Hanover and Caroline County Land Tax Lists, 1815; *Virginia Gazette and General Advertiser*, 7 February 1800. The fact that Dick and Randolph were tried in Henrico rather than Hanover arises from the testimony that they attended one of the meetings at Young's. To arrive at a current "market value" of the slaves executed for the conspiracy, something students often ask, is not easy. John McCusker favors using a "market basket of commodity prices" approach to make such a calculation, using a consumer price index (CPI) of 151 for the year 1800, and an estimated CPI of 2,639 for 2009. This produces a multiplier of roughly 17.5. Applied to the value of Gabriel or Thornton, each would command a price of approximately $8,700 in 2009 currency (John McCusker e-mail to author, 5 March 2009).

10. Testimony of Daniel at the trial of John, 11 September 1800, ExP II, box 8, folder 1; testimony of Prosser's Ben at the trial of Nat [Ned], 11 September, ibid. Egerton (86–87) says Mary Jones's John testified at the trials of Martin and Frank, but the informations filed by George William Smith (see note 1 above) in the cases of Martin and Frank (11 September 1800) identify the witness as Price's John. The evidence for Jones's hire of John to John Harvie appears in "[Joseph Selden and Gervas Storrs] To the keeper of the Jail of the County of Henrico," 5 September 1800, Henrico Judgements and Ended Causes. Richard Jones apparently handled financial affairs for Mary Jones.

11. Testimony of Prosser's Ben at the trial of Charles, 12 September 1800, ExP II, box 8, folder 1; testimonies of Toby and Prosser's Ben at the trial of Will, 11 September, ibid.; testimony of Prosser's Ben at the trial of Gilbert, 22 September, ibid., folder 2.

12. Testimony of Ben Woolfolk at the trial of Jack Gabriel, 29 October 1800, ExP II, box 8, folder 3; testimony of Woolfolk at the trial of John Fells, 30 October, ibid.

13. Testimony of Prosser's Sam at the trial of Jack Bowler, 29 October 1800, ExP II, box 8, folder 3; testimony of Ben Woolfolk at the trial of George Smith, 19 September, ibid., folder 2; testimony of Woolfolk at the trial of Sam Byrd, 27 September, ibid.; "Confession of Solomon . . . ," 15 September, ibid., folder 1; testimony of Prosser's Ben at the trial of Michael, 27 September, ibid., folder 2; testimony of Prosser's Ben at the trial of Gabriel, 6 October, ibid., folder 3; testimony of Daniel at trial of John, 11 September, ibid., folder 1; testimony of Woolfolk at trial of Billy, 1 October, ibid., folder 3; testimony of Woolfolk at trial of Lewis, 1 October, ibid.

14. "Confession of Solomon . . . ," 15 September 1800, ExP II, box 8, folder 1; testimony of Prosser's Ben at the trial of Solomon, 11 September, ibid.; testimony

of Prosser's Ben at the trial of Gabriel, 6 October, ibid., folder 3; testimony of Price's John at the trial of Gilbert, 22 September, ibid., folder 2; testimony of Price's John at the trial of Ben Woolfolk, 16 September, ibid., folder 2; testimony of Prosser's Ben at the trial of Ben Woolfolk, 16 September, ibid.; communications of Ben Woolfolk, 17 September, ibid. The trial records from Caroline County do not indicate that the recruits there had specific targets among the white population, but that probably results from the need to prove only agreement to join to obtain a conviction. Woolfolk provided much of this testimony, and he may not have been privy to individual wishes to attack a specific owner or other whites at the time or on the way to their rendezvous.

15. For the manumission activities of Quakers and Methodists, see McColley, *Slavery and Jeffersonian Virginia*, 141–62; Wolf, *Race and Liberty in the New Nation*, 39–129; and Peter Joseph Albert, "The Protean Institution: The Geography, Economy, and Ideology of Slavery in Post-Revolutionary Virginia (PhD diss., University of Maryland, 1976), 267–307. For the Methodist pronouncement in May, see "The Address of the General Conference of the Methodist Episcopal Church, to All Their Brethren and Friends in the United States" (Baltimore, 1800) (Evans no. 37957), in *Early American Imprints, Series I: Evans, 1639-1800* (digital edition published by Readex, A Division of Newsbank; access by subscription) [subsequent citations to sources found in this series will be by Evans number]; and Sylvia R. Frey, *Water from the Rock: Black Resistance in a Revolutionary Age* (Princeton, N.J.: Princeton University Press, 1991), 256–57. The Address, or a report of it, appeared in the *Federal Gazette and Baltimore General Advertiser* of 21 May 1800, and in the *Kentucky Gazette* of 1 September 1800, but it may not have appeared in Virginia papers. Frey indicates that the broadside itself was not circulated in the South (see Lacy, *Deliver Us from Evil*, 86–88).

16. Testimony of Price's John at trial of Frank, 12 September 1800, ExP II, box 8, folder 1; testimony of Billy at trial of Martin, 12 September, ibid.; testimony of Price's John at trial of Sam Byrd, 27 September, ibid., folder 2; testimony of Ben Woolfolk at trial of Abraham, 12 September, ibid., folder 1; testimony of Woolfolk at trial of Gabriel, 6 October, ibid., folder 3; testimony of David at trial of Isaac, 11 September, ibid., folder 1; testimony of Prosser's Ben at trial of Gabriel, 6 October, ibid., folder 3; testimony of Price's John at trial of Gilbert, 22 September, ibid., folder 2; testimony of Prosser's Ben at trial of Isaac, 11 September, ibid., folder 1; testimony of Woolfolk at trial of King, 25 September, ibid., folder 2; testimony of Prosser's Ben at trial of Isham, 15 September, ibid., folder 1; *Richmond Examiner*, 16 September 1800. The trial record of Burton's George on 13 September does not include any testimony, because he was acquitted. But, since the words reported by Callender in his published account of the trial are the same as those that are recorded in the trial of Isham on 15 September, and because the informations filed against the two brothers name the same two witnesses, it is likely the surviving testimony duplicates the unrecorded statements.

17. Testimony of Daniel at the trial of John, 11 September 1800, ExP II, box 8, folder 1; testimony of Daniel at the trial of Isaac, 11 September, ibid.; testimony of

Toby at the trial of Will, 11 September, ibid.; *Philadelphia Aurora*, 23 September 1800. See also the *Papers of Thomas Jefferson*, 32:137. As Sidbury (*Ploughshares into Swords*, 81n54) has already noted, Egerton (205n59) states, "There is . . . no evidence to support the assertion . . . that all blacks 'were to be forced to join the rebels or die like whites.'"

18. Testimony of Ben Woolfolk at trial of Randolph, 6 October 1800, ExP II, box 8, folder 3; "[Sam alias Sam Graham's] Information respecting the Insurrection," undated, ibid., folder 5. The threat against the two was serious. When Primus testified in two Caroline trials, he claimed he knew no one involved in a conspiracy, likely committing perjury when he did so. A man named Bristol also testified at one of the Caroline trials, but his statement was not recorded, nor was his owner identified, so he may not have been the same individual (see chapter 5).

19. Testimony of Prosser's Ben at the trial of Solomon, 11 September, 1800, ExP II, box 8, folder 1; testimony of Prosser's Ben at the trial of Gabriel, 6 October, ibid., folder 3; testimony of Toby at the trial of Will, 11 September, ibid., folder 1; testimony of Prosser's Ben at trial of Ben Woolfolk, 16 September, ibid., folder 2; testimony of Ben Woolfolk at trial of Sam Byrd Jr., 27 September, ibid.; testimony of Pharoah at trial of Solomon, 11 September, ibid., folder 1; testimony of Daniel at the trial of Isaac, 11 September, ibid.; Mullin, *Flight and Rebellion*, 149–50. Mullin thought the numbers were distorted for recruiting purposes. The claim of 400 horsemen engaged in Richmond is close to the total of 461 horses and mules taxed in the town in 1800, and is probably a similar type of claim to that of the 1,000 men enlisted in town—which is to say, everybody. The printer of the *Journal of the Senate of the Commonwealth of Virginia* . . . (Richmond, 1800 [1801]) (Shaw–Shoemaker no. 1586) correctly reported (p. 32) the 10,000 figure, but inflated the Richmond numbers to 10,000 and the Caroline recruits to 6,000 through typographical errors (see *Early American Imprints, Series II: Shaw-Shoemaker, 1801-1819* [digital edition published by Readex, A Division of Newsbank; access by subscription]. Subsequent citations to sources found in this series will be by Shaw–Shoemaker number).

20. Communications of Ben Woolfolk, 17 September 1800, ExP II, box 8, folder 2; testimony of Prosser's Ben at trial of Solomon, 11 September, ibid., folder 1; testimony of Ben Woolfolk at trial of Sam Byrd Jr., 27 September, ibid., folder 2; "Information from Mr Foster [from Gilbert] respecting the intended Insurrection Sepr 23d 1800," 23 September, ibid., folder 2. John Foster also reported that Price's John said that men put their marks on paper when they enlisted at a barbecue at Prosser's (see "Information respecting insurrection received of John Foster, September 9th 1800," ibid., folder 1). Lists mentioned in testimony play a role in charges by Egerton that Monroe suppressed evidence for political reasons (see chapter 5).

21. Testimony of Ben Woolfolk at trial of Sam Byrd Jr., 27 September 1800, ExP II, box 8, folder 2; "Communications of Ben alias Ben Woolfolk," 17 September, ibid. (my emphasis).

22. Testimony of Price's John at trials of: Frank, 12 September, 1800, ExP II, box 8, folder 1; Sam Graham, 29 September, ibid., folder 2; Sawney, 13 September, ibid., folder 1; Laddis, 16 September, ibid., folder 2; Sam Byrd Jr., 27 September, ibid.; Martin, 12 September, ibid., folder 1; George Smith, 19 September; and Gilbert, 22 September, ibid., folder 2; Sidbury, *Ploughshares into Swords*, 71. George William Smith listed Price's John as a witness at the trial of Prosser's Peter on 15 September, but no testamentary evidence from that trial seems to have survived. Given the limited range of John's testimony, it is likely he described Peter's standing and his joining Gabriel at one of the meetings at Young's spring. Egerton (66) places Peter, as well as Gregory's Charles and Billy, at the 10 August meeting at Young's spring, but trial evidence does not indicate the presence of the latter two.

23. "Information from Mr Foster [from Gilbert] respecting the intended Insurrection Sepr 23d 1800," 23 September, ExP II, box 8, folder 2. Sidbury reports there was a free black man named Toby who carried the post to Amherst in 1795 (see *Ploughshares into Swords*, 64n19).

24. King's case was tried on 25 September before the Richmond court, where he was found guilty. Nicholas appealed to the court for a recommendation of clemency, but the sitting aldermen refused. The decision was reported to Monroe, but someone noted as an endorsement that no trial testimony accompanied the case. On 3 October, Nicholas obtained a statement, signed by the mayor and recorder and three of the aldermen who sat on the case, which was a reconstruction of the testimony from notes and memory—an action taken "to do whatever with propriety they can do to gratify the wish" of Attorney General Nicholas—which was then submitted to the executive. Another, undated statement of some of the testimony of Woolfolk at this trial also exists. Both accounts contain similar statements of slaying the white people like sheep. The council granted a reprieve on 10 October, saving King from the mass executions that day, the first of several respites he received; he would be later transported (see ExP II, box 8, folders 2, 3, 5; and *Council Journals*, 1799–1801, 272).

25. Egerton, 53; Sidbury, *Ploughshares into Swords*, 87–92; William Mosby to Monroe, 10 November 1800, ExP II, box 8, folder 4; Christopher Hudson to Monroe, 24 September, ibid., folder 2; testimony of Nutty at the trial of Isham, 15 September, ibid., folder 1; W. Claiborne to Monroe, 15 February 1801, ExP I, box 3, folder 8. For a recent assessment of the emphasis on resistance in slave historiography, see Ben Schiller, "Selling Themselves: Slavery, Survival, and the Path of Least Resistance," *49th Parallel* 23 (Summer 2009): 1–23, http://www.49thparallel .bham.ac.uk/back/issue23/schiller.pdf. Schiller argues that making almost all actions into "defiant assertions of self and communal worth . . . risks constructing an essentialist history in which the enslaved remain no less dehumanised than they were in the racist accounts . . . justly consigned to the historical dustbin," and he makes note of Edward Baptist's observation "that valorising resistance effectively devalues survival and brands those that simply endured their enslavement

as inadequate, tragically implicated in the very mechanisms of social control and racial objectification that sustained their bondage" (ibid., 1–2).

26. "Confession of Solomon . . . ," 15 September 1800, ExP II, box 8, folder 1; testimony of Prosser's Ben at the trial of Gabriel, 6 October, ibid., folder 3. In the submission by Monroe to the General Assembly of the evidence of the conspiracy copied from the documents relayed to the executive, Leighton Wood apparently misread some scratched-out letters in Solomon's confession as an abbreviation for North and rendered Caroline as Carolina. He copied Caroline correctly three lines later. The mistake was not caught and was printed in the *Journal of the Senate* (1800 [1801]) (p. 26), from whence it entered Aptheker's account of the plot (see *American Negro Slave Revolts*, 226).

27. Testimony of Daniel at the trial of John, 11 September 1800, ExP II, box 8, folder 1; "Information from Mr Foster [from Gilbert] respecting the intended Insurrection Sepr 23d 1800," 23 September, ibid., folder 2; Caroline County Personal Property Taxes, 1784–96; Hanover County Personal Property Taxes, 1797–99; *The Papers of George Washington*, Retirement Series, ed. Dorothy Twohig et al. (Charlottesville: University of Virginia Press, 1998), 2:389–92, 430–31; Francis Corbin to Thomas Jefferson, 30 April 1814 (image 427), Thomas Jefferson Papers, Series I: General Correspondence, 1651–1827, Library of Congress, Manuscript Division, http://memory.loc.gov/cgi-bin/query/P?mtj:2:./temp/~ammem_OT41::. Egerton (43–44, 199n34) assumes that the unnamed man at Yorktown was Quersey, possibly a member of the French forces there, but no evidence links the two. Egerton notes that Corbin reported two unnamed whites on a tax list (for the year 1797 in text, 1799 in the note), apparently to suggest that Quersey was likely one of them. But the man named Dequasay, who was most likely Quersey, moved to Hanover soon after Corbin moved to Caroline. Dequasay is listed on the Caroline 1796 rolls, but Corbin not until 1797, his arrival probably coming after the 1796 list was compiled. I have not found the alleged French encourager other than in the records cited. Egerton says that Corbin became estranged from the Federalists, and hence pro-French/Republican, after Washington failed to give him the commission, but the only cited evidence of his political stances afterward was not expressed until 1818, and it reveals no connection to his disappointment with Washington. Politics had changed much over the preceding twenty years (see "The Corbin Family," *Virginia Magazine of History and Biography* 30 [July 1922]: 317).

28. Testimony of Prosser's Ben at the trial of Solomon, 11 September 1800, ExP II, box 8, folder 1; "Information from Mr Foster [from Gilbert] respecting the intended Insurrection Sepr 23d 1800," 23 September, ibid., folder 2. Egerton's interpretation of the conspiracy posits a coalition of enslaved blacks and poor whites. The existence of the two Frenchmen are key to his portrayal of the event, so much so that he tries to establish their identities in an appendix. He claims one of them was Charles Quersey, discussed above. The second, he argues, was Alexander Beddenhurst, or Weddenhurst, whom he states was identified by Gilbert "as a Frenchman." Gilbert never mentioned Beddenhurst, nor did he ever

suggest that Quersey was one of the two Frenchmen, instead maintaining that he never heard their names. Beddenhurst is only known through a bitterly partisan account of the aborted uprising published in the Fredericksburg *Virginia Herald* on 23 September 1800. It gives an anecdote of a man called General John Scott, reputedly one of the leaders in the plot, who was to lead the recruits out of Petersburg but who was captured while trying to board a stage to Norfolk. Scott reportedly carried a note "directing him to apply at the corner house of Coat's ally, Budd street, Philadelphia" for Alexander "Beddenhurst or Weddenhurst, who would furnish him with all things needful." Egerton never mentions Budd Street. It was later renamed New Market Street, and at the time was located some distance away, in the Northern Liberties. It did not touch Coates Alley, making the address less accurate than Egerton claims. Egerton also states that Scott was headed to John Boulanger's French boarding house, which he says sat on a corner of Coates Alley, and where he reported Beddenhurst rented a room. John Boulanger appears in Philadelphia directories in 1795 and 1796 as operating such an establishment, but at some distance to the south, at 40 Race Street, which runs parallel to Coates. Boulanger reappears in 1797 running a similar house at 171 North Front Street, a site closer to the alley, but after that he disappears from the city's directories. There is no evidence for either of Egerton's claims, that Beddenhurst rented a room from Boulanger or that he "was often," or ever had been, in Virginia. That Beddenhurst is the other Frenchman, or that he had ever been in Virginia, can only be conjecture. John Scott was reportedly the slave of a man named Greenhow, but was hired to someone named McCrea, who had tried to intercept the alleged absconding conspirator. But Scott was never named in any of the testimony, confessions, or lists compiled of the conspiracy, nor is there any slave with an owner identified as a Greenhow or McCrea. Indeed, for a man who was headed to Philadelphia to obtain arms, as Egerton claims (an unlikely effort, with the conspiracy collapsed), it is curious that Scott was never tried. Perhaps he expired from his dive into the river in his effort to escape, since the water was low, but no effort to seek compensation for him appears to have been made, as was often done for slaves who died while incarcerated or before they could be tried—as in the case of Jacob, discussed elsewhere. Given these problems, one might imagine other scenarios. Since the note was reported as stating only that Beddenhurst "would furnish him with all things needful," rather than, as Egerton presents it (i.e., he "would furnish [them] with [guns and] all things needful"), it is possible to draw other speculative conclusions from the same and additional evidence. A slave named John Scott at the Petersburg mill of Richard Bate ran away from him in the summer of 1799. Bate described the one-eyed, twenty-five-year-old man as being known as a waterman in Norfolk, where he was believed headed. What if Scott was simply making another attempt, this time carrying a note based on bits of information supplied by a sailor, white or black, who plied the waters between Philadelphia and Petersburg, Richmond, or Norfolk? Perhaps Beddenhurst was a sympathetic source of aid for a runaway reaching Philadelphia. Perhaps Scott had been taken up, sold to Greenhow, hired to McCrea, and then ran again. Perhaps he was one of the "usual suspects." As the arresting story of his capture spread, it may have picked up speculations about a role in the conspiracy. With Gabriel and Jack Bowler, the most significant conspirators still at large at the time, it would be reassuring to catch a "general." Given the crisis in Richmond, one could well imagine the rumors that could build around this incident—rumors that could well serve a Federalist editor's purposes, rumors that could lead to claims of a correspondence with Philadelphia, Petersburg, and Norfolk, all towns named in the anecdote. In addition to Scott, there was a Captain John McRae in Petersburg. Or he might be Alexander McRae, a Republican member of the council who, the summer before, had allegedly threatened to lead a mob in Richmond to "tear down every house in Brick Row" if a posse of Federalists harmed the print shop of Meriwether Jones, the employer of James Callender. If so, McRae might represent one of those "redoubtable democrats" whose presumed loose talk about equality might further inflame a Federalist editor's mind—or that of a political opponent who thought that such talk could have inspired slaves like John Scott or Gabriel. While there may have been two Frenchmen involved, and one might have been Quersey, there is no evidence, direct or circumstantial, that would warrant pinning Beddenhurst with the identity of the other (see Egerton, 44, 182–85). Among the Philadelphia directories examined where the name Boulanger was found were: Edmund Hogan, *The Prospect of Philadelphia . . . 1795* (Evans no. 28845), 74; Hogan, *The Prospect of Philadelphia . . . 1796*, 2nd ed. (Evans no. 30571), 74; *Stephen's Philadelphia Directory, for 1796* (Evans no. 31235), 19; and Cornelius William Stafford, *The Philadelphia Directory, for 1797* (Evans no. 32868), 30. Each of these works appears in *Early American Imprints, Series I*. Philadelphia directories were examined through 1802, the later ones appearing in *Early American Imprints, Series II: Shaw-Shoemaker, 1801–1819*. Several of these contained street locations. See also Jefferson M. Moak, *Philadelphia Street Name Changes*, rev. ed. (Philadelphia, 2002), 26, 37; and *Scott's Map of the Consolidated City of Philadelphia* (Philadelphia, 1855). I am indebted to Billy Smith for sending me a map of Philadelphia of the late-1790s constructed for his research, and for his caution about the state of Philadelphia's streets. For the confrontation involving McRae, see Durey, *"Hammer of Truth,"* 118–19. That "McCrae" and "McRae" could be the same name, see Thomas Booth to Capt. Alexander McCrae, 5 October 1800, ExP II, box 8, folder 3. Egerton actually gives McRae the name Alexander, but the newspaper report does not provide the first name. The Bate advertisement for John Scott appears in the *Norfolk Herald*, 3 August 1799. It can be found at the marvelous Geography of Slavery website, http://www2.vcdh .virginia.edu/gos/browse/browse_ads.php?state=VA&locale=32670&placetype =all&year=&month=&rows=10&numResults=642&page=47.

29. "Communications of Ben alias Ben Woolfolk," 17 September 1800, ExP II, box 8, folder 2; Norfolk *Epitome of the Times*, 6 October 1800; *Norfolk Herald*, 2 October 1800. Apparently, the group of 150 had gathered without anyone's reported notice until it was revealed by two white women who lived "with some negroes." It is also interesting that this scare did not emerge, or at least become

public, until Gabriel had been captured in nearby Norfolk, which brought the plot closer to home and probably provoked greater local scrutiny of suspicious characters. On 15 September, the Norfolk borough aldermen, "taking into consideration the alarming accounts received of an insurrection of the negroes in the City of Richmond," requested the borough militia to patrol, "as a timely precaution." They made no mention of local activities as a reason for their action. The Norfolk County court records are silent about any response to the gathering (see Norfolk City Hustings Court Order Book 10, 1800–1801, 25; and Norfolk County Order Book, 19 August 1799 to 18 May 1801, folios 153–96). Norfolk records reveal nothing about the gathering, because it did not happen in Norfolk. Egerton's account (68, 98–99, 216n12, 216n13) of the affair is confused. He first states that the slaves gathered toward the end of August, when the only report of the rendezvous states it took place during the first weekend in September. In response to the gathering, he reports that Thomas Newton called out the militia and "bound several over for trial," which trial he claims began in the Norfolk Courthouse in mid-October. He then claims that two men were tried but that the outcome of the trials was not known, since, he reports, the Norfolk County Court records are lost. He reasonably assumes that if the jailed would have been found guilty, a copy of the record would have appeared in the file of Condemned Slaves in the state archives in Richmond. But the incident actually occurred in and about Suffolk, which is in Nansemond County (where the records have been destroyed), rather than in Norfolk (where the records still survive), and from where the reports originated. His statement that Thomas Newton, of Norfolk, called out the militia, and that Newton bound over for trial some of the suspects, is an erroneous attribution based on an incorrect sense of the location of Suffolk. Egerton also identifies the report of the *Epitome of the Times* (he used the reprinted story appearing in the *Virginia Argus* on 10 October 1800) as having been based on the words of a magistrate, but that is only a surmise as well, and he presents some of the newspaper account as being the actual words of Newton, a tactic he uses elsewhere for interpretive purposes. There is no indication these were Newton's actual words, and it is unlikely they were.

30. Testimony of Prosser's Ben at trial of Isaac, 11 September 1800, ExP II, box 8, folder 1; testimony of Prosser's Ben at trial of Gilbert, 22 September, ibid., folder 2; "Communications of Ben alias Ben Woolfolk," 17 September, ibid.; testimony of Prosser's Ben at trial of Martin, 12 September, ibid., folder 1; testimony of Prosser's Ben at trial of Gabriel, 6 October, ibid., folder 3; testimony of Prosser's Ben at trial of Watt, 1 December, ibid., folder 4; testimony of Ben Woolfolk at trial of Gabriel, 6 October, ibid., folder 3; testimony of Prosser's Ben at trial of Jack Bowler, 29 October, ibid.; testimony of Prosser's Ben at trial of Laddis, 16 September, ibid., folder 2; testimony of Ben Woolfolk at trial of Dick, 6 October, ibid., folder 3; testimony of Ben Woolfolk at trial of John Fells, 30 October, ibid.; testimony of Prosser's Ben at trial of Charles, 12 September, ibid., folder 1.

31. Testimony of Daniel at trial of Isaac, 11 September 1800, ExP II, box 8, folder 1; "Confession of Solomon . . . ," 15 September, ibid.; testimony of Ben Woolfolk

at trial of Gabriel, 6 October, ibid., folder 3; testimony of Prosser's Ben at trial of Jupiter, 15 September, ibid., folder 1; "Information from Mr Foster [from Gilbert] respecting the intended Insurrection Sepr 23d 1800," 23 September, ibid., folder 2; "Communications made by Gilbert," undated, ibid., folder 5; Henrico Deed Book 2, 1785–88, 211. Randolph stated that Cowley was forty-five years old, which would make him about sixty in 1800. Egerton (175) cites an obituary in the Richmond *Commercial Compiler*, 10 February 1820, that reported Cowley's age at death at *"one hundred and twenty-five years"* (italics in original newspaper account). It misreported that Cowley, who purchased his own freedom, had been freed "by the Executive as a reward for his revolutionary services." One tip that Cowley's reported age was not accurate was the final admonition: "Let those who read this notice, beware of vice, and become votaries of temperance." Thus, the obituary was as much an advertisement for temperance as a notice of the elderly doorkeeper's death. It is not clear how many arms were in the capitol. In July 1799, a report stated that there were forty-six muskets, forty-five bayonets, and forty-three cartridge boxes out of fifty each formerly issued to a Richmond company, "in the care of the Keeper of the Capitol"—that is, Robert Cowley—but that all but one or two were "entirely out of repair . . . very rusty and appear to have been wholly neglected since they were issued." Twenty-seven more muskets and twenty-three bayonets were added to this stash by December, if not the nearly four thousand more muskets recently arrived under contract with the state. It is not clear if these were the arms seen by Gabriel the following summer or what their condition was by August 1800 (see *Calendar of Virginia State Papers*, 9:36, 64–65ff.).

32. Testimony of Prosser's Ben at trial of Isaac, 16 September 1800, ExP II, box 8, folder 2; testimony of Ben Woolfolk at trial of Gilbert, 22 September, ibid.; "Confession of Solomon . . . ," 15 September, ibid., folder 1; "Lucas or locust a white man," an undated list of suspects, ibid., folder 5. Palmer, in the *Richmond Times*, 28 December 1890, claims that the news of a slave uprising was a reference to an event on the Eastern Shore of Virginia, but I have found no indication of one in 1800. Aptheker, who faithfully reported such instances, notes none in *American Negro Slave Revolts*. One wonders if the Lucas/Locust offer could be an example of the kind of provocative exchanges that might have taken place between working white men and working black men. While it is not clear how Gabriel learned of the rumored revolt from Gregory's overseer—if he was told directly, rather than just overhearing a conversation—it also hints at what might seem to us to be an unlikely topic of conversation between a black man and a white man.

33. "Communications of Ben alias Ben Woolfolk," 17 September 1800, ExP II, box 8, folder 2. Since Jupiter had told Gabriel of access to the capitol on 8 August, and since Gilbert reported that the men had entered the capitol to look at the arms "one Sunday . . . early in the day," I assume it was Sunday, 10 August, obviously before the funeral and before the later assembly where Gabriel told the men that the muster was to take place on 30 August. Hence, this meeting seems

to have occurred between the inspection of the capitol and the post-funeral assembly at the spring. As noted, establishing an exact chronology is difficult.

34. "Communications of Ben alias Ben Woolfolk," 17 September 1800, ExP II, box 8, folder 2.

35. Testimony of Price's John at trial of Gabriel, 6 October 1800, ExP II, box 8, folder 3; testimony of Ben Woolfolk at trial of Gabriel, 6 October, ibid.; testimony of Prosser's Ben at trial of Jack Bowler, 29 October, ibid.; testimony of Price's John at trial of Jack Bowler, 29 October, ibid.

36. Testimony of Prosser's Sam at trial of Jack Bowler, 29 October 1800, ExP II, box 8, folder 3; testimony of Prosser's Ben at trial of Daniel, 15 September, ibid., folder 1; "[Sam alias Sam Graham's] Information respecting the Insurrection," undated, ibid., folder 5; testimony of Ben Woolfolk at trial of Thornton, 30 October, ibid., folder 3; testimony of Prosser's Ben at trial of Michael, 11 September, ibid., folder 1; testimony of Prosser's Ben at trial of Sam, 15 September, ibid.; testimony of Ben Woolfolk at trial of Gabriel, 6 October, ibid., folder 3; Sidbury, *Ploughshares into Swords*, 87; Egerton, 51. The ubiquity of juxtaposing liberty and death can be seen in a report in the *Boston Gazette*, 28 November 1791, of events in the early stages of the revolt in St. Domingue, where it was reported that the "Black Chief" stated, "This is our motto, liberty or death; for we will die or conquer."

3. The Deluge

1. J. Grammar to Augustine Davis, 9 August 1800, ExP I, box 2, folio 5; Proceedings of the Common Council, Petersburg, 1798–1805 (MS, Clerk of Common Council Office, Petersburg), folio 25.

2. Petersburg Register of Free Negroes and Mulattoes, 1794–1819, entry nos. 21, 35, 43, 80, 122, 133, 135, 154–99. In the register entry for Jesse Bird, no. 199, the affidavit of one Walker Halls is noted. No Walker Halls exists on the Essex tax rolls, but a Walker Haws does, so this is probably a misreading of a "w" as two "l's" by clerk Grammar. Walker Haws appears as a tithable on the Essex County personal property tax lists in 1791–92, but then disappears, only to reappear in 1795 on both King and Queen and Caroline County tax lists. In that year, he apparently received his inheritance of 1,394 acres from his father's Caroline estate, and acquired 100 more. He still held 1,494 acres in Caroline County in 1799, and finally settled in King William County (see Elizabeth Hawes Ryland, "Hawes Family of Caroline Co., Va.," *WMQ*, 2nd ser., 15 [April 1935]: 144, 147). The Caroline County connection is intriguing. Reuben Byrd, who registered as no. 198, became the second man of that name in Petersburg. Since at least 1795, a man named Reuben Byrd had been appearing on the Petersburg personal property tax lists, identified as a free black man. In 1803, this Reuben Byrd appears as a forty-six-year-old stonemason on a city list, the same census in which the second Reuben Byrd, and the one who registered in 1800, is listed as now being age twenty-six

and a carpenter. In 1810, when the elder Byrd finally registered, identified again as a stonemason but having aged only one year, he claimed to have been born free in Essex. For white discomfort with the growing free black population of Petersburg, see Nicholls, "Strangers Setting among Us: The Sources and Challenge of the Urban Free Black Population of Early Virginia," *Virginia Magazine of History and Biography* 108, no. 2 (2000): 155–79.

3. ExLB, 1794–1800, 376; James McClurg to Monroe, 10 August 1800, ExP I, box 2, folder 5.

4. *Richmond Examiner,* 5 September 1800; *Council Journals,* 1799–1801, 220, 226, 284–85, 322; ExLB, 1794–1800, 391; "[Mr. Thilman's] Information respecting an insurrection of the slaves [in] Han[o]v[e]r, 1800," undated, ExP II, box 8, folder 5; Robert Temple to Monroe, 12 October 1800, ExP I, box 3, folder 11; B. Temple Jr. to Monroe, undated, ibid. Located in ExP I, box 3, folder 1, are copies of the Hanover Oyer and Terminer court meeting of 20 October to establish the identity of Liberty, who had turned himself in, which reveal that the date of the original trial was 20 August. Included is a petition from owner Lydia Mallory, a letter of 28 October of Richard Littlepage, and another of 1 November to John Pendleton, which claims that Liberty had earlier been tried for a capital crime and that he was perhaps "among the greatest villains in this county." In spite of this, Liberty was eventually pardoned, on 23 December. Harry had been captured by two slave men within days of the jailbreak. Francis Baylor, of New Market in Caroline, pled for clemency for him, apparently ignorant of his escape (see Baylor to Monroe, 31 August, ExP I, box 2, folder 6). The cases of Liberty and Harry, and the published proclamation for them, helps place Thilman's undated account of the jail escape and the two bayonet-carrying men as occurring *before* the conspiracy was betrayed. Egerton (98) states that one of Thilman's slaves, a man named Holmy (a misreading of Holmes), was tried along with another, unidentified slave in the Hanover Court, for which no records survive. These two men, he argues, were the ones who broke out of jail, and he claims they "were never retaken." He assigns no specific date to the event, but treats it as having happened in October or November. Importantly, no proclamation was issued for Holmes and the other slave, which raises doubts about Egerton's tale. In *Flight and Rebellion* (154, 202n40), Mullin treats the assisted jailbreak as taking place in November because Thilman's undated account was filed in a folder dated "November 1800" at the time Mullin examined the record, and Egerton may have followed his lead. It has since been re-filed with other undated materials. There do not appear to have been any trials held in Hanover for the conspirators that led to convictions. Some Hanover slaves held by Thilman, like Randolph, Bristol, and Dick, were tried in Henrico, while other Thilman slaves, like Thornton, Scipio, and George, were tried in Caroline. These men were not tried in Hanover, because the evidence revealed their criminal conspiring took place at Young's spring at the Brook or on the Caroline side of Littlepage's Bridge. Where the alleged criminal conversations took place determined which court had jurisdiction. Most likely, it was for this reason that, based on information from Ben Woolfolk, Monroe

ordered a list of men taken up and then indicated where they were to be tried. Holmes and several others were to face trial in Caroline. None were ordered tried in Hanover (see the undated document endorsed "Information respecting the Insurrection. I requested Mickelborough Young a Gentleman of Caroline . . . ," ExP II, box 8, folder 5; the document ends, "The foregoing Negroes are implicated by the discovery of Ben alias Ben Woolfolk").

5. Testimony of Ben Woolfolk at trial of Thornton, 30 October 1800, ExP II, box 8, folder 3; testimony of Ben Woolfolk at trial of John Fells, 30 October, ibid.; testimony of Prosser's Ben at trial of Daniel, 15 September, ibid., folder 1; testimony of Daniel at trial of Isaac, 11 September, ibid.; testimony of Prosser's Ben at trial of Watt, 1 December, ibid., folder 4; *American Citizen*, 2 October 1800.

6. Mosby Sheppard to Monroe, 30 August 1800, ExP I, box 2, folder 6; Henrico County Deed Book 5, 1796–1800, 624; "A pay abstract of the Richmond Troop of Cavalry . . . 27 April 1801," Auditor of Public Accounts, Item 758: Insurrections, 1800–1801 [hereafter cited as Auditor's Item 758]; William Mosby to Monroe, 10 November 1800, ExP II, box 8, folder 4. Both Egerton (71) and Sidbury (*Ploughshares into Swords*, 109) attribute Mosby Sheppard with permitting the self-purchased emancipation of this man named Gabriel, citing Sheppard's account book of 1796. The deed of manumission of 1799 shows that Philip Sheppard purchased Gabriel from the estate and when reimbursed by Gabriel filed the deed, with Mosby Sheppard and Benjamin Sheppard serving as witnesses. The Henrico Order Book 9, 1799–1801, p. 80, also indicates that Philip was the formal manumitter. Mosby Sheppard was an executor of his father's will, a responsibility he renounced in 1803 (see Henrico Order Book 10, 1801–3, 567).

7. ExLB, 5 October 1800–18 October 1803, 34 [hereafter cited as ExLB, 1800–1803]; James McClurg to Monroe, undated, ExP II, box 8, folder 5. A copy of Monroe's statement to the assembly appears, as cited here, in the Executive Letter Book, but is also included in the *Journal of the Senate* (1800 [1801]), 11–13 (Shaw–Shoemaker no. 1583). In Egerton's account of Pharoah and Tom's warning to Sheppard (70–72), he places the conversation at the Sheppard farm at 11 *p.m.* Saturday night, 30 August, after the downpour began, using the violent storm as an important reason the two men concluded the plot would fail and that they would gain by disclosing it. Lacy K. Ford, in *Deliver Us from Evil* (52), gives a similar account. This is clearly in error, both as to location and time. The mistiming leads to the claim that word did not reach Monroe until Sunday, 31 August. Sheppard's warning is dated 30 August, and Monroe claimed he received it personally from him by "about two in the afternoon" that same day. Monroe then sent a warning to Petersburg, also dated 30 August. Clearly, Tom and Pharoah made their "discovery" before the storm. Egerton also reports that Monroe ordered the arms moved from the capitol to the penitentiary, and since Monroe "fancied himself a military tactician—appointed three aides-de-camp." He cites Harry Ammon, *James Monroe: The Quest for National Identity*, 185–86, as one of his sources, even though Ammon correctly states that Monroe learned of the warning from Mosby Sheppard on Saturday. Monroe did not appoint his military

assistants until 10 or 11 September (see ExLB, 1794–1800, 408–9), which softens Egerton's characterization of Monroe's military propensities. There is no support for Egerton's claim that Monroe ordered the arms removed from the capitol to the penitentiary in the sources he cited, nor is there any record elsewhere that can be found of Monroe's order, although a rumor to that effect reached the Brook *before* the plot was revealed.

8. Testimony of Pharoah at trial of Solomon, 11 September 1800, ExP II, box 8, folder 1; Samuel Mordecai, *Virginia, Especially Richmond in By-Gone Days*, 2nd ed. (Richmond, 1860), 113, 245; entry for Saturday, [August] 30, 1800, James Duvall Diary, 1799–1804, LVA. Solomon later admitted to making twelve swords, while Gabriel allegedly claimed twelve dozen had been made. One wonders whether the word "dozen" might have been inadvertently left out of the confession taken by Storrs and Selden, or if Gabriel exaggerated his stock of weapons. Egerton (55) attributes the idea of transforming the scythe blades into two swords to Will, the slave of John Mosby Sr., and is puzzled that the blacksmiths hadn't come up with the idea. One witness stated only that Will brought two blades to Gilbert to have them made into swords, which Solomon did at the charge of Gabriel, and another witness reported that Will told him that he had joined the conspiracy and "had to carry two Scythe Blades to Solomon to be made into Swords" (see the testimony of Prosser's Ben and the testimony of Holeman's Toby at the trial of Mosby's Will, 11 September 1800, ExP II, box 8, folder 1). No other evidence appears to exist that credits Will with the idea.

9. Mosby to Monroe, 10 November, ExP II, box 8, folder 4; ExLB, 1800–1803, 34; *Philadelphia Aurora*, 23 September 1800; Callender to Jefferson, 13 September 1800, in *Papers of Thomas Jefferson*, 32:136; entries for Saturday, [August] 30, and Sunday, [August] 31, 1800, James Duvall Diary, 1799–1804, LVA.

10. Testimony of Prosser's Ben at trial of Jack Bowler, 29 October 1800, ExP II, box 8, folder 3; testimony of Prosser's Ben at trial of Frank, 12 September, ibid., folder 1; testimony of Prosser's Ben at trial of Michael, 11 September, ibid.; Mosby to Monroe, 10 November, ibid., folder 4; ExLB, 1800–1803, 35.

11. Testimony of Prosser's Ben at trial of Jack Bowler, 29 October 1800, ExP II, box 8, folder 3; testimony of Prosser's Ben at trial of Michael, 27 September, ibid., folder 2.

12. Mosby to Monroe, 10 November 1800, ExP II, box 8, folder 4; Monroe to Mayor of Richmond [McClurg], 1 September 1800, ExLB, 1794–1800, 390.

13. ExLB, 1800–1803, 35–36; Monroe to members of Council of State, ExLB, 1794–1800, 391; George Tucker to St. George Tucker, 1 September 1800, Tucker/Coleman Papers, Correspondence, 4 June 1800–30 June 1803 (microfilm), Swem Library, College of William and Mary, Williamsburg, Va.

14. ExLB, 1794–1800, 390, 392; McClurg to Monroe, 1 September 1800, ExP II, box 8, folder 1. Writing of the 1861 conspiracy in Mississippi, Jordan states, "The term *examine* takes on the stench of euphemism for physical brutality" (see his prescient discussion of whippings and confessions in *Tumult and Silence at Second Creek*, 90–98 [quotation at 94]). The records of Gabriel's plot do not

reveal the use of physical torture, but that does not preclude its existence beyond the recorded verbal threats.

15. Testimony of Moses at trial of Martin, 12 September 1800, ExP II, box 8, folder 1; testimony of an unnamed white man at trial of Sam, 15 September, ibid.; testimony of William Gentry at trial of Michael, 11 September, ibid.; ExLB, 1800–1803, 37; *Council Journals,* 1799–1801, 224. William Gentry served as overseer to James Currie. His lands bordered on the estate of Jacob Smith, whose widow held George Smith (see Henrico County Processioners Returns, 73–74). Egerton (73) incorrectly reports the episode of Michael's capture as that of Isaac's.

16. Testimony of Ben Woolfolk at the trial of Gilbert, 22 September 1800, ExP II, box 8, folder 2; testimony of Ben Woolfolk at the trial of Lewis, 1 October, ibid., folder 3; "Acct of Martin Mims agt The Commonwealth for Maintenance of Negroes," 15 January 1801, Auditor's Item 758. The latter document establishes that Watt had been imprisoned by 15 November but was probably transferred to the Henrico jail on 22 November. Mims submitted an account prior to this one, but I have not found it. It might establish an earlier incarceration of Watt (see *Council Journals,* 1799–1801, 276). In the trial testimony of Gilbert, Woolfolk stated that Gilbert "commenced measuring himself with a rule, and began to write himself a pass," which Egerton (73), apparently not recognizing the physical descriptions in some passes or copies of free black register entries, renders as "commenced measuring himself [paper], and began . . ."

17. *Council Journals,* 1799–1801, 224–26; "[Mr. Thilman's] Information respecting an insurrection of the slaves [in] Han[o]v[e]r 1800," undated, ExP II, box 8, folder 5. Egerton (73) incorrectly, I believe, uses the Thilman statement to describe escape attempts after the conspiracy collapses, and chooses to refer to the arms the men carried not as bayonets but as "crude blades," apparently trying to suggest they were some of the refashioned scythe blades. Elsewhere (79, 210n40), Egerton claims that Gabriel threw away "his scythe sword" when he boarded the schooner to escape to Norfolk. He explains that "the scythe swords were tied to wooden handles and would have resembled a crude bayonet," apparently in an effort to discount "most of the newspaper accounts" that reported "Gabriel was carrying a bayonet fixed on a stick when he boarded . . ." However, the only apparent news report, the *Norfolk Herald* of 25 September 1800, states that Gabriel threw away "a bayonet and a bludgeon." In the same footnote, Egerton cites a letter of 24 September from Thomas Newton to Monroe, in which Newton reports the capture of Gabriel and recounts what he had learned from the slave crewmen. Newton relays that Gabriel "was arm'd with a bayonet fixed on a stick which he threw into the river." In his confession, Ben Woolfolk reported that Jack Bowler had fifty spears made of bayonets fixed on sticks for the initial surge into Richmond. It is puzzling why Egerton reports these weapons as scythe swords, unless he is trying to create more evidence for Gabriel's claim to have produced twelve dozen, most of which were apparently never found.

18. *Council Journals,* 1799–1801, 227–28.

19. ExLB, 1794–1800, 391–93; Robert Quarles to Monroe, 3 September 1800, ExP I, box 2, folder 7. Quarles's letter stated he received the letter by "Cooley" at 4:30 p.m. and it was returned "by Cooley." The force initially ordered to Prosser's Tavern appears to have been later redeployed to Priddy's or Gregory's Tavern, a newer establishment.

20. ExLB, 1800–1803, 37; ExLB, 1794–1800, 395–97.

21. Testimony of Ben Woolfolk at trial of Gilbert, 22 September 1800, ExP II, box 8, folder 2; William Prentis to Monroe, 6 September, ibid., folder 1. See Prentis to Monroe, 9 September, ibid., for evidence that Monroe replied to his earlier inquiry, contrary to Egerton's claim (100). Egerton's account concerning Petersburg officials is otherwise inaccurately reported. McClurg did not warn the Petersburg town fathers (99); Monroe did. William Prentis did not act on orders from Monroe to arrest Reuben and Jesse Byrd (100); he did so after receiving information from someone who had learned of Gilbert's charges from someone who attended Gilbert's trial. See the discussion below for the arrest first of four men, and then the arrest of six more and their subsequent release by Petersburg authorities, and see also Appendix C: Alleged Participants Not Prosecuted. The cases of the Byrds are discussed in chapters 4 and 5.

22. Gervas Storrs and Joseph Selden to Monroe, 8 September 1800, ExP II, box 8, folder 1; *Council Journals*, 1799–1801, 229–32; ExLB, 1794–1800, 399–402.

23. ExLB, 1794–1800, 399; ExLB, 1800–1803, 41; Sidbury, *Ploughshares into Swords*, 123–26; entry for Saturday, 6 September 1800, John Boyce Journal, 1798–1808, LVA. The executive reimbursed Cowley for his trip to Point of Fork and this ride into Chesterfield, the amount of £7.5.6 (see *Council Journals*, 1799–1801, 237).

24. *Council Journals*, 1799–1801, 233, 235. Not all printings of the proclamation for Gabriel carried a description. For example, see the 12 September 1800 issue of the *Virginia Gazette*. Two different proclamations soon appeared. The source of the first description of Gabriel is not known. He was initially described as being about 6 feet, 3 or 4 inches, bony faced, scarred on his head, and about twenty-four or twenty-five, with two front teeth missing, among other noticeable features (see *Norfolk Herald*, 16 September 1800). Later proclamations, which also included the notice for Jack Bowler, carried a description of Gabriel over the name of Prosser, where his missing teeth were not mentioned and his height was reduced to 6 feet, 2 or 3 inches (see the *Richmond Examiner* for 19 September 1800 or the *Virginia Argus* for 23 September 1800 for examples).

25. "Information respecting insurrection received of John Foster, September 9th 1800," 9 September 1800, ExP II, box 8, folder 1.

26. "Information respecting insurrection received of John Foster, September 9th 1800," 9 September 1800, ExP II, box 8, folder 1; Richmond City Common Council Minutes, 1796–1807 (microfilm), 98, LVA; *Council Journals*, 1799–1801, 235. On Foster's list someone placed an asterisk next to Jack Bowler's name, and another appears on the line with the names of Price's Bob and John. None appears

by Sam, who was thought to be able to identify many. It is possible that the two men may have been Bob and John, with another asterisk added by Jack Bowler's name as his involvement became more firmly established following Solomon's statement of 15 September, but Bob seems otherwise absent in the records, even though he was mentioned by Ben Woolfolk. Price's John stated that Sawney was the property of "Mr. Young," but in fact he was hired by William Young from the estate of William Lewis, another indication that Price's John had incomplete knowledge of the conspiracy, even though he recognized men at the meeting. At the same time, Sawney was identified at his trial as belonging to Young. For the clarification of ownership, see Auditor's Item 756. Egerton believes that Elisha Price's James and this man, John, who is identified on the list as "John the property of Mrs. Price," are one and the same, claiming that James was "commonly known by the nickname of John" (74), although he offers no evidence for this. In fact, in the 6 October petition for mercy from the Henrico magistrates on behalf of Elisha Price's James, he is called "Jim or James." Consequently, Egerton does not recognize "Price's John," who served as witness in many of the trials, as the man interrogated by Foster and others. And because of his misidentification, he reports James/John as being sentenced to hang but as being later pardoned. Indeed, James was. But, like Prosser's Ben, Price's John had no information filed against him and was never tried, probably because of the promise of his interrogators that "it was expected he would make some important discoveries by which he might save himself." He did so by surrendering the identity of several of the men who had gathered at Young's spring and escaped prosecution. This precluded the need for a formal pardon. Price's Bob was not tried. For those who were implicated but not prosecuted, see Appendix C: Alleged Participants Not Prosecuted.

27. ExLB, 1794–1800, 404, 408.

28. Col. W. Bentley to Monroe, 8 September 1800, ExP I, box 2, folder 7.

29. Joseph Jones to Monroe, 9 September 1800, ExP II, box 8, folder 1. Jones refers to a letter he sent Monroe the day before, which apparently has not survived. He says in a postscript that, "Just as I was abt sealg this letter I received yrs." This letter of Monroe's has not survived either. It may have been the same as the communication Prentis had just received from Monroe dated 8 September, which is no longer extant, and which may have been shared with Jones.

30. Jones to Monroe, 9 September 1800, ExP II, box 8, folder 1; William Prentis to Monroe, 9 September, ibid.; "Information of some supposed to be acquainted with the intended insurrection 1800," undated, ibid., folder 5; Petersburg Hustings Court Minute Book, 1800–1804, 7; Petersburg Deed Book 2, 1790–1801, 737; Deed Book 3, 1801–11, 7; Petersburg Will Book 2, 1806–27, folios 12, 31; Petersburg *Intelligencer,* 23 August 1805. A young woman named Louisa was noted as living with her grandfather, James Vaughan, in December 1815. Perhaps Vaughan had been released from prison early (see Petersburg Free Black Register, 1794–1819, no. 789). None of these men were tried (see Appendix C:

Alleged Participants Not Prosecuted). On 6 September, as noted above, Prentis had inquired about four "black persons of the following names": Jacob Brandum; Jos, or perhaps Jas, Bartlett; Maclin, or Martin, Bartlett; and John Pidgeon. In Monroe's missing reply of 8 September, he apparently notified Prentis that no evidence had yet appeared against the men. They were apparently then released. Jacob Brandum was a free man of color listed on the Petersburg personal property tax list in 1800, and as a carpenter on an 1803 census of free people of color in Petersburg. He appeared before the Petersburg magistrates on 6 October 1800, along with one Daniel Sullivant, on their recognizance on a breach of peace. The two men were discharged upon their appearance (see "List of people of Colour in Petersburg June 1803," Petersburg City, Free Negroe and Slave Records, oversized box 1, Lists of Free Negroes, 1803, LVA; and Petersburg Hustings Court Minute Book, 1800–1804, 11). By 1810, Cloe Brandon, a forty-six-year-old free woman of color who had been emancipated by Robert Pleasants in Henrico, was identified as Jacob's wife (see Petersburg Free Black Register, 1794–1819, no. 549). The Bartletts and John Pidgeon remain yet undiscovered and may have been slaves. These four individuals were not the same as the six men on the list carried by Capt. Sergeant to Monroe, discussed above.

31. Proceedings of Petersburg Common Council, 1798–1805, folio 26; Goochland Order Book 22, 1799–1801, 438, 482–84, 511, 523, 576–77; James Rush to John Mason, George Town, 10 November 1800, online image available at the Colonial Williamsburg website, http://research.history.org/JDRLibrary/Special _CollectionsDocs/Rush1.cfm.

32. ExLB, 1794–1800, 404–7; *Council Journals,* 1799–1801, 225.

33. ExLB, 1794–1800, 405–9.

34. Informations filed by George William Smith, Henrico Judgements and Ended Causes. In one of the anomalies of the record, on 1 December 1800, Smith obtained a certificate from the Henrico Court that he had prosecuted fifty-nine men, "all the criminals being charged with conspiracy and insurrection," since November 1799. He was also paid $25 for attending five called courts since November 1799 for other slave felons. He soon submitted a petition to the Assembly claiming that since 1 September he had prosecuted fifty-nine "Negroes or slaves" for conspiracy, besides five or six others for other felonies. His petition was accompanied with a certificate, dated 1 December 1800, from the Henrico Court clerk that the court had recommended Smith be paid $5 for each of the conspiracy trials. The delegates rejected the petition, and the Henrico Court subsequently paid him £59. The anomaly arises since the Henrico Order Book only records the trials of fifty-eight men for conspiracy. Smith may have simply miscalculated the total in his claim to the court, an error replicated in his petition, or he may have included the prosecution of Lucy Riddle's Jack for perjury at the conspiracy trial of Elisha Price's James (see petition of George William Smith with certificate of Adam Craig, 1 December 1800, Henrico Legislative Petitions; and Henrico County Order Book 9, 1799–1801, 396, 443, 454).

4. Revenge or Justice?

1. *Papers of James Madison*, 17:407–8; *Papers of Thomas Jefferson* 32:131.

2. Shepherd, *Statutes at Large of Virginia*, 1:125–27; Henrico Order Book 9, 1799–1801, 372. James Rind, the court-appointed attorney for Solomon, served as the defense attorney of record in all the Henrico cases. In 1785, he had witnessed Edmund Randolph's deed of manumission to Robert Cowley. For the procedures of the courts of oyer and terminer, see St. George Tucker, *A Dissertation on Slavery with a Proposal for the Gradual Abolition of It in the State of Virginia* (Philadelphia, 1796), 60–62.

3. Testimony of Prosser's Ben and Pharoah at trial of Solomon, 11 September 1800, ExP II, box 8, folder 1. No evidence exists of Lewis Barret ever being charged or tried, probably because Ben's knowledge of his involvement was secondhand, though he may have been picked up and interrogated. He remains unidentified, but could have been a slave of one of the three Barrets—Anderson, John, or the estate of William—who reported slave holdings on the Richmond personal property tax list of 1800. John Barret was an alderman.

4. Testimony of Prosser's Ben and Toby at trial of Will, 11 September 1800, ExP II, box 8, folder 1. Egerton (83) says that the second trial of the day was John's, the slave of Mary Jones. However, both the order book and the copy of the testimony of the day forwarded to the executive indicate Will was tried second, and John third. Court order books recorded the "orders" of the court and the order in which cases and petitions and matters of record were heard. Any evidence that the sequence of business was other than that recorded in the order book does not seem to exist. As noted elsewhere, Egerton has changed the recorded order of other trials for his narrative and interpretive purposes.

5. Testimony of Daniel and Charles at trial of John, 11 September 1800, ExP II, box 8, folder 1; testimony of Prosser's Ben and Daniel at trial of Isaac, 11 September, ibid.; testimony of Prosser's Ben, Pharoah, Ned, and William Gentry at trial of Michael, 11 September, ibid.; testimony of Prosser's Ben and Wilshire at trial of Ned, 11 September, ibid.; Henrico Order Book 9, 1799–1801, 372–75. Anne Parson's Ned was rendered as Nat in the copy sent to the executive and recopied for the document collection sent to the legislature. Each of the men tried on 11 September had been moved to the jail on 5 September (see "[Joseph Selden and Gervas Storrs] To the keeper of the Jail of the County of Henrico," 5 September, Henrico Judgements and Ended Causes; this document identifies Harvie as the hirer of Jones's John).

6. William Rose to Monroe, 12 September 1800, petition for Solomon, undated, ExP II, box 8, folder 1; ExLB, 1800–1803, 41. Henry Wiencek, who is working on a study of Jefferson and his slaves, kindly compared the handwriting in Solomon's petition with images of Callender's letters to Jefferson, and he believes it is likely the same hand, a conclusion also reached independently by Martha J. King at the Papers of Thomas Jefferson. My thanks to both.

7. The only account describing any of the executions appeared in the *Virginia Gazette* on 30 September 1800, and in both the *Virginia Argus* and the *Richmond Examiner* on 3 October. It exists only because rumors flew about that William Young, who had been implicated by Owen's Michael at the gallows, had promised $5 to each man who would enlist. This led to statements from William Young, John Mayo, and deputy sheriff John M. Sheppard, as well as a statement of the absurdity of the charge from two dozen of Young's most prominent neighbors and the Richmond elite of both political parties. The incident was picked up and used in the Philadelphia papers for their political purposes (see Nicholls, "'Holy Insurrection!'"). Mayo's George was a repeat runaway whose last disappearance began on 25 July 1799. By mid-May 1800, it was feared he had convinced his wife Polly to run from her Hanover master, too (see the *Virginia Gazette and General Advertiser* for 25 August 1790, 22 April 1795, 30 July 1799, and 28 October 1799; and the *Virginia Argus* for 2 September 1800). George also appears on an undated list of suspects (see Appendix C: Alleged Participants Not Prosecuted). Although he cites the newspaper account of Mayo's questioning of Michael, Egerton (104) states that, "When asked for a name, Michael 'collected himself' and went to his death silently," ignoring Michael's naming of Stockdell and Young. Interestingly, there is an undated petition to the Henrico Court from Elizabeth Stockdell, pleading for her slave Gilbert, alias "Eamonds(?)," who had not yet been tried. She claimed that a witness could counter the claim of the state's witness (Price's John[?]) that he had been at William Young's at a particular time, and asked for a delay in his trial. The petition was presented on 17 September, which created some confusion in the court about Gilbert's owner and explains some of the delays in trying Young's Gilbert (see petition of Elizabeth Stockdell (n.d.), filed with information against Gilbert (no. 22), 11 September, Henrico Judgements and Ended Causes; and Henrico County Order Book 9, 1799–1801, 388). Perhaps the confusion was compounded because the Stockdell's once owned the land that William Young purchased from John Young (see Henrico Deed Book 5, 1796–1800, 408). Stockdell's death on 13 July 1798 was noted in the *Virginia Gazette* for 24 July 1798 (cited in Henley Marriage/Obituary Index to Virginia Newspapers, LVA). An execution of a slave named Harris in 1796 is described by Benjamin Latrobe. A jailhouse convert, apparently, he walked to the gallows singing psalms and claiming he would soon be with God. Once there, he climbed into the cart, where he was blindfolded and tied up by a deputy sheriff who then drove off the cart, leaving Harris suspended and strangling (see *The Virginia Journals of Benjamin Henry Latrobe, 1795–1798*, ed. Edward C. Carter et al. [New Haven, Conn.: Yale University Press, 1977], 1:191–92; and Richmond Hustings Court Order Book 3, 1792–97, 492). Cf. Egerton's account of Harris's death (212n21). Only once did the court order more than five slaves executed at one time at the usual place in Richmond, but in that instance the reprieve to Solomon kept the number actually executed the next day to five. Officials may have discovered then that no more than five could have been executed at one time at the existing gallows.

8. Testimony of Prosser's Ben at trial of Billy, 12 September 1800, ExP II, box 8, folder 1; testimony of Prosser's Ben and Price's John at trial of Martin, 12 September, ibid.; testimony of Prosser's Ben and Patrick at trial of Charles, 12 September, ibid.; testimony of Price's John and Prosser's Ben at trial of Frank, 12 September, ibid.; testimony of Billy, Prosser's Ben, and Moses at trial of Martin, 12 September, ibid.; Henrico County Order Book 9, 1799–1801, 375–78. Egerton (86–87) wrongly attributes the testimony of Price's John at the trial of Martin to Jones's John, and claims there was a contradiction between it and that offered by Prosser's Ben as to Gabriel's attitude toward Martin's participation. There is no contradiction if Price's John was describing one of the few scenes he had observed and was apparently unaware of who some of the key individuals really were. Although owned by Sally Price, who lived in the Brook, his hiring in Richmond may have left him out of contact. Consequently, the witness did not understand how Martin and others were stepping forward as apparent plants to encourage others to follow their lead. Prosser's Ben, on the other hand, closely observed the interaction between the two brothers on different occasions. But misunderstanding who was the witness and what was being witnessed led Egerton to suggest that James Rind, the defense attorney, was inept or unobservant for not pointing out the discrepancy. He may have been, but this is not evidence of his abilities.

9. *Council Journals*, 1799–1801, 236–38; Monroe to Mayor of Williamsburg, 12 September 1800, ExLB, 1794–1800, 411. Thilman had personally paid the two men who captured Harry $10 each, and the council reimbursed him that amount and provided $20 more to be divided between the two (see scrap of letter, undated, signed B. Temple Jr., ExP I, box 2, folder 11).

10. *Richmond Examiner*, 12 September 1800; *Virginia Gazette and General Advertiser*, 12 September 1800; *Philadelphia Aurora*, 23 September 1800; *Virginia Argus*, 16 September 1800.

11. *Council Journals*, 1799–1801, 239; Adam Craig to Philip Norborne Nicholas, 13 September 1800, ExP II, box 8, folder 1; Storrs and Selden to Monroe, 13 September, ibid.

12. Because George was acquitted, no trial testimony was forwarded to the executive. But Callender's report of the trial, noted below, comes close to replicating the trial testimony given against Isham on the next Monday. The quotation here comes from Isham's trial record (Henrico County Order Book 9, 1799–1801, 378–79; testimony of Prosser's Ben and Price's John at trial of Sawney, 13 September 1800, ExP II, box 8, folder 1; informations against George [no. 14] and Frank [no. 13], 11 September, Henrico Judgements and Ended Causes; Thomas Newton to Monroe, 24 September, ExP II, box 8, folder 2, ibid.). Egerton (88, 213n31) wrongly dates the trial of Elisha Price's James as 13 September and says the case was repeated by mistake in the order book as one occurring on 30 September. The order book is correct. His misdating has consequences for his account of Ben Woolfolk's negotiations for a pardon, discussed below.

13. Callender to Jefferson, 13 September 1800, in *Papers of Thomas Jefferson*, 32:137; "Confession of Solomon . . . ," 15 September 1800, ExP II, box 8, folder 1.

Egerton (87) finds it ironic that "Mosby Sheppard, who had first sounded the alarm," was the one who certified the deaths of John and Solomon. Mosby Sheppard certified no one's death. Egerton confuses Mosby with John M. Sheppard, the ranking deputy sheriff who certified the deaths of Solomon, John, and all of the others executed in Henrico, except for the seven hanged outside of Richmond on 10 October. They were clearly two different individuals. Mosby was a private in the Richmond Horse, John M. the coronet. Mosby had served as one of Sheriff Bowler Cocke's deputies for one year, but was not renewed as a deputy when John Harvie succeeded Cocke in 1800. John M. Sheppard served several Henrico sheriffs as a deputy before moving to Hanover in 1801 or soon thereafter. Egerton also misdates the execution of the two men. Solomon was one of the five executed on 15 September. Jones's John was executed on Friday, 12 September. Solomon was reprieved until Monday, 15 September, a fact apparently overlooked.

14. ExLB, 1794–1800, 412–13.

15. Ibid., 413–14.

16. *Council Journals*, 1799–1801, 241; *Richmond Examiner*, 19 September 1800.

17. Henrico County Order Book 9, 1799–1801, 380–83; information against Peter (no. 9), 11 September 1800, Henrico Judgements and Ended Causes; testimony of Prosser's Ben and Thomas H. Prosser at trial of Jupiter, ExP II, box 8, folder 1; testimony of Prosser's Ben, Bristoe, Davy, or unidentified white man at trial of Sam, 15 September, ibid.; testimony of Prosser's Ben at trial of Daniel, 15 September, ibid. Although Peter was found guilty, the clerk did not include the trial testimony against him in the compilation provided to the executive of the trials held on 15 September. Davy's name was crossed out as the source of the description of Sam's surrender, and "A White man who took up the prisoner" inserted in its place.

18. Testimony of Prosser's Ben and William Burton at trial of Isham, 15 September 1800, ExP II, box 8, folder 1; petition of William Burton and others, 16 September, ibid., folder 2; *Council Journals*, 1799–1801, 245; "Copy of our Father's letter to our Mother, Richmond, September 16, 1800," Minor Family Papers, box 4, James Monroe Museum and Memorial Library, Fredericksburg.

19. Henrico County Order Book 9, 1799–1801, 383–87; testimony of Prosser's Ben at trial of Ned, 16 September 1800, ExP II, box 8, folder 2; testimony of Prosser's Ben at trial of Isaac, 16 September, ibid.; testimony of Prosser's Ben and Price's John at trial of Laddis, 16 September, ibid.; informations against Harry (no. 27), Ned (no. 29), Joe (no. 28), 11 September 1800, Henrico Judgements and Ended Causes. I believe Egerton (91) is correct when stating that Prosser's Ben had no direct testimony against these three men who belonged to Thomas Austin of Hanover.

20. "[Joseph Selden and Gervas Storrs] To the keeper of the Jail of the County of Henrico," 5 September 1800, Henrico Judgements and Ended Causes; information against Billy Chicken (no. 19), 11 September, ibid.; Henrico County Order Book 9, 1799–1801, 386. For a possible free man named Billy Chicken,

named by Gilbert but never prosecuted, see Appendix C: Alleged Participants Not Prosecuted.

21. Testimony of Price's John and Prosser's Ben at trial of Ben Woolfolk, 16 September 1800, ExP II, box 8, folder 2. Egerton (91, 214n43) believes Woolfolk was tried on 18 September, after he had confessed on 17 September and just before he was pardoned by the council. There were no Henrico conspiracy trials on 18 September; indeed, the court did not sit that day. Woolfolk was tried and found guilty on the 16th, confessed and named names on the 17th, and was pardoned by the council on the 18th. With his confession on 17 September there would have been no need to have witnesses against him at an 18 September trial, nor would he have pled not guilty. Because Egerton has consistently confused Prices's John as James, he believes the testimony against Woolfolk was "revenge" for the testimony Woolfolk supposedly gave against James at the 13 September trial which Egerton wrongly claims was erroneously recorded as occurring on 30 September. Misdating the trial of Price's James also leads Egerton to claim that Woolfolk used the occasion to offer to trade information for mercy, which led to his statements the following week. That negotiation did not take place until after Woolfolk was found guilty. The record shows that the testimony against Woolfolk was given by "Mrs. Prices" John. Correcting these errors forces a different sense of these trials and their protagonists, and their interactions.

22. *Virginia Argus*, 16 September 1800; *Richmond Examiner*, 16 and 19 September 1800. For a recent assessment of Baptists, evangelical Christianity, and slavery in early Virginia, see Randolph Ferguson Scully, *Religion and the Making of Nat Turner's Virginia: Baptist Community and Conflict, 1740–1840* (Charlottesville: University of Virginia Press, 2008). As noted elsewhere, Callender wrote to Jefferson on 13 September 1800, a letter which was not picked up to be mailed until a week later. Jefferson received it on 26 September. Meanwhile, Callender's amanuensis, Robert Richardson, had scribed another report of the trials, undated, which contained Callender's account of the response to his column in the *Examiner* attacking George Williamson. His reference to fifteen men having been executed dates this account as late as 18 September, but his report of the three carted men, discussed below, shows that it had to have been written on the 19th or later. If so, it could have been included with the original 13 September letter to Jefferson, since that letter's dispatch had been delayed. A Callender epistle to Jefferson, dated 29 September, refers to an enclosure of what he had sent Duane at the *Aurora*, and the editors of the Jefferson Papers identify this later account as a "probable enclosure." If so, Duane does not appear to have published it, and this (19[?] September) account does not appear in any other newspaper examined for this study (see *Papers of Thomas Jefferson*, 32:136–38, 174–76).

23. *Virginia Gazette*, 16 September 1800; Scully, *Religion and the Making of Nat Turner's Virginia*, 131–32. See also Nicholls, "'Holy Insurrection!.'"

24. "Communications of Ben alias Ben Woolfolk," 17 September 1800, ExP II, box 8, folder 2; Henrico Order Book 9, 1799–1801, 388; information against Stephen (no. 26), 11 September 1800, Henrico Judgements and Ended Causes;

"Information respecting the Insurrection. I requested Mickelborough Young a Gentleman of Caroline . . . ," undated, ExP II, box 8, folder 5; ExLB, 1794–1800, 417–18; "Rations of provisions and Spirits . . . Benjamin Jacob, Lieut.," Auditor's Item 758. It is unclear how many men were incarcerated by 30 September in Caroline. On 22 October, four of seven men then jailed were tried, but five men would face trial the next week, including John Fells, who was not named on the Woolfolk list, indicating that two more men were arrested after the first day of the Caroline trials (see Edmund Pendleton Jr. to Monroe, 22 October 1800, ExP I, box 2, folder 11).

25. *Council Journals*, 1799–1801, 245–47.

26. Petition of Andrew Dunscomb et al. to The Worshipfull Justices for Henrico County, 18 September 1800, Henrico Judgments and Ended Causes; Monroe to Major Dunscomb, 19 September 1800, ibid. (Monroe's letter would appear to be one heretofore not calendared); *Papers of Thomas Jefferson*, 32:175; *Council Journals*, 1799–1801, 249–50. Because the Henrico Court did not meet on 18 September, the petition of Dunscomb and the others may have been taken to the executive, thereby producing Monroe's response. However, the cart may have arrived ahead of the opening of the court on 19 September, which precipitated the executive intervention, if Callender is correct. In his account of the executions on Thursday, 18 September, Egerton (92) accurately quotes Callender that three men were in the cart, not realizing the polemicist was referring to the events of Friday. But apparently believing the intercession of the executive took place on the 18th, he veers the cart "north out of town," where he states five men were executed. Five men were executed on 18 September, but at the usual place in Richmond. By missing Callender's statement that after being returned to jail "these men have not been hung," Egerton, because George had been sentenced on 19 September to die near Prosser's Tavern on 3 October, then states, "Presumably that was where Isaac and Laddis were hanged later the same day; they were the sixteenth and seventeenth to swing from the noose" (92). They were not hanged until 10 October, and would die with Gabriel at the usual place, just where the court ordered. The petition to move the gallows to be near the magazine raises the question of where the gallows stood, an issue of some contemporary importance for identifying important sites in and about Richmond today related to the conspiracy. It has been assumed that the gallows were near the public magazine and the "burial ground for negroes" in Shockoe Valley, the place that appears on a map of Richmond created by the surveyor Richard Young sometime around 1810. However, the petitioners, according to the lot number they paid taxes on in 1800, would not have been able to look down into Shockoe, since most of their lots were west of Sixth Street. They lived closer to where Samuel Mordecai stated the gallows once stood: on the intermediate ground between John Harvie's home on the summit of Gamble's Hill and the penitentiary, a place he called "Gallows hill, the edifice on which was rendered in a great measure useless by the Penitentiary." A survey of Henrico and Richmond court records reveals that the only mention of the site

of the gallows in the 1780s was near Cocke's, on the west side of Richmond below the Brook Road's turn into town. Other Henrico-ordered executions through the 1790s were "at the usual place." Newspaper reports of executions of free people condemned by the General Court or the District Court only stated that they were executed at the gallows "near the city." After the Richmond Hustings Court found a slave man named Joe guilty of a felony in May 1792, it ordered his execution "on the gallows to be erected in this city," but it did not indicate a specific site and his subsequent pardon by the executive may have left those gallows unbuilt. Later municipal orders for executions then referred to the "usual place." In 1802, the Henrico Court found a slave man guilty and ordered him hanged at a gallows to be erected near the magazine, but the commuting of his sentence to transportation apparently left that gallows unbuilt too, until an ordered execution in 1804 led the Henrico Court to again order gallows to be erected at the site. Since the spot was on city land, the court sought and gained Richmond's permission, on the proviso that Richmond could share the use of the gallows. This seems to indicate that the eighteen men hanged in Richmond, including Gabriel, died on Gallows Hill, apparently "the usual place," but the record is not definitive (see Henrico County Order Book 1, 1781–84, 529–30, 532; Henrico County Order Book 2, 1784–87, 451, 515; Henrico County Order Book 7, 1796–98, 227; Henrico County Order Book 10, 1801–3, 328; Henrico County Order Book 11, 1803–5, 261; Richmond Hustings Court Order Book 3, 1792–97, 4, 492, 599–600; Richmond Hustings Court Order Book 4, 1797–1801, 46–48, 72, 220, 232–33, 245, 474; Richmond Hustings Court Order Book 5, 1801–4, 407; *Council Journals*, 1791–93, 133, 137; and Mordecai, *Richmond in By-Gone Days*, 97–98).

27. Testimony of Ben Woolfolk and Price's John at trial of George Smith, 19 September 1800, ExP II, box 8, folder 2; Henrico Order Book 9, 1799–1801, 388–89.

28. "Information from Mr Markham respecting Burwell Gates the property of Mr. George Brown respecting the insurrection, 15 September 1800," 15 September 1800, ExP II, box 8, folder 1; Monroe to Matthew Cheatham, 15 September 1800, ExLB, 1794–1800, 415; Mayo Carrington to Monroe, 17 September 1800, ExP II, box 8, folder 2; John Bracken to Monroe, 20 September, ibid.; William Bernard to Monroe, 20 September, ibid.; Capt. Christopher Hudson to Monroe, 24 September, ibid.; William Prentis to Monroe, 24 September, ibid.; *Council Journals*, 1799–1801, 254. Egerton reports (75) that Monroe "was forced to place 'stationary patrols along the river,'" but the patrols were the initiative of Carrington. He also claims (77) that the governor, "having no evidence to link Williamsburg with the plot . . . decided that the town was on its own and filed the request [of Bracken] away in his desk drawer." The council journal and a letter from Monroe to Bracken indicate that the request was granted, undercutting this colorful but imagined statement (see ExLB, 1794–1800, 427).

29. *Papers of Thomas Jefferson*, 32:145. Citing Monroe's letter, Ford states that Monroe estimated that "the death toll could easily run higher than fifty, and

perhaps even reach a hundred, if the executions proceeded unabated," but the figure of one hundred is an estimate of Egerton's (89), not Monroe's (see *Deliver Us from Evil*, 53, 556n21).

30. *Papers of Thomas Jefferson*, 32:160–61. For an analysis of Jefferson's appeal to necessity, see William G. Merkel, "To See Oneself as a Target of a Justified Revolution: Thomas Jefferson and Gabriel's Uprising," *American Nineteenth Century History* 4 (Summer 2003): 1–31.

31. Testimony of Prosser's Ben, Price's John, and Ben Woolfolk at the trial of Gilbert, 22 September 1800, ExP II, box 8, folder 2; William Prentis to Monroe, 24 September, ibid.; "Information from Mr Foster [from Gilbert] respecting the intended Insurrection Sepr 23d 1800," 23 September, ibid.; "Communications made by Gilbert," undated, ibid., folder 5. The undated statement of Gilbert's is the only one indicating the involvement of Byrd's uncles in Petersburg, and it does not give their first names. In Prentis's letter of 24 September, he states that at his trial Gilbert actually named Reuben and Jesse Byrd. There were two Reuben Byrd's and one by the name of Jesse at that time in Petersburg. Which of the two Reubens was arrested is not known, but it is likely it was the one who registered with Jesse on 29 August 1800. At one time or another, all three of these men claimed an Essex County origin (see Appendix C: Alleged Participants Not Prosecuted).

32. Henrico Order Book 9, 1799–1801, 389–91; information against Joe, [not numbered], 19 September 1800, Henrico Judgements and Ended Causes; Storrs and Selden to Henrico Sheriff and Keeper of the Jail, 13 September, ibid.; testimony of Prosser's Ben at trial of Tom, 22 September 1800, ExP II, box 8, folder 2. Although Egerton states (93) that both Prosser's Ben and Ben Woolfolk testified against Tom, only the testimony of Prosser's Ben was recorded, and there is no indication that Woolfolk testified. In 1816, Joseph Mosby, who identified himself as a neighbor of Izard Bacon in 1800, stated that Bacon "could not believe [George] was guilty as his Negroes knew well that as soon as the breath was out of . . . Bacon's body they were to be free." In his 1815 will, Bacon freed his slaves, but it took a petition to the legislature and a friendly suit by the slaves against the estate executor Charles Crenshaw, a relative and a Quaker, to effect the manumission. Two of the slave plaintiffs were named George. They left the estate as a group of over fifty and settled in Columbia, Pennsylvania (see "Petition of Izzard Bacon['s] Negroes by Charles Crenshaw, 14 December 1816," and "Memorial of Thos Ladd, Samuel Crew and Fleming Bates, trustees . . . 17 December 1818," Henrico County Legislative Petitions, FHL; and Leroy Hopkins, "Black Eldorado: The Emergence of Black Columbia [1726–1861]," *Journal of the Lancaster County Historical Society* 89 [Mickaelmas 1985]: 110–32).

33. "Information from Mr Foster [from Gilbert] respecting the intended Insurrection Sepr 23d 1800," 23 September 1800, ExP II, box 8, folder 2.

34. Richmond Order Book 4, 1797–1801, 473–74; King's Case, 3 October 1800, ExP II, box 8, folder 3; testimony of Ben Woolfolk and Mrs. Martin at trial of King, 25 September, ibid., folder 5. In the absence of trial testimony, it is not

clear if Brutus was being tried for his alleged involvement in the 1798 fire or for Gabriel's conspiracy. The statement Gilbert gave Foster pertains only to the arson. Of course, it might still appear in the order book under a charge of conspiracy and insurrection. The same caveat would apply to William Austin's Frank, who was not tried (see Appendix C: Alleged Participants Not Prosecuted).

35. Newton to Monroe, 24 September 1800, ExP II, box 8, folder 2; Richard E. Lee to Monroe, 25 September, ibid.; John Moss to Monroe, 28 September, ibid.; Miles King to Monroe, 18 April 1801, ExP I, box 3, folder 13; Richmond Order Book 4, 1797–1801, 274, 326. Thomas Newton provides the key account of Gabriel's flight and capture, while additional details exist in Richard E. Lee's letter. Newton and Lee, however, both misreported the name of John Moss (whom Billy, aka Will King, informed of Gabriel's presence) as Norris, a blacksmith, and as John Morse, an apprentice, respectively. Miles King, of Hampton, who referred to his ward's slave as Will, provides the key link between Billy/Will and Moss when he revealed that he had permitted the slave to go to Richmond "to get Sheldon Moss to hire him who had his wife." The effort apparently failed, leaving Billy at large, where he subsequently signed on with Richardson Taylor. John and Sheldon Moss received a tavern license in 1799 to run the Swan tavern. Sidbury (*Ploughshares into Swords,* 105) follows Newton's usage, while Egerton (106–7) follows Lee's rendering of "John Morse" but inexplicably identifies "Morse" as an African American. He then misidentifies John Moss as the sheriff of Norfolk. He labels Newton a Federalist who tried to get Gabriel to reveal the names in letters Gabriel was rumored to be carrying, something Egerton implies would be politically embarrassing. Newton, however, stood as a Jeffersonian elector that fall and had served as president of the Republican Society in Norfolk in 1793 (see Eugene P. Link, *Democratic-Republican Societies, 1790–1800* [1942; repr., New York: Octagon Books, 1965], 9–10). Why it took the *Mary* ten days to reach Norfolk remains a mystery, unless she was floated down the river, without sails, for refitting in Norfolk. Less steerable, it might also explain the vessel's stranding on the bar below Richmond. The only crew mentioned are the two slave men, perhaps a sufficient number if no sails had to be set. The length of time of the voyage may be why Ford says Gabriel floated down the James on a "flatboat" (see *Deliver Us from Evil,* 53).

36. Newton to Monroe, 24 September, ExP II, box 8, folder 2.

37. Ibid. Historians have ignored or not reported Gabriel's revelation of Gilbert's involvement, probably because the document, as conveniently presented in the *Calendar of Virginia State Papers,* 9:154–55, appears to be complete, having no ellipses to indicate what has been omitted. In the undated file (ExP II, box 8, folder 5) there exists a scrap of paper that reads, "Dear Sir, I am sick and have been so ever since I left Richmond." Newton reported that Taylor claimed to be ill and that he was about to inform on Gabriel. This scrap was apparently sent along as evidence of Taylor's claim. On the same scrap, in what seems to be Newton's hand, is written: "The above is all that could be found of Capt Taylors writing. Negro Isham. Inquire if Richardson Taylor has given his freedom

in Jas City & Wmsburg. Billy belonging to Miles King at Hampton." This scrap opens the door to checking some of Newton's information reported to Monroe concerning Richardson Taylor. The loss of James City and Williamsburg local records prevents checking on any manumission by Taylor, but personal property tax lists reveal that Taylor resided in Williamsburg between 1786 and 1791, in New Kent County in 1792, in the county of his birth in 1760, and in James City County between 1793 and 1796—the county in which he was raised. Sometime before 1794, he married Ann Shields of James City County. He next appears on the 1797–98 tax lists of Warwick County, where Richneck Plantation sat, a place with Foushee and Hylton connections, as Newton suggested in his letter (see *The Family Letters of Thomas Jefferson*, ed. Edwin Morris Betts and James Adam Beer Jr. [Columbia: University of Missouri Press, 1966], 155n2). As for Taylor's attachment to Methodism, if he had lost his enthusiasm, as Isham feared in 1800, it appears he returned to the fold, for he was listed as a Richmond subscriber to Jesse Lee's *A Short History of the Methodists in the United States* . . . (Baltimore, 1810). There is no evidence that he had been "a long time resident of Norfolk," as Egerton states (104, 177), and he did not simply disappear, as discussed in chapter 5. The part-owner of the schooner was probably Thomas Hooper, and the "Dr. Foushee" could have been John H. Foushee—two of the witnesses Taylor wanted summoned in his behalf at the suit of Thomas Henry Prosser in the fall of 1800 (discussed below). The Hylton could be either William or Daniel, the latter the future father-in-law of Prosser. Taylor's places of birth and upbringing appear in his 1834 pension application for Revolutionary War service; see Revolutionary War Pension and Bounty-Land Warrant Application Files, M804, Pension no. S15671, National Archives (microfilm), FHL (I am indebted to Angela Smith for calling my attention to this file). For Taylor's marriage to Ann Shields, see "Will of Col. James Shields of James City County," *WMQ*, 1st ser., 20 (July 1911): 36–38.

38. *Epitome of the Times*, 25 September 1800.

39. *Norfolk Herald*, 25 September 1800; ExLB, 1794–1800, 429; *Epitome of the Times*, 25 September 1800.

5. Putting a Period

1. *Virginia Argus*, 30 September 1800; *Virginia Gazette*, 30 September 1800. Egerton (107) uses the *Gazette*'s account—he cites the reprinting from the Fredericksburg *Virginia Herald* of 3 October—to try and establish the presence of Quersey and Beddenhurst in Norfolk. Ignoring the fact that Gabriel was reported as saying, "There were four or five others more materially concerned," Egerton reports that Gabriel claimed "that there were four others as deeply 'concerned in the business' as he was." Having changed an estimate into a specific number, he asserts that only Jack Bowler/Ditcher and Sam Byrd Jr. could be as "deeply involved" as Gabriel—that's two—and, wanting to name someone in Norfolk who Gabriel hinted existed, he declares, "The other two—those in Norfolk—had to be Quersey and Beddenhurst." Gabriel's statement actually means, I believe, that

beyond the four or five, he could even name some in Norfolk. No evidence exists of either white man's presence in Norfolk, nor does Egerton take into account Gabriel's claim of the significance of Gilbert, the record of George Smith's heavy involvement, or even that of Ben Woolfolk.

2. ExLB, 1794–1800, 426–30; *Council Journals*, 1799–1801, 257.

3. *Council Journals*, 1799–1801, 258–59. For an account of Virginia's efforts to arm itself beginning in the 1790s, see Giles Cromwell, *The Virginia Manufactory of Arms* (Charlottesville: University of Virginia Press, 1975).

4. Henrico Order Book 9, 1799–1801, 392–99; *Council Journals*, 1799–1801, 260.

5. *Council Journals*, 1799–1801, 261–63; Monroe to Madison, 8 October 1800, *Papers of James Madison*, 17:419–20. Egerton (111–12, 219n53) notes that Monroe had no vote in the council, but claims that "at length he persuaded the body to suspend further executions," which seems to be the case, but not until after eleven more men were executed. Apparently relying on the date of Monroe's letter rather than the date the proposal was discussed, he states that the discussion occurred "just before Gabriel was hanged." Because he mistakenly believes that Michael had been executed on 3 October, and Laddis and Isaac on 19 September, he is unaware of the full backlog of convicted men confronting the council when Monroe made his proposal on 3 October, when fifteen men stood convicted. Gabriel would join that number on 6 October. Subsequent pardons and reprieves would reduce the number of men executed on 10 October to ten, with others still to be tried or in jail with death sentences reprieved until a later date (see note 13 below, which lists the dates of death for the executed men). Egerton, in an apparent slip of the pen (112), says, "What to do with those who were pardoned presented a problem." He probably meant to write those who were "convicted" but who were "less criminal in comparison"—those individuals who had won reprieves from the executive pending a transportation bill which might be enacted. He makes the same error on page 101.

6. Testimony of Prosser's Ben, Price's John, and Ben Woolfolk at trial of Gabriel, 6 October 1800, ExP II, box 8, folder 3; Henrico Order Book 9, 1799–1801, 400; *Council Journals*, 1799–1801, 268; Monroe to Newton, 5 October 1800, in ExLB, 1800–1803, 1. Egerton's account of Gabriel's trial (109–10) contains several errors. Apparently striving for dramatic effect, Egerton says that Gabriel's trial took place after the other trials of the day, "just as the sun was slipping away." It was the first trial heard on 6 October. The case of Thomas Jordan Martin was opened but then carried over to 7 October because the court ran out of time, indicating Martin's was the last one heard that day. That is also the order of the cases as they appear in the Order Book. Because the court had pronounced that Gabriel should die on Tuesday, 7 October, Gabriel's request to have his execution put off until Friday, 10 October, required the intervention of the executive, and thus the involvement of both Monroe and the council on the following day. Hence, Justice Miles Selden could not have immediately agreed, "rather sourly," to reschedule his execution. No evidence exists that Gabriel wished the delay to occur so that

he could be hanged with fellow conspirators, as reported by Egerton, a request that Egerton incorrectly states (111) was denied. Gabriel was actually executed along with Laddis and Isaac at the usual place in Richmond, not as a result of Gabriel's request, but because the court had long before ordered them hanged at that spot. Egerton makes much of the mention of the Frenchmen in the testimony of Woolfolk and Prosser's Ben at this trial, but these accusations had emerged on the first day of the trials and had been reported in the papers starting on 16 September. The suggestion in Woolfolk's confession that Quakers and Methodists should be spared, a statement that surely was known to the court, had been made by 17 September.

7. Sidbury, *Ploughshares into Swords*, 74–82 (quotation at 79), 83n57, 88n68; Egerton, x, 38–41, 50, 109, 115 (quotation at p. x); Ford, *Deliver Us from Evil*, 555–56n13; Alfred F. Young, *Liberty Tree: Ordinary People and the American Revolution* (New York: New York University Press, 2006), 68–75. Young notes that in Philadelphia a meeting of the Democratic-Republican Society was portrayed by a hostile cartoonist as "filled with demonic lower-class figures, including blacks" (69). However, although these groups were infused with mechanics, artisan republicans in these Northern cities did not embrace the idea of opening "the skilled trades to free African Americans" (73). In arguing for a link between Gabriel and Richmond artisans of a republican persuasion, Egerton notes (38) the existence of "seven artisan clubs," that is, Democratic-Republican Societies, in the Chesapeake region, and states that "Richmond and Norfolk acted as host to several." He cites Link's *Democratic-Republican Societies, 1790–1800*, 13–16, in support of his claim, but Richmond does not appear on either Link's list of such groups or on his map of their locations. Link stated (16) that a 24 September 1794 issue of the *Connecticut Courant* "names additional societies in Virginia," but he does not indicate if they were not included by him in his master list. I have not found an issue of the *Courant* for that date among those in the Readex Early American Newspaper files. Link also states that Virginia probably hosted more Societies, but in locations where newspapers did not exist, or that the Societies were very small. It does not seem that his description would apply to a Society that might have been organized in Richmond.

8. Henrico Order Book 9, 1799–1801, 401–2.

9. Henrico Order Book 9, 1799–1801, 402–3. Egerton (108) misreports that the court agreed with Rind's objection. The slave testimony was admitted. See below for a further discussion of the legal issues of Martin's case.

10. ExLB, 1800–1803, 2; ExP I, box 2, folder 10. Egerton makes much of the political differences existing at the time and states (103–4) that Federalist mayor James McClurg was increasingly "left in the dark about the ongoing investigation" because Monroe was fearful of what might be leaked that would be politically embarrassing. However, when it came to the safety of Richmond, in this case and earlier, Monroe did not hesitate to work with McClurg (see Monroe to McClurg, 19 September 1800, ExLB, 1794–1800, 419; and chapter 6).

11. *Council Journals*, 1799–1801, 269–70.

12. ExLB, 1800–1803, 3, 56, 173; *Council Journals*, 1801–3, 29. Cowley was appointed keeper of the capitol and doorkeeper to the council on 30 April 1795, with an annual salary of £70 (about $234), and allowed the use of a small house. In 1794, he had looked after the governor's house in the interval between its occupancy by Henry Lee and that of Robert Brooke (see *Council Journals*, 1793–95, 223, 315). Subsequently, he would be paid for a variety of tasks, including guarding the Treasury, packing up and shipping muskets, storing arms at the capitol, distributing monies to Catawba and Chickasaw men passing through Richmond, providing a carpet for the council, numerous express hires, stocking the capitol with coal each fall, and other tasks. In July 1799, his base pay was raised to $300 (see *Council Journals*, 1795–97, 21, 215, 248, 309; *Council Journals*, 1797–98, 31, 65, 300; and *Council Journals*, 1798–99, 180 and passim). Whether Cowley was an active conspirator with sober second thoughts, or played along believing it would lead to nothing, or entirely something else, is not clear. Because Egerton (58) appears unaware of the surrender of the keys in April 1801, he misreports Cowley's salary as $200, a sum the legislature set in 1802 for the keeper of the keys to the capitol. The salary for the position to which Cowley had been appointed, as "door-keeper of the capitol and of the council, whose duty it is to keep the capitol clean, and obey the orders of the Executive," remained $300. Egerton's conclusions (58, 175) about Cowley's ambiguous position and role, and that he may have kept his options open until the final second, seem reasonable, though not because of his greatly inflated age. He was probably not thought to be 100 in 1800, given the demanding duties of his tasks and the presence of individuals, like his manumitter Edmund Randolph, who had a sense of his real age (see Shepherd, *Statutes at Large of Virginia*, 2:334). Cowley's continued employment as the council's doorkeeper was questioned in 1806, but a motion to have him replaced was defeated (see *Council Journals*, 1803–6, 379–80).

13. *Council Journals*, 1799–1801, 272; ExLB, 1800–1803, 4; Robert Sutcliff, *Travels in Some Parts of North America, in the Years 1804, 1805, 1806* (Philadelphia, 1812), 50. The certification of executions carried out by deputy Samuel Mosby corresponds with the court-ordered site for those executed at Prosser's Tavern. The same is true for deputy Benjamin Mosby's certification for those he executed east of Richmond, and for deputy John M. Sheppard's notations for his executions of Gabriel, Isaac, and Laddis, who were hanged "at the usual place." Egerton reports (110–11) that only seven men were executed that day, having claimed that Laddis and Isaac had been executed on 19 September, and Michael on 3 October. All three men were on the list of the condemned considered for pardons by the council on 3 October, but each of the three was denied. In order to establish who was executed, where and when, who was pardoned, and who was reprieved until pardoned or transported, the court records, executive papers, and executive journals have to be correlated. In most cases, specific slaves are named when pardoned or reprieved. Thus, on 19 September, the executive reprieved Laddis, Isaac, and Ned until the following Monday, 22 September, when they were again reprieved until 3 October. On 2 October, the council issued a

reprieve "to all the Negroes condemned to be executed tomorrow . . . until Friday the 10th instant," which also put off Michael's scheduled execution until 10 October. Ned was reprieved on 3 October until November, and would be pardoned in December. Assembling all the evidence produces the following schedule of the twenty-five executions in Henrico (with owner's names in parentheses). Five men on 12 September: Will (Mosby); John (Jones); Isaac (Burton); Michael (Owen); and Ned (Parsons). Five on 15 September: Solomon (Prosser); Billy (Gregory); Martin (Prosser); Charles (Gregory); and Frank (Prosser). Five on September 18: Sawney (Lewis); Peter (Prosser); Jupiter (Wilkinson); Sam (Wilkinson); and Isham (Burton). Ten on 10 October: Laddis (Williamson); Isaac (Allen); Michael (Goode); Sam Byrd Jr. (Clarke); Gilbert (Young); George Smith (Smith); Sam Graham (Graham); Tom (Prosser); William (Young); and Gabriel (Prosser). For the disposition of all the cases, see Appendix B: Men Tried for Conspiracy and Insurrection. On 14 October, the *Virginia Argus* accurately reported that ten conspirators had been executed on Friday, 10 October, including Gabriel and two others in Richmond, two "near Four-mile creek," and five "near the Brook." Among the latter were "Smith's *George* and Young's *Gilbert*."

14. *Virginia Gazette and General Advertiser,* 10 October 1800; Storrs to Monroe, 10 October, ExP II, box 8, folder 3. The *Gazette* is probably wrong. In the same account, it erroneously reported that fifteen men were to be executed that day, apparently unaware of the pardons or reprieves that had been granted that week. The identity of Peter Smith is not clear, but Storrs described him as a free Negro. Perhaps he was the man called Peter whom William S. Smith, who lived near Storrs, had freed in 1797 after collecting £45, and who was probably the free black man of that name prosecuted, but found not guilty, for hog stealing in January 1800 in the Henrico Court. It may have been more than proximity and Peter Smith's efforts that led Bowler to surrender specifically to Storrs. The magistrate had himself freed a man named Jacob in 1798. Moreover, while I have not noted Storrs "affirming" rather than swearing in court, he came from Quaker stock. His father, Joshua Storrs, a merchant, had married Susanna Pleasants in the Society of Friends Meeting in Henrico, and at his death in 1779 had ordered that his two slaves, Dick Joles and Cyrus, "shall enjoy their liberties in the most extensive manner." Storrs could not legally free them at the time without government approval, but Joles was ultimately freed in 1782, after private manumissions became legal. It is not clear what happened to Cyrus (see the Henrico County Deed Book 5, 1796–1800, 339, 519; Order Book 9, 1799–1801, 149; Henrico Wills, Settlement of Estates, etc., 1781–87, 30; Order Book 1, 1781–84, 104; the *Virginia Gazette* [Dixon and Nicholson], 11 December 1779; and the White Oak Swamp Friends Meeting Records, 1757–80 [microfilm], 52, 65, FHL).

15. Louisa County Order Book, 1799–1802, 284 (the Louisa County Court Minute Book, 1800–1801, 107, provides no additional details); testimony of Prosser's Ben at trial of Watt, 1 December 1800, ExP II, box 8, folder 4. On 8 November, Jefferson wrote Monroe that, while on a trip to Poplar Forest in Bedford County, he had heard concerns about the lack of any guard over the arms in the federal

armory at New London, just across the line in Campbell County. He claimed that "some in the neighborhood" suspected the "federal administration takes this method of offering arms to insurgent negroes" by not employing a guard. He urged Monroe to have the local militia form one from their ranks. Monroe failed to do so, and in January 1801 men in the area of the arsenal requested that the executive pursue measures to get the national government to either remove the weapons or create a guard. They noted their vulnerability in the midst of "a considerable number of slaves . . . [and] freed negroes and mulattoes . . . shou'd the spirit of insurrection reach that part of the country." In response to this request, Monroe ordered a guard from the Campbell militia to be sent there for what he expected would be about a six-week tour. But Monroe had other fears behind his orders, fears similar to those he held when the federal regiment was encamped near Richmond. He believed that arms were to be moved in order to prevent them falling into the hands of the Virginia government should the electoral process collapse in the House of Representatives. He sent Thomas Mann Randolph to survey the place and its contents. From Randolph he learned that the arms were to be moved to Harper's Ferry, but that it would take a huge number of wagons and several months to accomplish that task. Randolph also reported that the local guard ordered by Monroe had not materialized because of a dispute over the cost of rations, and that the people who lived in the immediate vicinity of the arsenal feared that "a wicked negro or a madman might blow them up any night and that a militia guard was not only the strength of the civil Officer but the surest control of the slaves." Local concern was immediate; the concerns of Jefferson and Monroe arose from political fears (see Jefferson to Monroe, 8 November 1800, in *Papers of Thomas Jefferson*, 32:248; Thomas West to Honable Exec of Virginia, 16 January 1801, ExP I, box 3, folio 7; ExLB, 1800–1803, 62; and Thomas Mann Randolph to Monroe, 14 February 1801, James Monroe Papers, Library of Congress, Manuscript Division [I am indebted to Bruce Kirby at the Library of Congress for providing a copy of this letter]).

16. Thomas Booth to Alexander McCrae, 5 October 1800, ExP II, box 8, folder 3; "To Mr. B. H., Gloster," 20 September 1800, endorsed with the affidavit "Thos Booth, 2 October 1800," ibid.; T. Buckner to Monroe, 4 October, ExP I, box 2, folder 10.

17. "6 Ap. 1801, Elzy Burroughs & als, Searching for a negroe for insurrection," Auditor's Item 758; petition of William Wilson, 23 December 1800, Gloucester County Legislative Petitions, FHL. Egerton (61) reports that John's recruiting was done in Norfolk, but this is an error. Egerton (74) also speculates that "brother X" might be Gabriel, but on the day of the letter's date Gabriel had been on the schooner *Mary* for six days and in hiding since 31 August. It more likely referred to a man known locally whose identity as a key planner could not be surrendered, perhaps an itinerant minister. On the basis of no real evidence, Egerton constructs a tale connecting Jacob to John Scott, the alleged "General" of the Petersburg recruits who was caught trying to get to Norfolk with the letter addressed to Beddinghurst, by claiming that Jacob had on occasion sailed

to Petersburg. Nothing supports this statement. To try and make these connections, Egerton uses the undated and misfiled, but clearly 1802 letter of William Prentis to Monroe (ExP II, box 8, folder 5) responding to an inquiry from Newton (see Newton to Monroe, 14 May 1802, ExP I, box 6, folder 2; and William Prentis to Monroe, 27 May 1802, ibid., folder 3). Prentis was asked about the "jugstopper" list of alleged conspirators, who turned out to be tobacco pickers, found in the cabin of a vessel belonging "to a free Negro, which passes between this town and Norfolk." Apparently, because Jacob was a slave, but with some freedom of movement, and Prentis identified the captain of the Petersburg craft as a free Negro, Egerton tries to resolve the discrepancy of the ship captain's status by asserting that "most contemporary newspaper sources incorrectly described Jacob as a free man." But he cites no newspapers to support his claim (204n36), and no media reference to Jacob has been found. He also states (113) that "most contemporaries thought him a freeman." But the only statement in the record about Jacob's status was made by Booth, who simply said he was "well known." Egerton (110) says Jacob was hunted down "by a floating posse of five ships and captured near Norfolk," but only Thomas submitted a bill for the use of a vessel, through Elzy Burroughs, and there is no evidence of where Jacob was actually caught. The tale is dramatic but speculative, spun largely out of an undated document, whose date—May 1802—can reasonably be established through the internal evidence of other documents of known dates (see Sidbury, *Ploughshares into Swords*, 142–43n75).

18. William Wilkinson to Monroe, 1 October 1800, ExP II, box 8, folder 3; claim of Willis Wilkinson, 4–14 October 1800, Auditor's Item 758; *Epitome of the Times*, 6 October 1800; *Norfolk Herald*, 2 October 1800; ExLB, 1800–1803, 1; Newton to Monroe, 9 October, ExP I, box 2, folder 10. See also the discussion in chapter 2, note 29.

19. ExLB, 1800–1803, 4–5. See also Appendix C: Alleged Participants Not Prosecuted. For the Petersburg case allowing slave testimony against a free man of color, see Hustings Court Minute Book, 1797–1800 (n.p.), 23 February 1798.

20. *Virginia Gazette*, 30 September 1800, 3 October 1800; *Virginia Reports: Jefferson—33 Grattan, 1730-1880*, annotated under the supervision of Thomas Johnson Michie (Charlottesville, 1903), 194; Henrico County Court Judgements and Ended Causes 1802, box 78, folder 6, March 1802, LVA; Henrico Order Book 10, 1801–3, 220; marriage bond of Richardson Taylor to Tabitha Worrock, 9 April 1802, Richmond City Marriage Bonds, 1797–1809, LVA [copy courtesy of Kevin Lett of Virginia Family Tree]; marriage bond of Richardson Taylor to Lucy Carter, 10 May 1806, Henrico County Marriage Bonds, FHL; "Stubbs v. Taylor," Henrico Chancery Court papers (1834-015), LVA (copy kindly provided by Brent Tarter). This suit establishes Taylor's departure for Lynchburg in 1810. His war service pension, cited in chapter 4, note 37, reveals he was in Kentucky by about 1817, and died there in 1835. Taylor also was a witness to George Nicholson's will (see Henrico Will Book 3, 1802–9, 11). James Rind, the court-appointed defense

attorney for the Henrico conspirators, was retained by Taylor when the latter was sued by Prosser. Among the witnesses Taylor wanted to appear on his behalf was Richmond mayor James McClurg, an indication that Taylor had likely appeared before him in fulfillment of the bond, and that the charge was probably dismissed. Cf. Egerton, 177.

21. Trial of Peter, Dinwiddie County, 20 October 1800, Condemned Slaves, 1800, Public Claims: Slaves and Free Blacks, Auditor's Item 756. Unless a capital case involved "conspiracy, insurrection, or rebellion," the courts of oyer and terminer could not set the date of execution to fall within thirty days of judgment. Peter's trial was held in the Dinwiddie County courthouse some miles southwest of Petersburg rather than in the town, as Egerton claims (100–101), which was also the site of his execution. There is no evidence he was a Petersburg slave, nor was he among those otherwise arrested in Petersburg, as assumed by Egerton (216n18), who never mentions the conspiracy to commit murder charge, although the only evidence of the trial does. One wonders whether the latter charge might hint at more disagreements over joining the conspiracy among those contemplating it, or if the animosity arose for other, unrelated reasons. None of the twelve men named as suspects in Petersburg were tried.

22. ExLB, 1800–1803, 6; *Journal of the Senate* (1800 [1801]), 12.

23. ExLB, 1800–1803, 4, 7; Richmond Hustings Order Book 4, 1797–1801, 483.

24. *Council Journals*, 1799–1801, 273–77.

25. Entries for 21 and 22 October 1800, James Duvall Diary, 1799–1804, LVA; Caroline County Order Book 1799–1802, 216–19; *Council Journals*, 1799–1801, 279; ExLB, 1800–1803, 12, 14; Edmund Pendleton Jr. to Monroe, 22 October 1800, ExP I, box 2, folder 11. According to the Caroline land tax lists for 1815, Duvall then lived sixteen miles south of Bowling Green, not far from the conspirators. If he lived at the same place in 1800, his interest in the trials may have arisen from knowing of some of the men being tried, rather than just a morbid curiosity.

26. Entry for 29 October 1800, James Duvall Diary, 1799–1804, LVA; Caroline Order Book 1799–1802, 220–22; testimony of Ben Woolfolk and Primus at trial of Jack Gabriel, 29 October 1800, ExP II, box 8, folder 3. On 27 October John Hoomes had requested Woolfolk's reappearance on 29 October, because "Ben [was] the only witness against" the accused. The recorded statements of Primus and Edmund over the last two days of the trials suggest Hoomes was substantively correct. Moreover, other potential witnesses, like Sam Graham, who gave a statement regarding the Hanover-Caroline conspirators, or Young's William, who had recruited in the area, had both been executed on 10 October. Primus was one of the two slaves who left the meeting at Littlepage's Bridge threatening to reveal the plot. Chased down, the two promised to reveal nothing. It would appear he kept his promise, but he may have committed perjury at these trials in order to do so (see chapter 2).

27. Caroline Order Book 1799–1802, 223–24; testimony of Ben Woolfolk and Edmund at trials of John Fells and Thornton, 30 October 1800, ExP II, box 8, folder 3. John Fells may not have been among those first arrested in Caroline. He was not named on the list of men to be taken up who lived in Hanover, Caroline, or King William, based on the statement of Woolfolk. But Woolfolk mentioned him in his testimony against Jack Gabriel on 29 October. Perhaps this led to a quick arrest and trial. Egerton's account (96–98) of the Caroline trials relates them out of order from their appearance in the Order Book in an effort to explain how the court failed to find Humphrey guilty. He claims that Humphrey testified against Jack Gabriel before his own trial, and since there is no evidence to reveal the reasoning of the court, Egerton surmises that one justice thought Humphrey should be rewarded for it. Indeed, it is not clear if Humphrey testified for or against Jack Gabriel, since his statement was not included in the trial testimony sent to the executive. The Order Book records the trial of Jack Gabriel as being heard *after* the court failed to find Humphrey guilty because of the dissenting vote. Similarly, but for reasons unknown, Egerton claims Thornton was first tried on 30 October, reversing the order of the Order Book, nor does he report that Edmund testified too.

28. Henrico Court Order Book 9, 1799–1801, 408–10, 416; testimony of Prosser's Ben, Price's John, and Prosser's Sam at trial of Jack Bowler, 29 October 1800, ExP II, box 8, folder 3. The trial testimony in Bowler's case is misdated and filed under 9 October.

29. *Council Journals*, 1799–1801, 274, 290; certificate of Jesse Smith, 23 October 1800, ExP II, box 8, folder 3; certificate of Thomas B. King, 24 October, ibid.; James Rind to Elisha Price, undated, ibid. James is the man Egerton wrongly identifies as Price's John. Nothing in the record reveals what skills James may have possessed, but the court valuation of £150, or $500, indicates he was valued as highly as the blacksmiths Gabriel, Solomon, and Thornton.

30. *Council Journals*, 1799–1801, 287–88, 311; "Application from Mr. Young for a pardon to Ned," 22 November 1800; John Hoomes to Monroe, 27 October 1800, ExP II, box 8, folder 3; Caroline justices' recommendation for mercy for Scipio, 8 November, ibid., folder 4. On 8 November, the council issued a blanket reprieve to all the conspirators scheduled to die on 14 November, until the second Friday in December. Egerton says (98) that Monroe pardoned Scipio at the request of Hoomes, which Monroe may have been inclined to do, but it actually took the petition of the collected justices to produce the executive pardon.

31. *Council Journals*, 1799–1801, 260, 272, 288; Larkin Stanard to Monroe, 30 October 1800, ExP II, box 8, folder 3.

32. *Council Journals*, 1799–1801, 288, 311, 322, 339.

33. Henrico Order Book 9, 1799–1801, 445; testimony of Prosser's Ben at trial of Watt, 1 December 1800, ExP II, box 8, folder 4; "Acct of Martin Mims agt the Commonwealth of Virginia for Maintenance of Negroes," 15 January 1801, Auditor's Item 758. Watt was valued at £55 at his trial, but sold for the equivalent of

£45 when transported. His purchasers noted that he suffered from frostbitten feet, probably acquired while in jail after his trial, which might explain the discrepancy (see *Calendar of Virginia State Papers*, 9:196–97). In his text, Egerton (113, 220n56) incorrectly reports that Watt was tried along with two others on 4 November, even though he gives the correct date of Watt's trial in his note. He states that "the court recommended that he instead be transported out of the state," but this is an assumption, since there is no record of a request for mercy for Watt in the court record and the legislature had not yet created the policy of exile, though Watt later would be transported. Instead, this seems to be a rare instance of executive action without at least the recorded recommendation of mercy by a court, but one that would also occur among the conspirators in the case of Williamson's Lewis and, apparently, Jack Bowler.

34. John Drayton to Monroe, 27 September 1800; ExP I, box 4, folder 10; ExLB, 1800–1803, 12. Because of a very difficult to read date, Drayton's letter has been filed as 27 September 1801 in the Executive Papers. Confirmation of its 1800 date comes from the copy Drayton submitted to the South Carolina legislature that fall (see S165009, box 31, Governor's Messages, no. 768, South Carolina Department of Archives and History, Columbia; I am grateful for the copy provided me by Steve Tuttle of that department).

35. *Virginia Gazette*, 30 September 1800; *Richmond Examiner*, 12 September 1800; *Virginia Argus*, 16 September 1800, 3 October 1800; list headed "Bob at Rockets, big man," undated, ExP II, box 8, folder 5; Joseph Jones to Monroe, 9 September 1800, ibid., folder 1. Sidbury has noted that Purcell had some connection with Jacob Valentine, a man examined before Richmond magistrates in 1797 for "encouraging an Insurrection among the Slaves of the City of Richmond," and wondered if Purcell was a possible link between the two plots. Also of interest is the naming of John Stockdell by Michael at the gallows, a surname that also appears in the scraps of paper taken as evidence in the case of Valentine. Stockdell's widow had a slave named Gilbert who was suspected in 1800. Such are the teasings of the historical record (see Sidbury, *Ploughshares into Swords*, 128, 178–83; and chapter 4, note 7).

36. Egerton, 102–4, 115, 185. For the dating of the Prentis letter of 1802, see note 17 above; for Scott and Beddenhurst, see chapter 2, note 28.

37. Philadelphia *Gazette of the United States*, 10 September 1800; Boston *Columbian Centinel*, 13 September 1800. For the coverage and controversies surrounding Gabriel's plot as reported in the press, see Nicholls, "'Holy Insurrection!.'" Some attention to Gabriel and the election of 1800 is given in Edward J. Larson, *A Magnificent Catastrophe*, 190–200; Susan Dunn, *Jefferson's Second Revolution: The Election Crisis of 1800 and the Triumph of Republicanism* (Boston: Houghton Mifflin, 2004), 153–58; and John Ferling, *Adams vs. Jefferson: The Tumultuous Election of 1800* (New York: Oxford University Press, 2004), 181–82.

38. Nicholls "'Holy Insurrection!'"; Norfolk *Epitome of the Times*, 2 and 13 October 1800.

6. Politics and Policies

1. See Appendix B: Men Tried For Conspiracy and Insurrection. Also, Randolph to Joseph Nicholson, 26 September 1800, quoted in William Cabell Bruce, *John Randolph of Roanoke, 1773–1833* (New York, 1922), 2:250. I am indebted to Steve Stathis for a transcription of the Randolph letter in the Library of Congress, which confirms that Bruce's rendering of the letter contains all that Randolph revealed about the plot in his letter (see note 8 below).

2. ExLB, 1800–1803, 33–42 (vernacularly known as Monroe's message). Monroe's message was also printed in the *Journal of the Senate* (1800 [1801]), 11–13, 33. The payrolls for the Caroline militiamen, their rations, house rent, and other associated costs, along with the bill from the Richmond Troop of Horse are scattered throughout Auditor's Item 758. See also *Journal of the House of Delegates of the Commonwealth of Virginia* . . . (Richmond 1800 [1801]), 28 (Shaw–Shoemaker no. 1585). In an heroic first effort to calculate the costs of the militia, Egerton (75) reports that the total cost of the 23rd Regiment from Chesterfield totaled $2,321, but it appears that he included a regimental summary list that duplicated most of the individual company accounts that also appear in the archives. The summary totaled $1172.75, all but one small claim consisting of payroll accounts. Another statement, of Col. John Mayo, is for tolls for militiamen crossing his bridge over the James River, not, as Egerton reports, for compensation "for a handful of drifters to guard his toll bridge." It is not clear how Egerton reached this conclusion, since the 6 October account was labeled "To Sundry Orders since 20th of September for 23rd Regmt for passing of guards to and fro on Toll Bridge." Mayo's bridge was not in complete working order much before this. Sometime in the summer, Prosser's Ben asked Michael how he intended to bring his men over the James from Manchester, "knowing the bridge to be impassable." Michael answered that they would use a boat, "that twenty or thirty could come in one Boat" (see Ben's testimony at trial of Michael, 27 September 1800, ExP II, box 8, folder 2). In an advertisement dated 18 October printed in the *Virginia Argus* of 21 October, Mayo announced that his bridge "is now in far better order than it has been for some years," and promised further improvements.

3. Calculated from "Register of Cert[ificates] & Warrants issued for Slaves Executed," Auditor of Public Accounts, APA 57, Ledger, 1779–1813, part 6, which includes transported and emancipated slaves; and "A list of Slaves reprieved and Sold by the Executive under the Act of Assembly intitaled [*sic*] 'An Act to empower the Governor to transport Slaves condemned when it shall be deemed expedient,'" General Assembly, Office of the Speaker, Executive Communication, oversized, 1803–6, folder 10, enclosure D, LVA. The value of the pardoned slaves was derived from the court evaluations in the Henrico and Caroline order books at the sentencing of the thirteen men later pardoned (see *Journal of the House of Delegates* [1799 (1800)], 83–88; and *Journal of the House of Delegates* [1800 (1801)], 64).

4. ExLB, 1800–1803, 34–35 (Monroe's message). Sidbury (*Ploughshares into Swords*, 132–35) concluded that Monroe's speech was essentially conservative in that it did not claim any incompatibility between slavery and republicanism, and reassuring in the sense that the forestalled uprising never posed any threat to the state's existence. I agree, but I believe it was also consciously shaped by republican ideological and political concerns about executive power, fiscal administration, and the importance of the militia in a republic.

5. ExLB, 1800–1803, 35–36 (Monroe's message).

6. Ibid., 36–67.

7. Ibid., 38–40. Egerton (148) reports that Monroe "indicated that several free blacks had been involved with Gabriel," but free blacks were not specifically mentioned by Monroe.

8. ExLB, 1800–1803, 41–42 (Monroe's message). Monroe's praise of the militia may have sought to deflect any criticism of the state's inability to arm its forces, such as the claim made by Callender to Jefferson in his letter of 13 September, but more importantly in the public columns of the *Philadelphia Aurora* of 23 September, that only thirty muskets were available to arm the four to five hundred men first mustered. Lacy Ford (*Deliver Us from Evil*, 58, 557n38) erroneously states that John Randolph made this claim about the unarmed militia to Joseph Nicholson in the letter cited in note 1 above. Egerton (147) reports that Monroe closed his address "with a request that the Assembly provide him with any 'recommendations' it might think proper 'on the issue' of the near revolt, as well as advice on the matter of transportation." Monroe asked for no "advice"—what could a true republican governor really expect to do without legislative authorization?—and he said nothing about transportation in his address.

9. Documents respecting the Insurrection of the Slaves, House of Delegates, Office of the Speaker, Executive Communications, 1800–1803, box 8, folder 7, LVA (this was printed in the *Journal of the Senate* [1800 (1801)], 26–33); Mosby Sheppard to Monroe, 30 August, ExP I, box 2, folder 6; "10 December 1800 Leigh. Wood. . . . Copying documents respecting the Insurrection," in Auditor's Item 758. The compilation of documents Monroe submitted ran to thirty-four handwritten pages. Wood was paid for scrivening twenty-nine pages. The last five pages are in a different hand, establishing that Wood was the major scribe for the legislative submission. Curiously, Egerton (79), in wanting to portray Monroe as a micro-manager of the state's response so that he could suppress and perhaps even destroy documents injurious to the Republicans, writes, "*Anticipating* a large number of trials—although not lengthy ones, for Virginia justice was also swift—Monroe signed pay warrants to Leigh Wood 'for copying 29 pages of documents on the Subject of the Insurrection'" (my emphasis). Obviously, Wood was employed to do this after the trials were over, and for the express purpose of the submission to the legislature. Monroe was an active administrator, but his nose was not in every thing involving the plot. Leighton Wood's civil service position is stated in the *Journal of the House of Delegates* (1800 [1801]), 12, where he and

two other clerks are recorded submitting a petition for higher wages. The appended documents were reprinted in issues of the Richmond *Recorder* between 2 and 13 April 1803.

10. Documents respecting the Insurrection of the Slaves, House of Delegates, Office of the Speaker, Executive Communications, 1800–1803, box 8, folder 7, LVA (also printed in the *Journal of the Senate* [1800 (1801)], 26–33).

11. *Virginia Gazette*, 11 December 1800. Sidbury used this letter, along with Monroe's message, an anonymous letter appearing in the Fredericksburg *Virginia Herald* on 23 September, and George Tucker's *Letter to a Member of the General Assembly of Virginia on the Subject of the Late Conspiracy of the Slaves; with a Proposal for their Colonization*, 2nd ed. (Richmond, 1801), as indicative of the range of attitudes revealed in response to Gabriel's threat (see *Ploughshares into Swords*, 235–39). For St. George Tucker's proposal, see *A Dissertation on Slavery*, 90–106; Wolf, *Race and Liberty*, 104–9; Philip Hamilton, "Revolutionary Principles and Family Loyalties: Slavery's Transformation in the St. George Tucker Household of Early National Virginia," *WMQ*, 3rd ser., 55 (October 1998): 531–56; and Jordan, *White Over Black*, 555–60.

12. *Journal of the House of Delegates* (1800 [1801]), 7; King and Queen Legislative Petitions, 2 December 1800 (microfilm), FHL.

13. *Journal of the House of Delegates* (1800 [1801]), 10, 19, 43.

14. Ibid., 43.

15. Ibid., 47–48. In his general orders of 15 September thanking the militiamen, Monroe had noted that "the slave who discovered this conspiracy has merited well of the community" (see ExLB, 1794–1800, 413–14). For the role of committee members as emancipators, see Petersburg Deed Book 2, 1790–1801, 667 (Harrison); Henrico Deed Book 5, 1796–1800, 519 (Storrs); and Richmond Deed Book 1, 1782–92, 456 (Copland).

16. *Journal of the House of Delegates* (1800 [1801]), 48.

17. Ibid., 59, 61, 67; *Journal of the Senate* (1800 [1801]), 57–59; ExLB, 1800–1803, 63, 68, 84–87, 91–93; ExP I, box 3, folders 9–10; Henrico County Deed Book 6, 1800–1803, 289–94; Sidbury, *Ploughshares into Swords*, 113.

18. *Journal of the Senate* (1800 [1801]), 51–52, 55–60, 63; Shepherd, *Statutes at Large of Virginia* 2:279. For the impact of the transportation act on Virginia jurisprudence, see Philip J. Schwarz, *Slave Laws in Virginia* (Athens: University of Georgia Press, 1996), chapter 4. Schwarz reports that some pardons issued before 1801 were conditional upon the owner removing the convicted slave from Virginia (102–3). That transportation was seen in part to be a cost-reducing measure was stated in 1802 by councilor Alexander Stuart, who said, "The true policy of the law I believe was, in the first place to guard against the inconveniences which might arise to the State in cases of insurrection, when offenders were so numerous that a general execution of them would not only exhaust the funds of the State, but in a great measure destroy the effect produced from example by familiarising the mind too much to such scenes" (see *Council Journals*, 1801–3,

233–34). In other words, too many executions were too costly and too inuring to the terror public executions were to create. To avoid crossing the line from justice to revenge was not part of Stuart's consideration.

19. *Papers of James Madison*, 17:420; Shepherd, *Statutes at Large of Virginia* 2:279–80; George Keith Taylor, *Substance of a Speech . . . On the Bill To Amend the Penal Laws of this Commonwealth* (Richmond, 1796), 13–15, 28–30 (Evans no. 31271); *American Citizen*, 2 October 1800; *Papers of Thomas Jefferson*, 32:145.

20. Shepherd, *Statutes at Large of Virginia* 2:275; McClurg to Monroe, 7 October, ExP I, box 2, folder 10; *Journal of the House of Delegates* (1800 [1801]), 61, 70–71. Ignoring chronology, misreading the House Journal and misidentifying the author of a letter, Egerton (148) quotes a 22 December epistle he states was sent from Thomas Brooke to Levin Powell complaining of a proposed law to repeal private manumissions. Egerton states that it was "formally entitled the 'free black' bill," and that it was derived from the Harrison Committee's third resolution, the one restricting places of residence for free people of color. He goes on to report that the measure was killed on 12 January 1801 by postponing further consideration until after the assembly had adjourned. Brooke is apparently referring to the plea of the King and Queen petition, since the Harrison committee's resolutions were not introduced until 31 December and none called for repealing the manumission law. The bill that was killed through postponement on 12 January 1801 was one "to enable courts of common law to give relief in certain cases." As noted above, the procedure to kill the residency bill was agreed to on 16 January. No measure seems to be referred to in the *Journal of the House of Delegates* (1800 [1801]) as the "free black" bill. Internal evidence indicates the author of the letter, "H. Brooke," is Humphrey Brooke, the clerk of the Virginia senate. My thanks to Steve Stathis for his assistance in securing an image of the Brooke letter from the Leven Powell Papers in the Library of Congress.

21. *Journal of the House of Delegates* (1800 [1801]), 48, 63, 78–79; Shepherd, *Statutes at Large of Virginia* 2:280, 295–96.

22. *Journal of the House of Delegates* (1800 [1801]), 50, 59, 61–62, 69, 71, 75–76; *Virginia Argus*, 9 January 1801. The proposed bill also appears in the Alexandria *Times, and District of Columbia Advertiser*, 23 January 1801. The publication of the early draft of this bill has apparently been overlooked by historians tracing the legislative history of the attempts to restrict manumissions in the years before 1806. See, for examples, Wolf, *Race and Liberty*, 121–22; and Albert, "The Protean Institution," 243.

23. Shepherd, *Statutes at Large of Virginia* 2:300–301. The Henrico justices in the Martin case were not alone in allowing a slave to testify against a free black defendant (see Petersburg Hustings Court Minute Book, 1797–1800, 23 February 1798 (n.p.), where Petersburg aldermen permitted a slave man named Moses to testify against a free black man named Stephen Walden Chaves, suspected of stealing tobacco from the Blandford Warehouse).

24. *Papers of Thomas Jefferson*, 32:482.

25. Benjamin Duval to Monroe, 26 December 1800, ExP I, box 3, folder 4; William Austin to Monroe, 27 December, ibid.; ExLB, 1800–1803, 51. Egerton (99) reports that Duval overheard the conversation in Norfolk rather than in Richmond.

26. Newton to Monroe, 29 December 1800, ExP II, box 8, folder 4; *Journal of the Senate* (1800 [1801]), 40.

27. ExLB, 1800–1803, 52; Richmond Common Council Minutes, 1796–1807, 103–7; Richmond Common Hall Records, no. 2, 134.

28. *Council Journals*, 1794–1801, 340–43; ExLB, 1800–1803, 63. Billy had been convicted in Henrico Court in October for robbery, but had claimed his benefit of clergy and had thus received thirty-nine lashes and a brand on his left hand. In December he was found guilty of breaking and entering and stealing tobacco from Rocketts's warehouse. He received the death sentence, since he had spent his only claim to the benefit of clergy (see Henrico Order Book 9, 1799–1801, 408; and Richmond Order Book 4, 1797–1801, 511). He was a hired slave of a woman of New Kent County.

29. ExLB, 1800–1803, 70–75, 90, 100–101; *Council Journals*, 1801–3, 29.

30. "1800, Commonwealth of Virginia to Paul Woolfolk," Auditor's Item 758; "Acct of Martin Mims agt the Commonwealth for Maintenance of Negroes," 15 January 1801, ibid. Paul Woolfolk also obtained the warrant compensating Paul Graham for the execution of Sam Graham in November (see "14 November 1800, Paul Graham, $366.66, Sls's Executed," Auditor's Item 756). Egerton (173) states that Ben Woolfolk was paid for his "services" on his release.

31. Henrico Deed Book 6, 1800–1803, 227.

32. "6 Ap. 1801, Elzy Burroughs & als," Auditor's Item 758; "Jas Spears, 15 June 1801," ibid. Egerton (150) misread the Spears account from Cumberland as being part of the charges submitted for the guard from Caroline, and states that an "irresponsible guard" lost the musket while moving the men to be transported from Bowling Green to Richmond. Two constables were sent from Richmond to accompany the four convicted men, who were placed on the stage run by John Hoomes for their trip to the Richmond jail.

33. *Papers of Thomas Jefferson*, 34:345–47, 35:683, 718–22; ExLB, 1800–1803, 136, 226, 272. I believe the correspondence arising from the joint resolution should be read within the context of the dilemma facing the executive over some of those found guilty of conspiracy, and following the expansion of the measure to include other capital crimes, of those whose crimes were thought to be less serious than actual insurrection. By the time Monroe wrote to Jefferson in June 1801, the men who had been reprieved in anticipation of a potential transportation law had already been sold to slave traders, to be taken out of Virginia. Thus, the effort did not really pertain to them, as is sometimes suggested. Nor was it seen as a means to avoid future executions of someone like Gabriel, the real leader of a plot. I don't believe Monroe and the executive had any qualms about his execution. Their concern seems to have been, as Monroe put it to Madison, with "those less criminal in comparison with others," such as the individual

who agreed to join but who never moved to act on the agreement by obtaining arms, appearing at a rendezvous, etc. Read in this context, Jefferson's statement in 1802 to Rufus King, the U.S. ambassador to Great Britain, about seeking the possibility of sending to Sierra Leone "slaves guilty of insurgency" but described by Jefferson at the same time as "not felons or common malefactors but persons guilty of what the safety of society, under actual circumstances obliges us to treat as a crime, but which their feelings may represent in a far different shape," makes more sense. Some were also troubled by the capital punishment for conspiracy for other reasons. In 1803, state council member William Foushee registered his dismay at the broad application by the local courts of the "law against insurrection &c; bringing almost every act of sudden impulse or individual conduct under the Terms Plotting & Conspiring an Insurrection," and hence the threat of the death penalty. Hanover petitioners in 1802 even noted the constant conversations among slaves about rebelling, but which they believed were never really intended to be acted upon, when they sought the executive's pardon for two men found guilty of conspiracy and insurrection there (see *Papers of James Madison*, 17:410; *Council Journals*, 1801–3, 375; and ExP I, box 7, folder 6 [pardon petitions for Tom and Glasgow]). For the latter, see the discussion in the afterword. For a contrary view by councilor Alexander Stuart, see note 18 above. For an intensive local study which demonstrates the complex nature of the relations between free blacks and whites, see Melvin Patrick Ely, *Israel on the Appomattox: A Southern Experiment in Black Freedom from the 1790s through the Civil War* (New York: Alfred A. Knopf, 2004). The petitions to the House of Delegates seeking permission to remain in the state after 1806 by those freed after that date also suggest the importance of face-to-face relationships for white support. For the threats perceived by white people in Virginia towns presented by freed blacks who relocated from rural areas, such as that studied by Ely, see Nicholls, "Strangers Setting among Us."

34. Petition of John G. Brown and William Morris, 24 December 1801, Greenbrier County Legislative Petitions, FHL; *Journal of the House of Delegates* (1801 [1802]), 41; Schwarz, *Slave Laws in Virginia*, 106, 110–11.

Afterword

1. For the importance and significance of slave funerals, and their perceived dangers, particularly during this era in Jamaica, see Vincent Brown, *The Reaper's Garden: Death and Power in the World of Atlantic Slavery* (Cambridge, Mass.: Harvard University Press, 2008). As discussed, the funeral of a slave child served as an important meeting time for Gabriel and his plotters, too. For the sheriff's claim, see Henrico Order Book 9, 1799–1801, 438.

2. Henrico County Will Book 3, 1802–9, 388; Henrico Order Book 10, 1801–3, 498.

3. Storrs to Governor, 10 October 1800, ExP II, box 8, folio 3; Henrico Personal Property Tax Lists, 1800–1803; Richmond City Personal Property Tax Lists,

1805–12; Richmond Hustings Deeds 4, 1804–6, 149; Henrico County Deed Book 7, 1803–6, 270. As noted below, there is no direct evidence that those who served the state at the trials or by betraying the conspiracy were threatened by their neighbors, but it was reasonable to expect that some were. A man named Lewis Bolahs, or Bowlagh, who grew up near Richmond and was about twenty-six or twenty-seven in 1800, was sold via the interstate slave trade to New Orleans. He exposed a plot there in 1812 and was subsequently freed by the Louisiana legislature, but fled for fear of his life. He left New Orleans by entering the U.S. Navy, and ended up back in Virginia, where he petitioned the General Assembly in 1824 for permission to remain in the state, in or near Richmond, where he said "all his attachments, all that can render his life desirable to him" existed. Because of his act in New Orleans, he feared going to "Hayti" or to "Messurado" (the site of Monrovia, Liberia), because "he would be an object of persecution in any Society governed by persons of colour." Without his family, he felt isolated in any other part of the United States (see Petition of Lewis Bolahs, 13 December 1824, Richmond City Legislative Petitions, LVA). He did not name his previous Virginia owner or when he had been sold, which prevents discovering if he were present during Gabriel's Conspiracy before being sold to New Orleans.

4. See Appendix C: Alleged Participants Not Prosecuted; Henrico Deed Book 6, 1800–1803, 227; and Richmond City Hustings Court Order Book 7, 1806–8, 202. Sidbury (*Ploughshares into Swords*, 113n46) incorrectly renders Woolfolk's new owner as Wilson Cary Miles. The other slave witnesses, but not Woolfolk, had just been tried for the same crime. None had been found guilty.

5. Henrico Deed Book 6, 1800–1803, 289–94; petition of Pharoah Sheppard, 14 December 1810, Richmond City Legislative Petitions, LVA; Henrico Deed Book 11, 1814–15, 354; Sidbury, *Ploughshares into Swords*, 105–15; Egerton, 174–75; Hanover County Personal Property Tax Lists, 1802–18; Henrico Personal Property Tax Lists, 1802–21. The law permitting Pharoah Sheppard's son to remain in the state appears in "Acts Passed at a General Assembly of the Commonwealth of Virginia . . ." (Richmond, 1811), 101–2 (Shaw–Shoemaker no. 24341a); since it was not included in the digital edition of *Early American Imprints,* this document was accessed via microcard. For an account of the bloody reprisals following Nat Turner's rebellion, see Thomas C. Parramore, "Covenant in Jerusalem," in *Nat Turner: A Slave Rebellion in History and Memory,* ed. Kenneth S. Greenberg, 58–76. Both Egerton and Sidbury offer explanations for the betrayal of the plot by Pharoah and Tom. Egerton, erroneously believing the revelation took place very late on Saturday night after the brunt of the storm, suggests that Pharoah concluded that the effort was hopeless and, bringing Tom along, acted for his own gain. Sidbury correctly reports that their revelation took place before the storm, and tries to explain their decision on the basis of a hoped-for manumission, fear of the white reprisals that would follow, and of their relatively privileged position in slavery. At the same time, Sidbury argues that they waited until the last minute, which could possibly allow them to benefit from either a white victory or defeat. Evidence of skepticism about the number of recruits who would appear,

among even the inner circle, suggests that the two men could have feared that the undertaking would be disastrous but did not reach that conclusion until the last few days. Whispers probably ran in all directions, geographically and politically, and some probably reflected doubts about the enterprise's chances of success or how deep and broad the commitment actually was among the men of the Brook and the outlying cells.

6. Henrico Order Book 10, 1801–3, 328; *Council Journals*, 1801–3, 237, 262, 270; documents associated with "Negroes Condemnd from Hanover . . . May 8, 1802," in ExP I, box 7, folder 6 (Pardons R–W) (my thanks to Brent Tarter for providing copies of the documents pertaining to this appeal). Although he believes that good evidence exists for a conspiracy in the hinterlands of Petersburg and in and about Norfolk in 1802, Egerton discounts the existence of this Henrico plot because the evidence for it sounded too much like a rehash of Gabriel's plan—a conclusion, as Egerton notes (141), that reinforces one reached by Bertram Wyatt-Brown in *Southern Honor: Ethics and Behavior in the Old South* (New York: Oxford University Press, 1981), 426. The second petition, mentioned above, is partly reproduced by Wyatt-Brown on p. 416.

7. Henrico Order Book 12, 1805–7, 454–55, 465–66.

8. Petition of Izzard Bacon['s] Negroes by Charles Crenshaw, 14 December 1816, Henrico Legislative Petitions, FHL; "Memorial of Thomas Ladd, Samuel Crew and Fleming Bates, trustees appointed . . . for slaves intended to be emancipated by the last will of Izard Bacon," 17 December 1818, ibid.; petition of John Winston, 11 December 1820, ibid.; Leroy Hopkins, "Black Eldorado on the Susquehanna," *Journal of the Lancaster County Historical Society* 89 (Mickaelmas 1985): 110–32. A similar large manumission touched the Hanover neighborhood involved in the plot when Samuel Gist died in 1815 (see Philip J. Schwarz, *Migrants against Slavery: Virginians and the Nation* [Charlottesville: University Press of Virginia, 2001], 122–48).

9. Ira Berlin, *The Making of African America: The Four Great Migrations* (New York: Viking, 2010), 106. Important recent work on the internal slave trade appears in Walter Johnson, *Soul By Soul: Life Inside the Antebellum Slave Market* (Cambridge, Mass.: Harvard University Press, 1999); Michael Tadman, *Speculators and Slaves: Masters, Traders, and Slaves in the Old South* (Madison: University of Wisconsin Press, 1989); Steven Deyle, *Carry Me Back: The Domestic Slave Trade in American Life* (New York: Oxford University Press, 2005); and Robert H. Gudmestad, *A Troublesome Commerce: The Transformation of the Interstate Slave Trade* (Baton Rouge: Louisiana State University Press, 2003). The distances slaves were moved after being sold, and the volume of slave sales, sharply distinguished the interstate slave trade from the earlier expansion of slavery from the Tidewater to the Piedmont in Virginia. For a discussion of the hoped-for security to be found in the "whitening" of Virginia, see Ford, *Deliver Us from Evil;* and Michael L. Nicholls, "Recreating a White Urban Virginia," in *Lois Green Carr: The Chesapeake and Beyond—A Celebration* (Crownsville: Maryland Historical and Cultural Publications, 1992), 27–36.

10. *Virginia Argus*, 30 June 1801, cited in Henley Marriage/Obituary Index to Virginia Newspapers, LVA; Henrico Order Book 11, 1803–5, 30; Henrico Deed Book 11, 1814–15, 552; Edward Biddle and Mantle Fielding, *The Life and Works of Thomas Sully (1783-1872)* (Philadelphia: Wickersham Press, 1921), 254; Mrs. Thomas Nelson Carter Bruns, comp., *Louisiana Portraits* (New Orleans: National Society of the Colonial Dames of America in the State of Louisiana, 1975), 213; Henrico Will Book 4, 1809–15, 104; *Richmond Enquirer,* 11 September 1810, 9 October 1810. For Prosser's various land and slave transactions, see Henrico Deed Book 6, 1800–1803, 75, 473; Deed Book 7, 1803–6, 409; Deed Book 8, 1806–10, 246, 279, 287, 361–62, 376; Deed Book 9, 1810–12, 10, 53, 474, 519; Deed Book 10, 1812–14, 20; Deed Book 15, 1817, 219–20, 222; Deed Book 16, 1817–18, 402, 552; Deed Book 17, 1818, 308, 492, 495, 670; Deed Book 18, 1818–19, 507; Deed Book 19, 1819, 292, 588, 590; Deed Book 39, 1837–38, 141; Richmond City Deed Book 16, 1819–20, 321; Henrico Personal Property Tax Lists, 1810–11; Richmond City Personal Property Tax List, 1811; Fourth Census of U.S., Wilkinson County, Mississippi (1820); Wilkinson County, Miss., Land Book D, 45, 303, 362; and Wilkinson County, Miss., Land Book F, 154. For the great importance of slave labor as the significant and portable source of wealth and collateral for Southern planters, see Gavin Wright, *Old South, New South: Revolutions in the Southern Economy since the Civil War* (New York: Basic Books, 1986), chapters 1 and 2; and Bonnie Martin, "Slavery's Invisible Engine: Mortgaging Human Property," *Journal of Southern History* 76 (November 2010): 817–66.

11. Monroe to Jefferson, 11 June 1802, in Thomas Jefferson Papers, Series I: General Correspondence, 1651–1827, Library of Congress, Manuscript Division, available at http://memory.loc.gov/cgi-bin/ampage?collId=mtj1&fileName=mtj 1page026.db&recNum=545. For a discussion of George Tucker's views, see Sidbury, *Ploughshares into Swords*, 135–38; and Ford, *Deliver Us from Evil*, 57–59. The centrality of slavery in the politics of the early republic and the importance of the issue of slavery's expansion have recently been reemphasized in Matthew Mason, *Slavery and Politics in the Early American Republic* (Chapel Hill: University of North Carolina Press, 2006); and Robert Pierce Forbes, *The Missouri Compromise and Its Aftermath: Slavery and the Meaning of America* (Chapel Hill: University of North Carolina Press, 2007). For an argument for recognizing the Civil War as "the greatest slave rebellion," see Steven Hahn, *The Political Worlds of Slavery and Freedom* (Cambridge, Mass.: Harvard University Press, 2009), 55–114.

Appendix A

1. Henrico County Land Tax List, Upper District, 1800; Henrico County Deed Book, 1750–67, 869; John Pendleton Kennedy, ed., *Journals of the House of Burgesses, 1761-1765* (Richmond: Virginia State Library, 1907), 307–8, 317–24, 326–27, 362, 364; Henrico Court Orders, 1763–67, 640; Henrico County Will Book 3, 1802–9, 1; Henrico County Deed Book, 1767–74, 311; Henrico County

Deed Book 3, 1789–92, 463; Henrico County Deed Book 5, 1796–1800, 464; *Virginia Gazette and Richmond and Manchester Advertiser*, 4 October 1796, cited in *Marriages and Deaths from Richmond, Virginia Newspapers, 1780–1820* (Richmond: Virginia Genealogical Society, 1983), 125; Henrico County Personal Property Tax List, Upper District, 1800.

2. Petition of Nathaniel Wilkinson, 18 December 1800, Henrico County Legislative Petitions, FHL; Henrico County Land Tax List, Upper District, 1800; Henrico County Deed Book 5, 1796–1800, 556–58; Henrico County Personal Property Tax List, Upper District, 1800.

3. Henrico County Deed Book 2, 1785–88, 212, 235–37; "Copy [of the] Will of Fendall Southerland dec'd for Doct: F. Gregory," dated August 24, 1789, probated in King William County, Va. (see Mss2 So885 a 1, VHS); Henrico County Land Tax List, Upper District, 1800; Henrico County Personal Property Tax List, Upper District, 1800.

4. Henrico County Deed Book 4, 1792–94, 184, 555; Henrico County Deed Book 5, 1796–1800, 408, 613; Henrico County Land Tax List, Upper District, 1800; Henrico County Personal Property Tax List, Upper District, 1800. For the prior ownership of Young's main tract, see Henrico County Deed Book 2, 1785–88, 607, 609; and Henrico County Deed Book 3, 1789–92, 67, 174. He is not to be confused with another William Young, who resided in the Lower District, east of Richmond.

5. The locations of these owners and their slaves have been garnered from the Henrico Deed Books, Land Tax lists, and Processioners Returns, cited elsewhere.

6. Henrico County Order Book 9, 1799–1801, 5, 84, 304.

7. Hanover County Personal Property Tax List, St. Paul's Parish, 1800.

8. These slave holdings are based on the 1800 Personal Property Tax Lists for Hanover, King William, and Caroline Counties.

9. Slave holdings are taken from the 1800 Personal Property Tax Lists for Hanover. Hanover Court records have generally not survived for this period. Locations are derived from the Hanover County Land Tax Lists, 1815. For Graham's later location, see Caroline County Wills, 1742–1830, 69. For Austin's, see Richmond *Virginia Gazette* (Hayes), 2 March 1782. For Martha Whitlock, see will of David Whitlock, 28 March 1798, in Hanover County Chancery Causes, Thomas Dix v. heirs of David Whitlock (1860-003), Chancery Records Index, online images available at the Library of Virginia, http://www.virginiamemory.com/collections/chancery.

Index

Bristol (C. Carter's?), 40, 168, 169n6, 186n18

Bristol (P. Thilman's), 157, 159n10; trial and verdict of, 98, 194n4

Brook, the. *See* Upham (Ufnam) Brook

Brook Bridge, *14*, 15

Brooke, John: lands of, 15, 153; slaves of, 80, 153, 156

Brooke, Moses (J. Graham's), 160

Brooke, Robert, 43, 111, 213n12

Brooke, Thomas, 223n20

Brook Road, 13, *14*, 16, 35, 52, 100, 141, 151, 152, 154, 207n26

Brown, George, slaves of, 161

Brown, John, 2

Brown, John G., 136, 139–40

Brutus/Julius (Wm. Anderson's), 28, 158, 159n13, 164n33; accusations against, 88; trial and verdict of, 89, 209n34

Buchanan, John: lands of, 15; slaves of, 160

Buckner, Thomas, 102, 165n41

Burroughs, Elzy, 102, 138, 216n17

Burton, Thomas, 154; lands of, 15, 16, 153; slaves of, 33, 94, 153, 157, 185n16

Burton, William: lands of, 15, 153; slaves of, 74, 75, 78, 81, 153, 156, 168

Byrd, Jesse (free man), 35, 53, 161, 166n52, 198n21, 208n31; accusations against, 88, 104, 117

Byrd, Reuben (free man), 35, 53, 161, 166–67n53, 193–94n2, 198n21, 208n31; accusations against, 88, 104, 117

Byrd, Sam, Sr. (free man), 23, 35, 167n53; arrest, 84, 104–5, 117, 133

Byrd, Sam, Jr. (Jane Clarke's), 153, 157, 163n9, 164n24, 166n52; Egerton on, 210–11n1; execution of, 100; French crisis rumors heard by,

46–47; objectives of, 38, 43; plan as envisioned by, 27, 33, 41–42, 177n14; as recruiting "plant," 42–43; recruitment by, 23–24, 35, 41, 89, 101, 133; trial and verdict of, 94

Byrd family, 151, 166–67nn52–53

Calendar of Virginia State Papers, 1–4, 5, 6

Callender, James Thomson: anti-Federalism of, 20, 190n28; on August 30 storm, 57; letters to Jefferson, 78, 83, 180n20, 201n6, 205n22, 221n7; *The Prospect Before Us,* 21; reporting on conspiracy, 28, 31, 40, 74, 75, 76, 83–84, 185n16, 206n26; sedition trial and jailing, 21, 22, 74, 115

Caroline County, *14*, 16–17, 25, 28, 32, 35–36, 50, 54–55, 57–58, 61, 66, 70, 82, 96, 136, 151, 153, 159n8, 178n17; arrests in, 77–78, 84–85; recruits from, 40–41; trials in, 107–9, 111, 118, 143, 154–55, 158, 159nn14–15; unnamed white man from, 44–46, 88, 113

Carrington, Edward, 21–22, 207n28

Carrington, Mayo, 86–87, 165n40

Carter, Charles: lands of, 16, 54; slaves of, 36, 37, 40, 108, 109, 154, 155, 158, 159n14, 168, 169n6

Cartersville, Virginia, 86, 165n40

Cary, Wilson Miles, 143

Catawba Indians, 23, 177n14

Charles (R. Gregory's), 156; aspirations, 37, 47; execution of, 75, 79, 153; trial and verdict of, 75

Charles (Mrs. [Ann] Smith's), 65, 160, 163n16

Charles (Wm. Winston's), 168; testimony of, 73

Charles City County, *14*, 76, 155

Charlottesville, Virginia, 35

Chase, Samuel, 21

Chaves, Stephen Walden, 223n23

Cheatham, Mathew, 63

Chesterfield County, *14*, 21, 35, 36, 63, 64, 66, 69, 70, 72, 99, 121, 141, 151, 153, 167n54

Chickahominy River, 13, *14*, 15–17, 76, 101, 151, 152, 155, 164n32

Chickasaw Indians, 177n14

Claiborne (W. P.) estate, slaves of, 106, 158

Clarke, Jane: lands of, 23, 177n14; slaves of, 23–24, 94, 100, 133, 153, 157

Clarke, John, 136–37

Clopton, John, 97

Coleman, Daniel (free man), 53

conspiracy, law of, 9, 31–32, 71, 130–31

Cooley, Bob. *See* Cowley, Robert

Copland, Charles, 20, 128, 129

Corbin, Francis, 45, 188n27

Court of Oyer and Terminer, 18, 54, 70, 72, 89, 94, 194n4, 201n2, 217n21

Cowley, Robert (free man), 64, 96, 161; armory key lent by, 48, 89, 96, 99, 137, 164n31; duties, 48, 62, 64, 177n14, 213n12; manumission of, 201n2; role in conspiracy discussed, 99–100, 167n56

Craig, Adam, 77

Crenshaw, Charles, 208n32

Cumberland County, 15, 38, 66, 86, 101, 138, 151–52, 155, 165n40, 224n32

Dabney, Benjamin, 127

Daniel (J. Brooke's), 153, 156; later life, 142; trial and verdict of, 78, 80

Daniel (Wm. Burton's), 40, 168

Daniel (N. Wilkinson's), 156; trial and verdict of, 80–81

Daniel (J. Williamson Jr.'s), 168; testimony of, 39–40, 45, 73

Davey (unknown), 168

David (A. Barrett's), 168

David (Stras or Southall's), 160, 162n6

Davies, William, slaves of, 161

Davis, Augustine, 20, 52, 53, 76, 84, 124–27

Davis, David Brion, 10

Davis, Thomas J., 9

Davy (unstated), 80, 161, 164n27

Deep Run, 15, 16

Dequasay, Charles, 45, 164n35. *See also* Quersey, Charles

Dick (J. Smith's), 157; pardon of, 95; trial and verdict of, 94

Dick (P. Thilman's), 47, 157, 159n10; pardon of, 99; recruitment of, 36; trial and verdict of, 98, 194n4

Dinwiddie County, *14*, 127, 166n52, 217n21; execution in, 106, 117; trial in, 70, 106, 158

Drayton, John, 112–13, 219n34

Duane, James, 76, 205n22

Dunscomb, Andrew, 85–86, 175n3, 206n26

Dunsmore, John, 53

Duval, Benjamin, 134, 135

Duvall, James, 57, 107–9, 217n25

Edmund (P. Woolfolk's), 161, 164–65n36, 168; testimony of, 109, 169n5, 217n21

Egerton, Douglas R., *Gabriel's Rebellion*, 6–7, 8–9, 11; on Byrd, 177n14; Caroline trials account, 218n27, 224n32; chronology errors, 194–95n4, 195n7, 197n17, 201n4, 203n12, 205n21, 206n26, 211–12nn5–6; on Cowley, 192n31, 213n12; erroneous testimony attributions, 203n8, 205n21, 209n32; errors on Gabriel's capture, 209n35;

on Gabriel's conspiracy number
claims, 210–11n1; Gabriel's trial
account, 211–12n6; on Gabriel's
weapon, 197n17; on Gilbert, 197n16;
on lack of evidence of coercion,
186n17; on later plot, 227n6; mis-
identifications, 184n10, 199n26,
204n13, 215–16n17, 218n29; on
Monroe's crisis handling, 207–
8nn28–29, 211n5, 221–22nn7–9;
on Monroe's message, 220n2,
221–22nn8–9; on Palmer's scrapbook, 172n11; on Peter's trial,
217n21; on plot revealers' possible
motivations, 226–27n5; political
ideology ascribed in, 32, 97, 188–
90n28, 212n7, 212nn9–10; on possible identification of Frenchmen,
188n27; on proposed manumission
law, 223n20; on Prosser, 174n3; on
Sheppard, 195n6; sifting evidence
charge against Monroe, 113–14;
on significance of religion in plot,
179–80n20; on Taylor, 210n37;
on weapons, 196n8; on women's
exclusion from conspiracy, 44; on
Woolfolk, 178n17, 183n5; on Young's
spring meeting, 187n22
election of 1800, 1, 4, 5, 19–22, 84,
107, 114–16, 138
emancipation/manumission/abolition:
African colonizaton, 139, 148;
anti-manumission petition, 127; of
Bacon's slaves, 146; of Gist's slaves,
217n21; master's power in, 18–19;
Monroe's views, 148; "private citizen"'s letter on, 124–27; Quakers'
and Methodists' support, 39; of
state witnesses, 27, 142–45; Tucker's
proposal, 6, 8, 125, 139; Virginia
laws on, 132–34, 144, 145, 208n32
Emanuel (D. Wood's), 153, 158; trial
and verdict of, 109

Epitome of the Times, The, 91, 102,
115–16
evangelical Christianity, 4, 6, 7. *See
also* Baptists; Methodists
evidence of conspiracy, 59, 107; accounts of recruitment, 9, 31–32, 71,
83–84; date range, 30–31; mixed
messages on, 66–67; Monroe's se-
lective documentation, 123; public
presentation of, 70; range of, 130–
31; swords as, 62–63

Federalists, 5, 20–21, 115–16, 122,
190n28
Fells, John (C. Carter's), 37, 47, 55,
109, 158, 159n14, 206n24, 218n27;
trial and verdict of, 165n36, 169n5
Ferguson, Robert, 8
Fluvanna County, 43, 61, 62, 95, 143
Ford, Hezekiah, slaves of, 168
Ford, Lacy K., 8, 97; *Deliver Us from
Evil*, 195n7, 207–8n29, 221n7
Foster, John, 45, 64–66, 72, 82, 88,
89, 99, 163n16, 163n19, 167n56,
186n20, 209n34
Foushee, Dr., 91, 159n13
Foushee, John, 28
Foushee, William, 28, 85, 94, 137,
225n33
Fox, John, slaves of, 161, 164n22
France, foreign relations with, 46–47
Frank (Wm. Austin's), 161, 164n33,
209n34
Frank (Wm. Burton's), 168
Frank (T. H. Prosser's), 26, 42, 57, 58,
156; execution of, 75, 79; recruit-
ment by, 35; trial and verdict of, 75
Frank (unstated), 161, 164n25
Frank (N. Wilkinson's), 156; later life,
142; trial and verdict of, 78
Franklin, Elijah, 154
Fredericksburg, Virginia, 16, 23, 81,
131, 154

free blacks in Virginia, 19, 39; Petersburg registration of, 53, 77; registration requirements, 133–34; Richmond registration of, 77–78; rights of, 126–27, 128, 131–34

Frenchmen, mentions of, 38, 39, 45–47, 73, 84, 88, 89, 96, 97, 113–15, 123, 125, 188–90nn27–28, 211–12n6

Gabriel (T. H. Prosser's), 157; accusations against, 63, 64, 65, 73, 79; Aptheker's characterization, 5; benefit of clergy plea, 26; as blacksmith, 6, 26, 63; bullets made by, 47, 96; capture of, 90–92, 93, 197n17, 209n35; described, 26, 198n24; Egerton's characterization, 6–7, 32; execution of, 100, 212n6, 213n13; Gilbert accused by, 24, 89, 91, 209–10n37, 211n1; gunpowder secured by, 47; jailed, 93–94; at large, 61, 76–77, 78; as leader, 1, 3, 25, 37, 42, 49–51, 58, 109, 177n14; monetary value, 36, 218n29; motivations, 97; Mullin's characterization, 6; objectives of, 38; Palmer's characterization, 4; postponement of attack by, 57; recruitment by, 32, 33, 41, 44–45, 75; reprieve, 98; reward for capture of, 64, 76, 94, 198n24; skills and knowledge, 25–26, 97; swords made by, 27, 47–48, 51, 62–63, 96, 196n8; trial and verdict of, 38, 40–41, 96–98, 123–24; visit to state capitol, 48, 54, 99, 192–93n33

Gabriel, Jack (C. Carter's), 55, 158, 159n14; recruitment by, 37; trial and verdict of, 108–9, 109, 169n6, 218n27

Gabriel's Conspiracy: accounts and studies, 1–9, 76–77; African culture influences in, 8; aftermath, 134–40, 141–49, 226n3; alleged participants

not prosecuted, 160–67; beginnings, 23–29; betrayal, 55–57; capture of conspirators, 59, 60–61, 90–92, 93; center, 13, *14*, 15–18; "conquering the white people" goal, 3–4, 23, 33, 38–39, 51, 60, 67, 73, 75, 80, 82; conspirators' resolve, 50–51; date, 50, 52; evidence, 1, 9, 70; execution accounts, 202n7, 206n26; execution dates, 213–14n13; execution list, 156–57; execution locations, 74, 85–86, 100, 202n7, 206–7n26; execution number, 117, 214n13; expenses for containing, 1, 106, 107–8, 117–19, 137–38; fictional accounts, 7; French relations and, 46–47; geography of, 13–18, 34–35, 151–55, 173–74n1; goals, 1, 9–10, 27, 32, 37–42, 43, 80; key state witnesses, 71–72, 142–45; in larger context, 7–8; later conspiracy scares, 145–46, 227n6; leadership, 25–26; military and strategic needs, 44–47; military ranks in, 36–37; Monroe's account and documentation, 119–24; national importance, 114–16; number of participants needed, 31, 40–42, 96; outcome, 1, 129–40; "outside influences," 3, 4, 6; pardons in, 142; plan details, 27–29; preparation for, 30; public notices, 76; public's later response, 93; purported lists of conspirators' names, 41–42, 186n20; range of intended victims, 38–40; range of verdicts, 71, 72–73, 142; recruitment for, 23–25, 31–47; recruitment methods, 32–37, 39–40, 42–43; recruitment sites, 36, 40, 42, 48, 52, 65, 153; regiment demobilization and, 22; rejected ideas, 43; rescheduling, 57, 58–59; research problems and errors, 8–11; rumors about, 52–53; secrecy of, 3,

29, 30, 34, 39–40, 43–44, 49; slave witnesses list, 168–69; suppression, 59–70; timing, 29, 30–31, 48–51, 55; trial outcomes, 117–19, 156–58; trials, 71–90, 94–99, 101, 104–9, 112–13; weapons acquisition plans, 47–49; weather preventing, 1, 6, 57–58, 195n7; witness interrogations, 27, 63, 143, 196n14; women excluded from, 43–44

Galt, William, slaves of, 28–29, 65, 160, 163n18

Garland, Edward, slaves of, 108, 158, 159n17, 163n11, 168

Garthright, Elvey, 76

Gates, Burwell (G. Brown's), 86, 161, 167n54

Gaufney [Gwathmey?], Richard, slaves of, 161, 164n26

Gentry, William, 60, 73–74

George (I. Bacon's), 157; manumission of, 146, 208n32; trial and verdict of, 89

George (Wm. Burton's), 153, 156; objectives of, 39; trial and verdict of, 75, 78, 81, 83, 185n16, 203n9

George (Hatcher's), 160

George (J. Mayo's), 74, 160, 163n8, 202n7

George (J. Smith estate's). *See* Smith, George (J. Smith estate's)

George (P. Thilman's), 158, 159n15; trial and verdict of, 108, 194n4

George (Mrs. David Whitlock's), 155, 161, 164nn32–33

Georgetown, District of Columbia, 20

Gilbert (Elizabeth Stockdell's), 202n7

Gilbert (Wm. Young's), 29, 35, 37, 41–42, 48, 49, 153, 157; accusations against, 24, 65, 89, 91, 209–10n37; accusations by, 160–61, 164n29, 164n31, 164n35; confession of, 24, 35, 37, 45, 46, 63, 64–65, 66, 77, 89–90, 90, 99, 113, 123,

163nn19–20, 164n24, 167n56; execution of, 25, 100; at large, 60–61, 197n16; as recruiting "plant," 42–43; recruitment of, 24; skills and knowledge, 24, 28, 212n7; speech impediment, 24, 37, 45, 89, 178n16; trial and verdict of, 88–89, 89, 94; trial postponement, 81, 84

Giles, Captain, 92

Gist (Samuel) estate: manumission of slaves, 227n8; slaves of, 36, 154

Glasgow (P. Thilman's), 145–46

Gloucester County, 101–3, 117, 165nn41–42

Goochland County, 15, 26, 35, 40, 43, 55, 61, 62, 66, 68, 87, 95, 101, 112, 153, 163n17, 164n25, 165n40, 200n31

Goodall, Parke: slaves of, 168; tavern, 57, 174–75n3

Goode, Thomas: Prosser and, 183n8; slaves of, 35, 94, 100, 153, 157, 159n7

Goodwyn, Peterson, 127

Graham, Duncan, 155

Graham, John, slaves of, 77–78, 160, 163n13

Graham, Paul: lands of, 24–25; slaves of, 24–25, 35, 65, 66, 94, 137, 155, 156, 157, 159n4, 168, 178n17

Graham, Sam (P. Graham's), 42, 155, 157, 159n8, 163n15, 169n6; accusations against, 65, 66; accusations by, 160; execution of, 100, 141, 217n21, 224n30; trial and verdict of, 94

Grammer, John, 52–53

Gregory, Roger: informed of conspiracy, 56; lands of, 15, 152–53; overseer of, 49; patrols, 58; slaves of, 47, 60, 74, 75, 153, 156; statement requested of, 107

Gregory's Tavern, *14*, 16, 47, 56, 75, 152, 174n3

Griffen (B. Hurt's), 87, 161, 167n55

Ground Squirrel Bridge, *14*, 17, 40

Gunn, John, slaves of, 161, 164n28

Halls [Haws?], Walker, 53, 193n2

Hamilton, Alexander, 20, 115

Hanover County, *14*, 16, 35, 39, 50, 58, 144, 151

Hanover Court House, Virginia, *14*, 16, 23, 36, 54–55, 155, 164n32

Hanover Town, Virginia, 23, 29, 35, 104, 154

Harper's Ferry, Virginia, 215n15

Harrison (unknown), 146

Harrison, Benjamin, 67, 127

Harrison, Edmund, 127, 129, 132

Harry: capture of, 76, 194n4, 203n9; escape from jail, 54, 61

Harry (T. Austin's), 156; trial and verdict of, 82

Harvie, Col. John, 61; slaves of, 36, 73, 159n1, 160, 162n5, 184n10

Henrico County, 64; 1800 tax census, 17; as center of conspiracy, 13, *14*, 15–18, 30–35, 57–61, 151–55; divisions of, 17; executions in, 117; men tried in, 156–57; Quakers in, 39; trials in, 70, 71–90, 94–100, 107, 109, 112

Henry, Patrick, 51

Heron, James, 111

Higginson, Thomas Wentworth, 4

Hobson, Mathew, 154

Holeman, John, slaves of, 40, 73, 168

Holmes (P. Thilman's), 161, 165n37, 194–95n4

Hooper, Mr. [Thomas], 91, 210n37

Humphrey (E. Garland's), 158, 163n11, 168; testimony of, 108–9, 169n7; trial and verdict of, 108, 218n27

Humphrey (Mrs. Sutton's?), 160

Hungary Baptist Meeting House, Brook neighborhood, 16, 24

Hurt, Benjamin, slaves of, 161, 167n55

Hylton, Daniel L., 147, 210n37

Hylton, Lucy Bolling, 147

Isaac (J. Allen's), 48–49, 156; execution of, 85–86, 100, 211n6, 213n13; trial and verdict of, 82, 94

Isaac (Wm. Burton's), 153, 156; execution of, 74–75; recruitment by, 40, 55; trial and verdict of, 73, 74

Isaac (T. H. Prosser's), 146

Isham (Wm. Burton's), 153, 156; accusations against, 78; execution of, 81, 85; objectives of, 39; trial and verdict of, 81, 203n9; wife, 44

Isham (*Mary* crewman), 90–91, 105

Jack (Col. J. Harvie's), 160, 162n5

Jack (Mrs. Riddle's), 168, 200n34; testimony of, 169n4

Jack (Stras or Southall's), 160, 162n6

Jacob (Wm. Wilson's), 101–3, 117, 138, 161, 165n42, 189n28, 215–16n17

Jacob (T. Woodfin's), 157; pardon of, 95; recruitment of, 33–34; trial and verdict of, 94

James (E. Price's), 153, 157, 199n26, 218n29; monetary value, 36, 218n29; pardon of, 110; reprieve, 98–99, 110; trial and verdict of, 94–95, 169n4, 200n34

James (P. Tinsley's), 161, 164n31; visit to state capitol, 48, 54, 89, 96, 99

James River, *14*, 15, 21, 23, 35, 43, 64, 66, 77, 78, 86, 101, 131, 220n2

Jefferson, Thomas, 1; Callender's letters to, 78, 83; election of 1800, 20, 114–16; ideas about African colony of freed slaves, 225n33; Monroe's letters to, 72, 87, 138–39, 148, 182n1, 214–15n15, 224n33; response to crisis, 8, 87–88

Jeffersonian republicanism, 4, 20, 84, 114–16

Michael Plunkett
Afro-American Sources in Virginia: A Guide to Manuscripts

Sally Belfrage
Freedom Summer

Armstead L. Robinson and Patricia Sullivan, eds.
New Directions in Civil Rights Studies

Leroy Vail and Landeg White
Power and the Praise Poem: Southern African Voices in History

Robert A. Pratt
The Color of Their Skin: Education and Race in Richmond, Virginia, 1954–89

Ira Berlin and Philip D. Morgan, eds.
Cultivation and Culture: Labor and the Shaping of Slave Life in the Americas

Gerald Horne
Fire This Time: The Watts Uprising and the 1960s

Sam C. Nolutshungu
Limits of Anarchy: Intervention and State Formation in Chad

Jeannie M. Whayne
A New Plantation South: Land, Labor, and Federal Favor in Twentieth-Century Arkansas

Patience Essah
A House Divided: Slavery and Emancipation in Delaware, 1638–1865

Tommy L. Bogger
Free Blacks in Norfolk, Virginia, 1790–1860: The Darker Side of Freedom

Robert C. Kenzer
Enterprising Southerners: Black Economic Success in North Carolina, 1865–1915

Midori Takagi
"Rearing Wolves to Our Own Destruction": Slavery in Richmond, Virginia, 1782–1865

Alessandra Lorini
Rituals of Race: American Public Culture and the Search for Racial Democracy

Mary Ellen Curtin
Black Prisoners and Their World, Alabama, 1865–1900

Philip J. Schwarz
Migrants against Slavery: Virginians and the Nation

Armstead L. Robinson
Bitter Fruits of Bondage: The Demise of Slavery and the Collapse of the Confederacy, 1861–1865

Francille Rusan Wilson
The Segregated Scholars: Black Social Scientists and the Creation of Black Labor Studies, 1890–1950

Gregory Michael Dorr
Segregation's Science: Eugenics and Society in Virginia

Glenn McNair
Criminal Injustice: Slaves and Free Blacks in Georgia's Criminal Justice System

William Dusinberre
Strategies for Survival: Recollections of Bondage in Antebellum Virginia

Valerie C. Cooper
Word, Like Fire: Maria Stewart, the Bible, and the Rights of African Americans

Michael L. Nicholls
Whispers of Rebellion: Narrating Gabriel's Conspiracy